NOT YOUR AVERAGE CEO

Nicole Gallicchio-Elz
Danielle Cuomo, MBA

ISBN: 979-8-218-36835-7

Printed by Ingram in the United States of America.

First printing edition 2024

CONTENTS
Not Your Average CEO

INTRODUCTION
Unlocking Potential: A Dual Journey with a CEO and COO

Plenty of books exist on becoming a CEO, achieving marketing success, or breaking your sales records. You probably read one, or even dozens. But, we realized that they all are lacking that elusive piece. That missing piece that understands that we are all intrinsically different and the world in which we work has transformed. Those books lack the details and action steps to take to improve your company and professional growth as a CEO or executive.

Navigating today's business landscape takes many skill sets - more so than ever before, a broad knowledge base, an adoption of technology, and a deep understanding of how things are changing. So, we sought out to find advice that is unconventional and current with today's modern workforce. Those tips and pieces of advice that are game-changers once you have heard them. We began writing this book by asking the question, *"What does being 'Not Your Average CEO' mean to you?"* And as you may imagine, it means something different to every leader. Over the past few years, we have asked hundreds of executives - across all industries, in all regions of the world - what this phrase means to them and what advice they have received that was different and unheard of.Each answer was unique and will make you a better, stronger CEO.

Throughout this book, you'll find industry experts' unique perspectives on the aforementioned question and gain insight into how you can stand out as a leader. This book acknowledges that the business environment has evolved into a diverse and interconnected global marketplace, influenced by technological advancements, cultural shifts, and changing consumer behaviors. Moreover, being a Not Your Average CEO requires a deep awareness of the current state of the world. The corporate terrain is characterized by rapid digital transformation, disruptive technologies, evolving market trends, and heightened customer expectations. This necessitates staying informed, continuously learning, and adapting strategies to remain competitive and relevant.

And, all the while, standing out.

As every ambitious leader knows, taking the advice of others can only create growth potential. These pages carry the ideologies of growth aspects in an all-encompassing and instructive way. You'll find minimal fluff in this book. Instead, you'll receive a practical, detail-oriented, and informative guide for hitting the ground running in building your empire and a successful company. We've included executive tips and summaries throughout the book that are based on our practical experience over our nearly two decades of running an organization.

And, we would be remiss to not include how managing remotely fits in these days. The benefit of remote management lies in its flexibility and convenience for employers and employees. With the rise of technology and AI, more and more workers seek remote work options to balance their personal and professional lives. However, with this shift comes a new set of expectations from employees. They want perks like flexible schedules, opportunities for growth, and a positive work culture that fosters collaboration and innovation. It is leading in a different world.

This book will talk about how executives can regulate impulse control, as every good CEO knows that it's essential to take a step back and let the dust settle before making rash decisions. Impulse control is vital for effective leadership, as is taking advice from all sides. By doing so, leaders can create a workplace environment that not only meets the needs of their employees but also drives success for the company as a whole. This book will help you learn how to leverage your skill set, team, new and innovative technologies, and strategic plans to elevate your business.

Collaboration, cohesion, and consistency are the three keys to prosperity in business. All aspects of your business should be talking the same talk and walking the same walk on a high level. When you aim for the top, it sparks creativity and innovation. This type of high-level thinking means that your team is buzzing with smart ideas, ready to face challenges and shake things up – all things that your average CEO wouldn't do!

CHAPTER
ONE

Unleashing Your
Strengths and
Confronting Weaknesses

SELF-DISCOVERY
Unleashing Your Strengths and Confronting Weaknesses

Not Your Average CEO demands a self aware leader that is receptive to feedback, as this ensures a continuous cycle of growth and is the beacon for improvement. Such a leader recognizes that their journey is not solitary, but one that intertwines with the collective development of their team and organization. Yes, we all have our strengths and weaknesses but what makes us strong and resilient as leaders is being mindful of both. As executives, we must remember to stop and take a moment to assess what is happening around us. This includes a constant reexamination of our own personal strengths and weaknesses. Our flaws and assets both evolve, and staying on top of the changes and evolution is prudent. Making the incorrect assumption that you know everything or are always right, will be your pitfall in leadership, stunt growth and tarnish your overall legacy.

Some initial steps you can take to assess and understand your strengths and weaknesses include:

- **Goal evaluation:** Not only setting specific, measurable, achievable, relevant, and time-bound (SMART) goals, but also re-evaluating these goals. As you work toward your objectives, assess your progress and identify areas where you thrive and areas that need improvement. Keep in mind your goals are fluid.
- **Journaling:** Keep a journal to record your thoughts, feelings, and experiences. Regularly reviewing your journal can help identify patterns and recurring themes related to your strengths and weaknesses.
- **Utilizing self-assessment tools:** Instruments like StrengthsFinder, Myers-Briggs Type Indicator (MBTI), or DISC profiling can provide structured insights into your personality traits and strengths. This will allow you to understand your natural and adaptive behavioral styles, ultimately improving your communication with others.
- **Peer comparisons:** Compare your skills and attributes with those of your peers or colleagues in similar roles. This comparative analysis can reveal areas where you excel or areas of opportunity.
- **Asking those you trust for feedback:** Others may offer valuable insights that you might not see yourself. You don't know what you don't know. Don't be afraid to listen to what others have to say!

Relating to the last bullet point, remember that if you have a closed-off attitude, you are stunting growth and expansion not only of your company but the world around you. Being mindful and open to receiving feedback can be a difficult step for most executives, especially the CEO. We may not feel comfortable asking employees for specific input or being vulnerable and receptive to making changes. Some may ask, "Well, what's the big deal? Why do I need to re-evaluate my strengths and weaknesses? Things are working *okay* now, so why make changes?"

True, it can be challenging to ask for feedback from those that you supervise. Perhaps you feel they won't be comfortable being as candid and transparent with you, for fear of their job security. Make sure that they know that nothing will be "held against them." You may even want to do this in a 360 review or make the feedback anonymous. This means that respondents can provide feedback without fear of retribution, giving way to a more candid assessment. Clearly communicate the measures taken to protect anonymity – perhaps you are using a tool like SurveyMonkey that ensures participants can submit responses without revealing their identities – or you are involving a third party like an HR representative or external consultant to collect the feedback.

Executive tip: At Virtual Assist USA, we have done these types of anonymous reviews on the CEO and COO over the years. Having done this several times, we would advise that when you are reviewing feedback, concentrate on identifying recurring themes or patterns rather than trying to pinpoint specific contributors. This helps you glean insights without fixating on individual responses. And use open-ended questions. Frame questions to encourage qualitative responses rather than seeking specific details. This makes it harder to identify individuals based on their writing style or specific examples.

To be successful, you must be an expert on your own weaknesses and strengths. Recognizing and addressing weaknesses is the catalyst for improvement and growth. Effective CEOs and executives leverage this self-awareness – not only to navigate challenges but also to capitalize on opportunities. Understanding the interplay between individual strengths and weaknesses allows for strategic adaptation, personal growth, and professional development.

So how do we do it?

Being a CEO or executive means that you're likely spending a lot of time in solitude, despite a busy world around you. Pushing through the hard stuff can feel lonely and overwhelming. To thrive in this role and maintain your unique vision, it's crucial to maintain a keen awareness of your mental, physical, and emotional state. This self-awareness serves as the compass guiding you through the complexities, enabling the achievement of milestones and the continuous expansion of boundaries. Success in the CEO position demands not just strategic foresight but also a resilient and well-balanced approach that acknowledges and addresses the many different demands of leadership. Take a moment to listen and assess your current state.

CEOs and executives - the most successful ones - often exhibit a compulsive and excessive dedication to their work, occasionally to the detriment of their well-being and personal life. In contemporary terms, a "workaholic" may not only be driven by long hours at the office but can also be characterized by an incessant need to stay connected and engaged with work-related tasks, even outside traditional working hours. This behavior is often fueled by a blend of professional ambition, a demanding work culture, and the ubiquity of technology that enables constant connectivity. Modern workaholics may find it challenging to establish clear boundaries between work and personal life, leading to potential burnout and negative impacts on overall life satisfaction.

So, how can the modern workaholic maintain homeostasis?

Simple. Tell your inner workaholic to stop working at specific times.

For example, take the weekends off entirely or stop working after six in the evening. Of course, that's not always feasible and, a lot of times, can trigger more anxiety. But if you slowly interject processes and boundaries, it is possible.

You might think: "OK, a few more hours and I can get back to work. What do I have to do? Can I just make a list? *Should* I make a list? What's next?" Or you could be worried about urgent emails or missing a sales call.

Despite these racing thoughts, take breaks when you need to take breaks. Set one hard limit for taking a midday lunch. Be flexible with yourself when you need to take a day off. Work needs to be just one part of a balanced and healthy life. Training the mind to shut down and restart at the end of the day is physiologically essential to grow and care for your overall well-being.

Make a promise to yourself, and don't break it. When you are not creating a healthy balance in your work life, you're limiting yourself from not only reaching your full potential but from living a full life – you know, the one outside of work. To advance both in our personal and professional lives, we have to build trust within ourselves. Start with a single commitment and stick to it.

To be less of a workaholic, consider making the following commitments and setting corresponding goals:

1. Establish Work-Life Boundaries:

Commitment: I will define clear boundaries between work and personal life.
Goal: Set specific work hours and designate time for personal activities. Avoid checking work emails or engaging in work-related tasks during personal time. Use the "Do Not Disturb" feature on your phone. You may even go so far as to put your phone in a basket or cabinet when you are finished with work, so that it is "out of sight, out of mind."

2. Prioritize Well-Being:

Commitment: I will prioritize my physical, mental, and emotional well-being.
Goal: Set regular breaks during the workday, even if it's "just" for 5-10 minutes. During this time, engage in physical exercise, practice mindfulness, and ensure sufficient time for adequate sleep. One helpful tip is to take a 15-minute break. During this time, go outside and walk straight for 7.5 minutes. Then turn around and come back. Now you've taken a 15-minute break for yourself – and got some exercise in the process.

3. Set Realistic Goals:

Commitment: I will set achievable and realistic goals for work tasks.
Goal: Break down large projects into manageable tasks, prioritize based on importance, and avoid overloading the schedule with unrealistic expectations. And delegate! Don't worry, we will deep dive into that later on in the book.

4. Take Up Hobbies and Interests:

Commitment: I will identify some hobbies and interests outside of work.
Goal: Identify activities or hobbies that bring personal fulfillment and schedule dedicated time for them. This can include pursuing creative interests like watching a YouTube tutorial on drawing, playing pick-up sports like pickleball, joining a book club at the library, or spending quality time with loved ones.

7. Evaluate Workload:

Commitment: I will regularly assess my workload and adjust as needed.
Goal: Periodically review work commitments, deadlines, and projects. This "review of your tasks" should be one of your tasks. If the workload becomes overwhelming, consider reprioritizing tasks or seeking support to maintain a balanced workload.

Remember, the key is to create sustainable habits that contribute to a healthier work-life balance. Adjust these commitments and goals based on your unique circumstances and personal preferences.

If you continue to do the same things over and over again, you're never going to break that habit, and you are never going to advance.

Now where to begin?

It starts with a calendar.

Use a calendar to set accurate expectations and utilize proper time management. Account for your time in the day by putting something on your calendar and sticking to it. Look at your week ahead and see where you can take some time away from work that's important to you. Start a new initiative in your personal life or take some time to advance your career by taking a class, such as one on LinkedIn Learning. Use the time for your health by going to yoga, taking a walk in the woods, or playing hockey. Put it on the calendar and stick to it. Say yes to the things you want to, and say no to the things that you don't. Slowly but surely, work will no longer feel like work.

Gaining a firmer grasp of your own emotions and mental health is crucial to emotional intelligence and self-awareness. Having high emotional intelligence is an invaluable asset when you manage people and interact with others frequently in your career. Effective leaders always exhibit high emotional intelligence. They understand their own emotions, manage stress well, and can empathize with and motivate their team members.

Even though pressure is inevitable, burnout is not. It's easy to understand how prolonged stress in the workplace could lead to mental and physical wellness problems if not addressed. While this book is going to cover many areas of leadership development, this first piece is a crucial one.

Positive responses to pressure and decreased risk of burnout can be achieved by recognizing the onset of stressful emotions and taking frequent pauses to relieve pressure. We know from experience that executives are especially vulnerable to burnout. It is characterized by a sense of overwhelm, persistent fatigue, reduced efficiency, and a decline in overall job satisfaction. CEOs and executives facing burnout often find it challenging to cope with the demands of their leadership roles, and it can negatively impact their decision-making abilities, creativity, and overall well-being. This underscores the importance of adopting proactive measures and implementing effective strategies to address and alleviate the challenges associated with workplace stress.

"Burnout comes from a need to prove yourself. There's so many reasons why we want to be at a certain level in our business, that almost undermines what we are going through. So we are almost designed to be at a certain level that we're going to disregard our well-being in order to get there and that can come from wanting to prove to someone that you can be successful to maybe even wanting to prove that you're worthy or you're good enough or that you can actually do it. What happens is that because it's such a driving factor to achieve something, especially everywhere you look everything's about achieving your next level, especially in the online space. We talk about hitting your next level, stepping it up, and this constant drive to do more and more and more to get to that next level, rather than becoming very intentional with your time and your energy in order to have success."

Ashleigh Camilla, CEO, Mindset and Business Energetics Mentor

Being Self-Aware

Every day, our actions at work are heavily influenced by our thoughts and emotions. Self-aware people know what they want, understand their strengths and shortcomings, and know how to manage their presentation. This level of self-awareness is essential for success in any workplace. It allows individuals to identify areas for improvement and take steps to address them while leveraging their strengths to achieve their goals. Self-awareness also helps individuals navigate complex social dynamics at work, such as managing relationships with colleagues and superiors. By understanding their own emotions and reactions, self-aware individuals are better equipped to communicate effectively and constructively resolve conflicts. Overall, self-awareness is a key component of emotional intelligence, which as we discussed is a critical factor in professional success. By cultivating this skill, individuals become more effective leaders, collaborators, and contributors in any workplace.

People who are very self-aware even have the ability to reinterpret the circumstances they are facing in their minds so that they see things in a positive light rather than a negative one. While we may all believe we are self-aware, and have a grasp on how we feel, in our experience on average less than 20% of people are self-aware. Self-awareness development is a continuous process and the key to thriving in the workplace. People frequently misunderstand this term, because they believe it applies only to them and has no bearing on those around them.

We understand at work that we must give tasks our full attention, but we must also remember to keep self-awareness in our thoughts. Being mindful of your own actions, emotions, and productivity makes us better leaders, considerate workers, and much more. If you lack a sufficient amount of self-awareness in the job, it may be challenging for you to effectively manage your time and maintain top performance on a consistent basis. If you are able to plan ahead and organize your day in a way that makes the most of your strengths while minimizing your flaws, it will be of great assistance to you.

For instance, if you know that you are most productive first thing in the morning, organize your day in such a way as to minimize the number of meetings and other interruptions and concentrate on the things that are most important to you. You owe this to yourself – and your company, your colleagues and your future.

A self-aware person influences and helps others, particularly in the workplace. Encouraging the individual to consider how others are feeling improves their relationships. And it's something that ought to be introduced early on in someone's career. Those who are given self-awareness training are better able to evaluate their leadership abilities and foster a stronger sense of teamwork. Self-aware people evaluate their skill sets to contribute more effectively and create a collaborative workplace culture.

Self-trust is equally important as it helps you to believe in yourself and your abilities, giving you the confidence to pursue your goals with determination. Dedication and repetitiveness are also crucial as they help you to stay focused on your goals, even when faced with obstacles or setbacks. Committing yourself fully to your goals increases the likelihood of achieving them. In addition, repetition helps to reinforce positive habits and behaviors that are necessary for success. Therefore, by developing self-awareness, self-trust, dedication, repetitiveness, and commitment, you can create a strong foundation for success in all areas of your life.

It's time to think deeply about yourself.

Start by identifying the blind spots you have. To reach this level of self-awareness, you must carefully assess your situation, your feelings, and yourself to determine what's missing. Knowing your blind spots helps you identify areas for improvement and helps you set goals.

Executive Tip: One way to do this is to ask your employees to tell stories about you. Really! Encouraging employees to share stories or metaphors about their experiences within the organization and you as a leader can reveal underlying issues or perspectives that may not be apparent through traditional feedback channels.

High-performing leaders also recognize their limitations and seek support or delegate tasks accordingly. Self-aware *and* high-performing leaders are more adaptable, empathetic, and able to make better decisions based on their self-knowledge.

Self-awareness is a key player in executive structure and connectivity. When self-aware, we can reflect on ourselves as leaders, build better relationships, and foster company and team cultures. When you sharpen your self-awareness skills, you will become more empathetic due to improved emotional intelligence. Being mindful of the present moment when you are self-aware allows you to accept events as they arise rather than lingering on the past or making projections about the future.

A few unique ways to improve your self-awareness:

- **Have patience:** Although your first instinct might be to reprimand a colleague for making a mistake or vent your frustrations on your team, self-awareness will help you exhibit patience, especially during conflict. When faced with conflict, don't react - just wait. Practicing waiting during conflict allows dust and emotion to settle before reacting. This may be a tough practice, but trust us, it's worth it.

"Spin it to win it. Always try to find a way to bring the messaging back to a positive one. Take each response as an opportunity to spin your messaging into showing people who and what you are really about."

Emily Green, CEO, Grace Communications Agency

- **Pay attention to your own emotions:** To do this, you need to identify your triggers. These are things that cause you to feel anxious and stressed out or they can be positive associations. Your negative triggers can include something as simple as bad weather, rude people, or even how you feel when you wake up. But they can also be more complex, such as someone using the same language in a sentence that was used in a previous argument with a different person. This can cause you to feel a certain way and perhaps even shut down. Examples of positive triggers could be certain smells or music. Taking note of what makes you feel good about yourself and others around you is eye-opening. Regardless, acknowledging your own emotions and taking a step back to assess and process them, can have a positive twist in the outcome of an event.
- **Use communication and teamwork:** Being self-aware helps understand how your actions, words, and behaviors impact others. It allows you to communicate effectively, listen actively, and build strong relationships with colleagues, employees, clients, and stakeholders. Recognizing your biases and triggers allows you to navigate conflicts and work collaboratively towards shared goals.

- **Fine tune decision-making:** Self-awareness enables better decision-making. When you understand your values, beliefs, and emotions, you can make decisions that align with your authentic self. Make a list of the 10 values that are most important to you in your work as a CEO.
- **Demonstrate emotional intelligence:** Self-awareness is a cornerstone of emotional intelligence, which is crucial in the business environment. Understanding and managing your own emotions, as well as recognizing and empathizing with the emotions of others, allows for better interpersonal relationships, conflict resolution, and effective leadership.
- **Possess adaptability and resilience:** In a dynamic and rapidly changing business environment, self-awareness enables you to adapt to new circumstances, embrace challenges, and navigate setbacks. Understanding your own reactions to change and stress empowers you to develop coping mechanisms, build resilience, and bounce back from setbacks more effectively.
- **Reflect:** Take time to reflect on what you're doing right, and what you could be doing better. This is a great way to figure out where you need to focus more energy in order to accomplish goals.

Collaboration and self-awareness go hand in hand. Understanding both yourself and others is essential for creating a harmonious work environment. A good place to start is sometimes taking a step back and reassessing not only your feelings but those around you.

"If you put yourself in someone else's shoes... just for a minute... you'll escape your own feelings and maybe gain an understanding of their needs, emotions, and a clearer path to a positive resolution."

Emily Green, CEO, Grace Communications Agency

This is a great practice and path to reflection and coexisting for success.

Self-awareness is an ongoing journey that requires a willingness to explore your own thoughts, emotions, and behaviors to continuously grow and improve as a professional and leader. Just remember that if you want to improve in any area of your life, the first step is to be honest about where you are today and what you need to do next.

Collaborating and coexisting for success

Co-existing and having the right people in the right seats creates a necessary foundation for success within a company and the leadership team. Just as self-awareness is important for a CEO, it's important to be aware of all of those traits for your leadership team, too. When individuals are placed in roles that align with their strengths and passions, they are more likely to be engaged and motivated, leading to higher productivity and job satisfaction. We must recognize that our strengths lie in certain areas, and we should focus on those to maximize our potential.

This also means that we should surround ourselves with people who complement our strengths and can help us grow in areas where we may not be as proficient. By doing so, we create a well-rounded team that can achieve great things. Additionally, understanding our capabilities allows us to set realistic goals and expectations for ourselves, which can lead to a more fulfilling and satisfying life. Having a diverse team with varying perspectives can lead to more creative problem-solving and decision-making. Understand that it is important for leaders to not only focus on hiring the right people but also on investing in their development and providing growth opportunities. Doing so makes employees feel valued and supported, increasing loyalty and retention. Ultimately, a strong foundation of co-existing with the right people in the right seats sets the stage for long-term success both within the company and its leadership team.

Collaboration and coexistence among your executive team are crucial for creating a positive and productive work environment.

When individuals on an executive team work together effectively and harmoniously, they can achieve shared goals and drive success. When these individuals collaborate, they can leverage each other's strengths, skills, and expertise. This synergy allows teams to achieve more collectively than what individuals could accomplish on their own.

Here are some key aspects to consider for successful collaboration and coexistence in the workplace:

Respect and empathy: Treat your colleagues with respect, regardless of their role or position. Treating colleagues respectfully, irrespective of their position, is not just a matter of courtesy but a strategic investment in building a harmonious, productive, and sustainable work environment. Show empathy by understanding and considering their perspectives, needs, and emotions. Create an inclusive environment where everyone feels valued and heard. Sometimes all this takes is an extra 1-2 minutes in a conversation. Pay close attention to tone, nonverbal cues, and body language when speaking with colleagues.

Effective communication: Clear and open communication is essential for collaboration. Encourage open dialogue, active listening, and constructive feedback. Articulate expectations, share information, and encourage team members to express their ideas and concerns.

Shared goals and vision: Establish shared goals and a common vision that aligns with the organization's mission. Ensure that all team members understand and are committed to these objectives. Regularly revisit and communicate the purpose and progress of the team's work to maintain alignment.

Recognize and leverage strengths: Acknowledge and appreciate the unique strengths and skills of each team member. Encourage individuals to contribute their expertise and take ownership of their responsibilities. Create opportunities for people to utilize their strengths while also fostering growth and development in areas where they may have weaknesses.

Collaboration tools and processes: Provide the necessary tools and resources to facilitate collaboration. Utilize technology platforms for efficient communication and project management. Establish clear processes for decision-making, task allocation, and problem-solving to ensure transparency and accountability.

Conflict resolution: Conflict is inevitable in any workplace. Encourage open and respectful discussions to address conflicts when they arise. Provide a safe space for team members to express their concerns and work towards mutually agreeable solutions. Seek mediation or involve leadership when necessary.

Promote diversity and inclusion: Embrace diversity in all its forms, including differences in background, perspectives, skill sets, and experiences. Foster an inclusive culture where everyone feels welcome and valued. Encourage diverse voices and ideas, as they can lead to innovative solutions and better outcomes.

Develop teamwork and collaboration: Create opportunities for team members to collaborate and work together on projects and initiatives. Encourage cross-functional collaboration and knowledge sharing. Recognize and reward collaborative efforts and outcomes.

Continuous learning and growth: Encourage a growth mindset within the team, where individuals are open to learning and adapting. Support professional development initiatives, provide training opportunities, and encourage knowledge sharing within the team.

Lead by example: As a leader or team member, model the behaviors and values you expect from others. Demonstrate collaboration, respect, and professionalism in your interactions. Encourage a culture of collaboration and coexistence through your own actions and decisions.

By fostering a collaborative and inclusive workplace culture, organizations can harness the collective strengths of their employees, drive innovation, and achieve success in a supportive and harmonious environment.

The Road to Self-Discovery

Stepping outside the box and comfort zone is challenging without practice. Even just taking one small side step from our busy, fast-moving lane is difficult. Yet, stopping and looking around is essential to a harmonious balance in work and life. It is important to find space and time to reflect on who we truly are, what is important, what we aspire to become and our purpose in life, or your "ikigai".

Ikigai is the Japanese term that means "life purpose." Ikigai encompasses the process of establishing one's individual life purpose by considering their talents, passions, career, and how they can contribute to the greater community. Proponents of this doctrine maintain that discovering this unique and tailored sense of meaning can result in a more satisfying life and extended longevity. There are many components to the road to self-discovery and the results that follow are life altering: happiness, success, expansion, and balance.

Executive Tip: Grab a piece of paper and break it into six sections, leaving room for 3-5 bullet points underneath each.

Section one titled "I love...".
Section two, "I am good at...".
Section three, "The world needs"
Section four, "Reasons for my being"
Section five, "Income and resources"
Section six, "What brings me peace"

Fill in all the sections and take a step back. Review where all of these overlap.

This overlap is where you should focus your efforts and professional and personal fulfillment.

Many of us find it hard to understand our true purpose. Taking steps to self-discovery can help realign your world both professionally and personally.

Simply implementing one of the following into your life will build a solid foundation of personal and professional growth.

Checking Out:

"Life comes at us pretty quick. If you don't have a whitespace, a touchstone, a place where you can ground yourself, you're not paying attention. A whole month, or year can fly by. You will find yourself saying, 'Wow, how did I get here? Or was this all the progress I made?' That is where Zen for Success comes in, checking out so you can check in on your day to day life, checking in on all the roles that we have. It might be mother versus father, things of that nature."

Jeff Eschliman, CEO

Goal Setting:

Define clear, achievable goals for different aspects of your life. Working toward these goals can reveal your true desires and motivations. Regular views and repetitive focus on goals sets the tone of your daily life and business. Choosing goals and setting specific times to review the progress is imperative. These goals act as beacons, guiding your actions, decisions, and priorities.

Manifestation:

Using manifestation techniques such as vision boards or positive affirmations can help clarify your goals and desires, making them more tangible. Manifestation is the belief that what you put out into the universe is what you get back, and like attracts like. Psychological foundations for clarifying your goals and maintaining a positive belief system will align your worlds, exponentially increasing your likelihood of success.

"If the answer was strategy, everyone would be making millions, which is why it's what is going on behind the strategy, a.k.a. your inner belief system, that amplifies the success of that strategy."

Ashleigh Camila, CEO, Mindset and Business Energetics Mentor

As a business owner, receiving rejection emails, having clients decide not to move forward with you, or having consumers leave your website without completing a transaction from their shopping carts might be discouraging. However, remember that "no" only means another opportunity is waiting.

Believe that if someone doesn't want to work with you, it's because someone better is on the way or there is a specific reason why it is not meant to be, since the universe is always on your side and never against you.

If you're having trouble letting go of the outcome, try writing down one positive aspect of the fact that this chance didn't pan out. Since the law of opposites states that one cannot exist without the other, this "no" may be the best possible outcome. Doing this will also help you align with the 'right' type of customer or client for you.

Learn from the "no." By reflecting on the reasons behind the rejection, you can gain valuable insights and identify areas for improvement in your approach or product. Embrace the opportunity to grow and adapt, as each "no" brings you closer to finding the perfect fit for your business. By relinquishing the fixation on specific results, CEOs can transform their leadership into a strategic dance, where adaptability, empowerment, and innovation become the choreography. This shift not only places emphasis on strategic thinking over micromanagement, but also turns setbacks into stepping stones for organizational learning.

Meditation:

Regular meditation practice can provide a calm and focused state of mind, enabling self-reflection and introspection. It helps in understanding your thoughts and emotions. This can be a very difficult and frustrating step for the busy mind of a leader, but here is a tip to help. When the thoughts become a flood, change the flood to a flowing river that comes and passes by. Allowing the thoughts to enter and exit with every breath will begin to steady the mind and allow for meditation to be simpler to achieve.

Finding Your Focus Zone:

You know that groove when you are completely zoned into your work and blinders come on to the outside world? That is the amount of focus required to propel your strengths steps ahead. It's the sweet spot where your creativity flourishes, and your productivity soars. In this space, distractions fade away, and you harness the full power of your concentration. It's not just about finding your focus. It's about cultivating an environment that allows your genius to thrive. Embrace this focus zone as the launching pad for your most impactful and innovative endeavors.

Pro tips to get in the optimal focus zone:

- Research continuously shows that it takes between 20-25 minutes to focus once switching from one task to another.
- Take steps to minimize distractions. Find an environment that has successfully allowed for extreme focus. Replicate this or use this environment regularly for harboring and achieving long term focus.
  - The phenomenon where auditory and scent memories are linked is often referred to as "cross-modal memory" or "cross-modal association." In this context, it

describes the connection between memories of sounds and scents, where experiences from one sensory modality trigger memories or associations with another. This interconnectedness of sensory memories is a fascinating aspect of human cognition, illustrating how different sensory cues can be linked in the brain, evoking rich and interconnected memories.

"I'm at my absolute best and most productive when I'm parked by the beach, windows slightly ajar, with the water not even 10 feet from my door. I give myself between one to two hours with the predetermined projects at hand and a goal to obtain. This is where my creative side shines and my focus zone is maxed. It is a distinctive environment that repeatedly brings me into focus. The auditory memory sounds of the waves and the scent memories of the ocean helps immerse me in a state of heightened concentration. The more often it happens, the quicker I am able to bring myself into a focus zone."

Nicole Gallichio-Elz, COO

- Breaks are essential for maintaining focus. Plan short breaks between work sessions to recharge. Consider techniques like the Pomodoro Technique, which involves working in focused intervals (e.g. 25 minutes) followed by short breaks.
  - Strategically plan this around food and beverage breaks as well. Oftentimes, drinking tea or coffee will set a recharge moment. Staying consciously hydrated as well is significant.
- Identify the most important and high-priority tasks. Tackling crucial tasks first allows you to invest your peak focus and energy where it matters most, setting a positive tone for the rest of your work. You must go into the focus zone with clearly identified goals, even if it is just brainstorming on a specific topic.

New Experiences:

Remaining stagnant in one location can be draining and attribute to burnout. Traveling to new places and trying new experiences can push you out of your comfort zone and reveal hidden aspects of your personality. Experiencing new things can change your perspective and provide greater insights.

Physical Health:

Maintaining a healthy lifestyle through exercise and proper nutrition can enhance your mental and emotional well-being, making it easier to explore your inner self.

Remember, these results of self-discovery look different for everyone. It is important to define what each of them look like for you, and incorporate them into your goal setting. Ultimately, recognizing and embracing the uniqueness of your self-discovery journey and using it as a foundation for setting meaningful goals can lead to a more purposeful and fulfilling life. It's about honoring your individuality and shaping your aspirations and objectives in a way that resonates with the person you've become through your journey of self-discovery.

CHAPTER TWO

Harmonizing Excellence: Building the Ultimate Team

TEAM FOUNDATIONS
Understanding the Importance of Your Team

The average person thinks about a successful company and immediately thinks about the CEO. They tend to think about one singular person that is in the top role. When in reality, while the CEO is the conductor, the team behind the CEO makes sure the train runs smoothly.

Seamless operations start with the Chief Operating Officer (COO) and the communication between the CEO and COO. This balance creates a thriving environment. Some of these roles may be crossed and become "not your average" responsibilities but ultimately a fluid wave of communication is essential. Some obstacles could be, which role handles client or team complaints, as this may also be a cross over responsibility. Another decision could be who runs and executes certain team meetings. Let's go through how we can overcome some of these obstacles and pave the way for stability in unstable environments.

Building a strong leadership team is crucial for the success of any organization. This is well-known. The executive team is responsible for setting the vision and direction of the company, as well as making critical decisions that impact its future. Finding the right individuals to join this team can be challenging, but it is the essential ingredient to ensure that the organization can achieve its goals and growth objectives. Building a strong leadership team requires carefully considering each member's skills, experience, and personality traits— but also how they harmonize together. It is essential to identify individuals who are not only talented in their respective fields but also possess strong communication skills, strategic thinking abilities, and a passion for the company's mission. Identifying someone who can complement your strengths and improve upon your weaknesses is also important.

For those who are currently solo entrepreneurs, the next step in expanding your business should be someone who is operational in skillset. Surprisingly, you may not need to hire someone with 25 years of experience as a COO. What you do want to look for, however, is someone who is opposite in behavioral style. The operational role is ideally suited for someone who is detail-oriented, analytical, proactive, and has strong follow through. Even if you are process-oriented as a CEO, your number one responsibility on a day-to-day basis should be growth and vision. Passing along any process work, such as, but of course not limited to, tracking billable analytics, implementing team processes, smoothing out client journeys, and ensuring day to day operations are buttoned up, to someone else will free you up to execute the higher level visionary and "big picture" work. You want your COO to have the skill sets you lack or are uninterested in. Developing a yin and yang harmony is the key here, and continues to be important as you expand outward from a two person team.

Contrary to what many people think when hiring, having a complementary partner in business can be a game-changer. Going with your "gut" and someone who you "get along with" isn't always going to be the right choice, or the smartest choice. Finding someone who has a different behavioral style is what brings balance to the team. As a CEO, it's important to recognize your strengths and weaknesses and delegate tasks accordingly. It's also important to recognize that everyone has their own unique strengths and weaknesses, and as we discussed earlier, there are ways to do that. Identifying a partner who will balance out your skill set is incredibly beneficial. The CEO/COO collaboration is the compass guiding the company through. The CEO provides the visionary melody, setting the strategic direction and overarching goals. Meanwhile, the COO adds the rhythm, orchestrating the operational cadence to ensure efficiency, consistency, and seamless execution. Prioritizing this communication is crucial because it synchronizes the heartbeat of the organization. This will lead to increased productivity, better decision-making, and ultimately, more success in achieving your goals.

It is also important to ensure that you share a common vision and values with your partner. Without this alignment, working together towards a common goal will be difficult. Additionally, communication is key in any partnership - and in this role, it is important to make sure you are open and honest with each other about your expectations and needs. Take the time to set expectations and constantly revisit managing communication between each other. We all perceive situations differently and respond to them in our own unique ways. Assessing your language and approach in communication will only enhance the effectiveness of your message and contribute to better understanding and collaboration. You can achieve great things together by finding the right partner and fostering a strong working relationship. Building a strong executive team is a critical undertaking that requires a combination of time, patience, and practice. It is a process that necessitates self-awareness and a comprehensive understanding of your entire business process. By having a clear vision of your organization's goals and objectives, you can identify the specific areas where you need to strengthen your executive team and hire the right individuals to fill those roles.

Hiring Decisions

To determine the aspects of an executive team you need to hire for, it is important to have a comprehensive understanding of your entire business processes. This involves conducting a thorough assessment of your organization's current state, identifying areas of improvement, and defining the strategic direction you want to pursue. By examining each department and function within your company, you will identify the key leadership positions that will have the greatest impact on driving growth, innovation, and overall success.

During the hiring process, align the desired skills and qualifications of potential executives with your organization's strategic objectives. This requires a careful evaluation of candidates' experiences, expertise, and track records to ensure they possess the necessary qualities to contribute to achieving your business goals. Additionally, consideration of cultural fit and the ability to collaborate effectively with other team members is essential in building a cohesive and high-performing executive team.

When hiring someone to be your right-hand, here are some questions that you can ask to uncover if you'll be the right match:

1) How would you resolve conflict with your supervisor? And, conversely, how would you resolve it with those whom you supervise? What are the differences in approach?
2) How important is it for you to match communication styles with your team, and what happens if you don't?
3) How do you balance visionary needs with the need to be process-oriented?
4) What would be your top three priorities as a new COO?

Patience is a vital attribute when assembling an executive team. It is not a process that can be rushed, as finding the right individuals who align with your vision and values takes time. It is essential to conduct thorough interviews, check references, and assess candidates through various means to ensure they possess the requisite skills, experience, and cultural fit. Rushing the process can lead to hiring the wrong individuals, which can harm the team's dynamics and overall organizational performance.

Furthermore, it is an iterative process that requires practice and continuous improvement. It will likely involve making adjustments along the way, learning from past experiences, and refining your hiring and team building approach.

Overall, building a strong executive team requires time, patience, careful planning, thoughtful recruitment, effective leadership, and practice. Being self-aware and understanding your entire business processes are key to identifying the areas in which you need to strengthen your team. By carefully evaluating candidates and aligning their skills with your strategic objectives, you can assemble a high-performing executive team that drives the success of your organization. Remaining patient and continuously improving your approach to team building will contribute to long-term success and enable your executive team to thrive.

Being Kind Can Come At A Cost

Alignment in behavior, values, morals, and work ethic is crucial for both employees and leadership within an organization. Begin with fundamental principles and ensure your team can harmonize effectively. Despite common misconceptions, being kind can come at a cost—it may impact your corporate culture, team dynamics, and ultimately, financial outcomes. As leaders with external pressure, we can often just want to forgo conflict, and being kind is much easier than being the boss no one likes. This, however, can severely impact the company in a negative way and set a precedent that can be hard to break. There are numerous examples of when being kind can come at a cost, so we will move through several examples.

Misalignment Example: Envision this scenario—a team meeting is underway with the Chief Operating Officer (COO), and a team member raises a question related to a specific process. The COO responds in accordance with the established process. However, the situation takes a turn when the team member asserts, "Well, the CEO said it was okay if I just took this shortcut."

In this instance, the CEO likely intended to alleviate the workload for the employee - "being kind" - but the unintended consequences of this scenario create multiple hot spots with the potential to impact costs significantly. Beyond merely signaling a misalignment with the executive team's vision, it establishes a concerning precedent within the team that circumventing hierarchical structures is acceptable when questions arise. This, in turn, creates optics of instability and a sense of doubt within the team.

Furthermore, sidestepping established processes can have financial implications for the company. Processes exist for a reason—they provide structure, ensure efficiency, and mitigate risks. Bypassing them introduces the possibility of errors and can result in substantial costs. Thus, acknowledging and adhering to established procedures is crucial for maintaining a stable foundation and safeguarding the financial well-being of the organization. Once you bypass a policy for anyone, do you have to do it for everyone?

Mishiring Example: In the hiring process, it's tempting to rely on gut feelings and choose someone likable, the kind of person that you'd like to go have a beer with, or the person in genuine need of a job who is having money struggles. Opting for the "easy" route and prioritizing kindness in hiring can prove to be a costly mistake. Selecting the wrong individual for a position can incur expenses reaching tens of thousands of dollars. In this context, being overly kind upfront is an aspect that warrants caution. Making strategic and well-informed hiring decisions is crucial to avoiding financial setbacks and ensuring the right fit for both the individual and the organization.

Searching For Your Team

Define the team's purpose and goals: Clearly articulate the purpose and goals of the executive team. Determine each team member's specific roles and responsibilities based on the organization's strategic objectives and the skills needed to achieve them. Write them down,

29

starting with high-level key performance indicators. You can do this by taking the time to write a formal job description.

Identify key competencies and skills: Identify the core competencies and skills required for the executive team members to be successful in their roles. Consider factors such as industry knowledge, leadership abilities, strategic thinking, communication skills, and cultural fit with the organization.

Recruit top talent: Develop a comprehensive recruitment strategy to attract top talent. Leverage professional networks, industry connections, and executive search firms to identify potential candidates. Conduct thorough interviews, assess candidates' qualifications, and seek references to ensure a good fit. If you are a solo-entrepreneur, it is important to consider how you are going to hire. Will this be a contracted role? Are you prepared to start with a payroll system - and all of the compliance and regulation that goes with it? Investing money with a recruiter is something to consider as well. There are a lot of ways to recruit "for free" if you put in the time and effort. Using Linkedin and Indeed are going to be your first key steps when recruiting, as well as drafting an attractive job-ad.

Build a diverse and inclusive team: Aim to build a team that embraces diversity in terms of professional backgrounds, perspectives, and experiences. Diverse perspectives can lead to more innovative solutions and better decision-making. Create a supportive environment where all team members feel valued and can contribute their best. Building a diverse and resourceful team is crucial for driving innovation, creativity, and better decision-making.

Here are some additional strategies to develop those diverse skill sets:

Set the tone from the top: Leaders should actively champion for team members to expand on their skill sets and demonstrate their commitment through their actions. Make it clear that diversity in thought is a priority and that all team members are valued for their unique perspectives and contributions.

Create a culture: Developing your unique company culture can be tricky, especially as the company grows and new personalities are introduced. In later chapters, we will discuss building your company culture, but for now, establish a culture where everyone feels safe, respected, and encouraged to share their ideas and opinions. Create an environment that values diverse perspectives and encourages collaboration. An example of this would be creating cross-team trainings. Instead of focusing solely on the development needs of a specific team, cross-team trainings aim to bring together members from different departments or units to enhance their skills, knowledge, and collaboration abilities collectively.

Encourage open dialogue and active listening: Create an environment where open dialogue is encouraged and all team members feel comfortable sharing their perspectives and experiences. Practice active listening and ensure everyone's voice is heard and respected during team meetings and discussions. Encourage constructive feedback and learn from different viewpoints. Establish regular team meetings, both in-person and virtually, to discuss strategic initiatives, share progress updates and address challenges. Foster a culture of collaboration, where team members can leverage each other's expertise and work collectively towards shared goals.

Promote career development and mentorship: Offer career development opportunities and mentorship programs that support the growth and advancement of all team members who show interest. Be able to showcase to candidates where their career path would take them, rather than just saying "growth opportunities." Be able to show them what it means in practice.

Here are more steps to consider for achieving a culture of collaboration:

Provide leadership and mentorship: As the leader of the executive team, provide clear direction, guidance, and support. Set a positive example through your own leadership style and behaviors. Promote a culture of continuous learning and development by providing mentorship opportunities and investing in the growth of your team members.

Set clear expectations and performance metrics: Define clear expectations for each executive team member, including performance goals, targets, and metrics. Regularly review and assess individual and team performance against these expectations. Provide constructive feedback and support professional development opportunities to help team members excel.

Executive Tip: Polite constructive feedback with suggestions and specific instructions will be received in a beneficial manner.

We cannot go back and change what mistakes or errors were made but we can learn from them and move forward in an appropriate manner.

Imagine one of your top executives is presenting a project to the team and the graphs are off, there are spelling errors, and some of the data seems to be skewed. A knee jerk reaction here would be to get upset at the lack of attention to detail and the unprofessionalism in the presentation. But where would that get the company and the employee? Working through the meeting to pull together the overall message and data is the first step. After the meeting has concluded, it would then be appropriate to speak to the employee about what happened, and provide feedback as to what the clear expectations are from presentations. The last part is the support part. Schedule a 15 minute meeting before the next presentation with the employee to review the progress.

Continuously evaluate and evolve: Regularly assess the performance and dynamics of the executive team. Identify areas for improvement and take proactive steps to address any gaps or challenges. Embrace a culture of continuous improvement and adaptability as the team and organization evolve.

Evaluating and finding unique strategies customized to your organization's needs creates a continuous expansion of possibilities. This involves regular assessments of the organization at multiple levels. At our company, Virtual Assist USA, Nicole Gallicchio-Elz said, "The need to look outside the box to evaluate the remote company was non-negotiable. Typical implementations of hiring a full-time manager, would not have solved our overarching problems. Writing down the issues we needed to solve and assessing roles that needed to be filled, enabled me to develop a supervisor program that elevated employees while creating the proper hierarchy and solid foundation the team needed to be successful. This took thought, testing, adjustments, honesty, and flexibility to work. But being open to the unknown was imperative, not only for me as the COO, but for the team members as well."

Building a strong executive team takes time, effort, and a strategic approach. By following these steps and creating a culture of collaboration and excellence, you can establish a high-performing executive team that drives the organization's success. Remember that your ultimate mission should always be centered around growth and vision, even if you are process-oriented. Working with someone who complements your style can help you achieve these goals more effectively and efficiently.

Establishing How to Work with Your Team

Once you have made a decision on who your executive team is going to be, it will take hard work, consistency, and written procedures to not only maintain a healthy working executive culture, but to grow it. Let's move through steps that should be actively set in place for the harmony of the executive team to thrive.

Establish a schedule: Operating on a dedicated schedule fosters collaboration, consistency, respect, time management, and accountability. This structured framework ensures that all team members are aligned in terms of time commitments and priorities. Regularly scheduled meetings, both formal and informal, provide a platform for effective communication, updates, and collaborative decision-making. This helps to build a cohesive and well-coordinated executive team.

At minimum, the established structure should be as follows:

- Weekly Meetings
- Quarterly Goal Setting
- Quarterly Financial Review
- Annual Review
- Annual Forward Planning
- Employee Reviews

Create an agenda: Developing a well-defined agenda for meetings is essential to maximize time. efficiency, and productivity. The agenda should outline key topics to be discussed, allocate appropriate (approximation) time for each agenda item, and identify responsible parties for presentations or reports. By providing a roadmap for the meeting, the agenda ensures that discussions stay focused, time is utilized efficiently, and all necessary points are addressed. This contributes to a sense of purpose and direction within the executive team.

Pay attention to the atmosphere and culture: The vibe between the executive team can be felt throughout the company. Employees sense when things are not aligned and the culture shifts, even slightly. Emphasizing shared values and goals helps to align individual efforts with the overarching vision of the organization. Promoting a culture of recognition, where achievements are acknowledged and contributions are valued, contributes to a motivated and engaged executive team. This positive atmosphere, combined with a shared sense of purpose, forms the foundation for a thriving and harmonious executive team culture that will live through the company.

The 'what if' plan: A company's success should not depend solely on one person. It is too great a risk. To spread the risk, there should be cross training, procedures, and documentation, and the 'what if' plan. What if there is an emergency? What if there is a natural disaster? What if the payroll system fails to work? What if there is a sudden medical emergency? The list goes on. Set a time to create a 'what if' plan that has laid out steps to the next course of action in multiple scenarios.

At minimum, the 'what if' plan should include specific steps and contingency plans for:

- Payroll or bank issues
- Tech issues such as your email system being down
- Personal or family medical emergencies

- Losing a large account/client/line of business
- Security issues and breaches
- Lawsuits
- Deaths
- Long term illness
- Short term and long term leaves

Accountability, accountability, accountability: Setting expectations at the start is the most suitable time to set the stage for holding everyone accountable. That includes you. Without accountability and action items, there is no way to reflect on anything. If you are unaware of who is doing what, then how can you expect to put steps forward? During meetings, whether they are the daily, weekly, or monthly, always put quantifiable action items on the list. This does not have to be the whole list, but at least 75% of your list should be quantitative items.

Some examples of these items:

- Brainstorm on upcoming goals - this does not necessarily have to be a tangible item to be quantitative in nature!
- Look into new technology platforms and automations to improve operations and lead generation
- Return all emails within a certain time frame
- Network with at least 15 people this month– even if it is simply a message on Linkedin or joining a new group.

While the recruiting and establishment of a team looks differently to everyone, the framework remains the same. Stable footings and foundations lead to incredible opportunities for building skyscraper companies. Creating well documented procedures, an open culture, a supportive community, and consistent processes drive growth and harmonization for an executive team.

CHAPTER THREE

A New Era: Unleashing Innovation for a Future Fueled by Technology

EMBRACING TECHNOLOGY
Prepare for an Innovative Future

Technology is everywhere, but surprisingly, not all companies utilize it to its best and highest capability. What may come as a shock is that embracing technology no longer means simply getting a Facebook account or creating a website on WordPress. It dives much deeper into exploring all that technology can offer your company. From automation to AI, technology has vastly changed the face of most businesses over the last decade, but even more so over the past two years. Understanding where technology can take your company over the next five to ten years will put you ahead of the competition and into a forward-thinking mindset.

Embracing technology means being open to new ideas and innovations that can make our lives easier and more efficient. It means understanding the benefits of technology and how it can be used to improve our daily routines, whether using smart devices, or relying on mobile apps to automate processes. But embracing technology also means being aware of its potential drawbacks, such as privacy concerns and the negative impact on social interactions. It's important to strike a balance using technology to enhance our lives while being mindful of its limitations. Ultimately, embracing technology means staying informed and adaptable in a rapidly changing world where technological advancements constantly reshape how we live and work. As we navigate this digital age, embracing technology will become increasingly crucial for staying connected, productive, and informed as a CEO or executive.

Beyond the Office Walls: Unlocking Remote Productivity With Technology

By working remotely, you can develop collaboration among your team members, regardless of their physical location. This promotes cohesion and also allows for a wider pool of talent to be tapped into. With the right tools and communication channels, virtual teams can be as effective as those working in side-by-side cubicles.

Consistency with technology is also crucial in building a solid brand identity and customer loyalty. It comes into play not just in your team building, but in your marketing as well. By utilizing virtual marketing and customer engagement platforms, you can ensure that your messaging is consistent across all channels. Additionally, virtual events and webinars can expand your reach beyond geographical limitations and provide valuable opportunities for networking and lead generation. Being a Not Your Average CEO means staying ahead of the curve by embracing technology and utilizing virtual space to its fullest potential.

It's crucial to keep technology costs in check. The sheer number of platforms makes it simple for prices to rise, especially when there are annual and monthly subscription fees as well as per-user fees. As platforms continue to grow and develop further, they also begin to create new capabilities; therefore, it is essential to integrate and make use of a variety of purposeful softwares and platforms. By doing so, businesses can streamline their operations and increase efficiency. Remember, it's important to prioritize which platforms are necessary and which ones can be eliminated to avoid overspending. We will talk more about that in later chapters, as well, as it relates to revenue and profits.

Adopting Automations

Until just a few years ago, a majority of business was conducted in person and most processes were done manually. Especially post-pandemic, businesses have shifted towards digitalization and with that comes automations in virtually all facets of a company. The use of online platforms has revolutionized the way business is conducted, making it more efficient and cost-effective. The use of automation, artificial intelligence, and machine learning has further enhanced business operations by automating tasks such as customer service and data analysis.

Some common tasks that are frequently automated include:

- **Data Entry and Processing:** Automation tools are used to enter, organize, and process large volumes of data quickly and accurately.
- **Email Marketing Campaigns:** Businesses automate email campaigns to reach their audience with personalized content, track engagement, and analyze results.
- **Customer Support:** Chatbots and automated response systems are employed to handle routine customer queries, provide instant responses and free up human agents for more complex issues.
- **Appointment Scheduling:** Automation tools like Calendly and TimeTrade are used to schedule appointments, meetings, and calls based on availability, reducing manual coordination efforts.
- **Social Media Posting:** Tools automate social media posts, scheduling content across platforms and optimizing posting times.
- **Invoice and Billing Processes:** Automation is applied to generate, send, and track invoices, as well as manage billing cycles efficiently. Certain systems can be set up to create automated reminders.
- **Employee Onboarding:** The onboarding process, including document submission, orientation materials, and training modules, can be automated to ensure a smooth experience for new hires.
- **Expense Reporting:** Automation simplifies expense tracking and reporting, reducing manual effort and minimizing errors in financial records.

- **IT and System Monitoring:** Automated tools monitor network performance, system health, and security, providing real-time alerts and minimizing downtime.
- **Inventory Management:** Businesses automate inventory tracking, ordering, and restocking processes to optimize supply chain management.
- **Recruitment and Applicant Tracking:** Automation streamlines recruitment by managing job postings, screening resumes, and even conducting initial candidate assessments.
- **Content Curation:** Tools automate the process of discovering, curating, and sharing relevant content across digital platforms.
- **Lead Scoring:** Marketing automation tools help score and prioritize leads based on predefined criteria, aiding sales teams in focusing efforts on high-value prospects.
- **Performance Analytics:** Automated analytics platforms provide insights into key performance indicators (KPIs) across various business functions.
- **Workflow Automation:** Businesses use workflow automation to design, manage, and optimize end-to-end business processes, reducing manual intervention.

Start with thinking about which functions are currently within your company. Are there any areas that could benefit from further automation? Consider the potential benefits of implementing artificial intelligence and machine learning technologies. These can help streamline processes, improve accuracy, and reduce costs. Explore the possibilities of incorporating virtual or augmented reality into your business operations. This can enhance customer experiences and provide innovative solutions to common problems. It's also important to stay up-to-date with emerging technologies and industry trends. Attend conferences, read industry publications, and network with other professionals to gain valuable insights and knowledge. By adopting a forward-thinking mindset and embracing technological advancements, your company can stay competitive.

The AI Component

The potential benefits of implementing artificial intelligence (AI) and machine learning technologies are vast and varied. AI is radically altering how people interact with technology. Whether you see it as a threat or a helpful tool, its use in a wide range of fields is quickly growing. AI has become a useful tool for increasing output, upgrading quality, and optimizing performance in the field of content creation. AI technologies should not be viewed as a replacement for humans but rather as a way to improve existing workflows, current processes, and brand content. In this next section, we'll look at some practical ways to collaborate with AI to maximize the value of your day and stand out from the crowd.

AI should be seen as a complement, not a substitute. So where can AI be a complement and maximize value?

Writing and Keyword Assistance: AI can be a great "writing assistant", assisting in numerous parts of text development. Grammar and spell-checking can be provided by AI-powered technologies like Grammarly, guaranteeing that your work is error-free and flows properly. AI algorithms can also suggest alternative language, improve readability, and improve the general flow of your writing. Some advanced AI writing systems can even generate complete paragraphs or drafts based on certain prompts, providing content creators with a useful starting point. Still, it should not be seen as a replacement, as there are many aspects to writing that AI cannot replicate authentically.

Content Optimization: AI technology allows content authors to optimize their work for search engines and target specific audiences. AI technologies can provide valuable advice for optimizing titles, headers, meta descriptions, and other components that impact search engine rankings by evaluating keywords, search trends, and competitor data. AI systems can also assess user activity data and provide recommendations to boost engagement, such as shortening paragraphs or integrating visual information. Make sure to also get ideas for your content creation from sources other than AI.

Many creators find that coming up with ideas for content is a challenge. If everyone is looking at the same feeds, the same information created by AI, and the same scroll, then the experience is going to be extremely monotonous. If you are developing content, your primary objective should be to provide your audience with something fresh and original. And in order to do this, you need to get outside of your comfort zone and look for inspiration. Ask yourself, are you saying something inspiring, important, or interesting? Does your content create engagement with your audience? AI can assist with writer's block and provide overall content suggestions. It can get the ideas flowing but should only be used in tandem with your creative ideas. Be unique and find those true hooks and pain points for your audience.

Personalization and User Experience: Delivering personalized content experiences is crucial for engaging audiences. AI algorithms can analyze user data, such as browsing behavior and preferences, to create personalized recommendations and tailor content to individual users. By leveraging AI, content creators can enhance user experiences, boost customer satisfaction, and increase conversions. AI-powered chatbots can also provide real-time assistance to website visitors, addressing their queries and guiding them to relevant content.

Performance Analytics: Measuring the data of all aspects of your business is essential for refining your strategies and understanding what resonates with your audience. AI-powered analytics tools provide in-depth insights into content performance by tracking metrics such as page views, click-through rates, bounce rates, and social media engagement. By leveraging AI analytics, business owners can identify trends, optimize their content marketing strategies, and allocate resources effectively.

Automations: From workflow automations with your website and retarget marketing to inbox and calendar management, to cybersecurity and fraud detection - AI is strong in automating numerous parts of your day. Think about how you use social media in your current role. AI can be utilized for social media retargeting by helping to create custom audiences on social media platforms through website interactions analysis and targeting users with specific ad content. It can help with lookalike audiences too, as AI identifies users similar to those in the retargeting pool, expanding the reach of retargeting campaigns.

You may have heard how AI will disrupt healthcare with the use of AI-powered robots to assist with surgeries and machine learning to make medical diagnoses. Certainly, you've heard of how self-driving cars will transform the transportation industry.

But what about smaller companies? Is AI industry-agnostic?

Small business owners can benefit from automation unprecedentedly with recent AI platforms. Integrating AI and other platforms can allow the lead journey and onboarding to be completely automated. Your AI arsenal can now include automated emails, retarget marketing, call-to-action buttons, customization of engagement, and more. AI has allowed for the development of presentations to be automated within minutes, ad copy to be written instantaneously, videos to be customized and AI generated, all while making the small business owners workflow more fluid and efficient.

Overall, there are countless areas and industries that could benefit from further automation through the use of artificial intelligence and machine learning technologies.

Voice Revolution: AI Voice Assistants

AI voice assistants have emerged, fundamentally altering the ways in which people interact with technologies. Voice assistants that can understand and follow verbal orders are becoming increasingly integrated into our daily lives. However, as their sway grows, a vital discussion has gained steam, which centers on the ethical and privacy concerns of the broad adoption of AI voice assistant technology.

The evolution of artificial intelligence voice assistants like Amazon's Alexa, Apple's Siri and Google's Assistant has taken them well beyond their original function as simple tools. These digital companions promise ease and productivity by understanding spoken language and responding appropriately in different settings. But along with their tremendous potential has come a flood of ethical and privacy concerns, undoubtedly requiring further investigation and caution when using these technologies.

Did you know AI could do this to maximize your work day?

- **Find Bids for RFPs:** AI can scour databases, websites, and relevant platforms to identify potential bids that match the Request for Proposals (RFPs) criteria. This automates and expedites the process of discovering opportunities for businesses.
- **Content Creation:** AI-powered language models can generate content for various purposes, including websites, presentations, scripts, logos, email topics, blogs, and videos. Users can provide a text prompt, and the AI will produce coherent and contextually relevant content.
- **Task Automation Upon Form Submission:** Integration with websites allows AI to perform a chain of tasks automatically when a form is filled out. This could include data entry, sending emails, updating databases, and other routine tasks, which streamlines workflow processes.
- **Personalized Newsletters:** AI analyzes user preferences and behavior to customize newsletters, ensuring each individual receives content tailored to their interests. This enhances engagement and provides a more personalized experience.
- **Automated Article Completion:** AI can assist in finishing articles by generating suggestive text based on the existing content. This can be particularly useful for content creators facing writer's block or needing inspiration.
- **Calendar Integration with Video Links:** Connecting AI with your calendar enables the automatic insertion of relevant video links based on scheduled events. This ensures seamless access to resources and information during appointments or meetings.
- **Keyword Recommendations and Ad Optimization:** AI algorithms can analyze data to generate recommended keywords and optimize advertising campaigns. This helps businesses target the right audience and improve the effectiveness of their ads.
- **Inbox Management:** AI can assist in organizing emails by taking items out of the inbox and returning them when requested. This feature aids in task management and serves as a virtual reminder system.
- **Excel Operations:** AI can perform complex operations in Excel, such as creating formulas, reformatting data, and cleaning datasets. This accelerates data processing tasks and enhances efficiency in spreadsheet-related work.
- **Text-Based Creativity:** AI-powered text-based tools can be utilized to create diverse content, including movies, music, games, simulations, and more. This opens up creative possibilities for content creators and developers.

AI automations have the potential to revolutionize the modern workday by streamlining processes, reducing manual tasks and improving productivity. Use it to your advantage and proceed with caution. Because if you find the correct formula, your productivity will skyrocket.

Exploring the Synergy Between Human Virtual Assistants and AI

Let's go a bit more in-depth with these tasks and be a bit more specific. With the introduction of AI, certain tasks can be executed by your human Virtual Assistant with a click of a button.

Of course, trusting the AI output without human review is extremely risky. But AI does make your Virtual Assistant's tasks more efficient and effective— in fact, with the aid of AI your VA can now execute a diverse range of tasks within 30 minutes.

Please keep in mind that time may vary depending on the current state of your processes and access to AI tools.

1. **Rapid Email Triage:** Your VA can leverage AI-powered email management platforms like Google Workspace or Microsoft Outlook, which employ smart algorithms to categorize and prioritize emails based on urgency, sender history, and content. Depending on the inflow of your email, your VA can use these AI email management tools to conduct the human aspect of your email triage within 30 minutes a day. If your VA is also responding to emails, creating templates in your voice for the easy and efficiency of responding will also cut down time.
2. **Efficient Calendar Management:** AI-driven calendar tools such as Calendly or Doodle analyze your schedule, preferences, and relevant data to schedule meetings and appointments swiftly. These platforms consider availability, time zones, and preferences to optimize your calendar efficiently. One of our favorite AI programs, Motion, can ensure you are getting the most out of your time. Your VA can help you organize your tasks, appointments, and projects by importance and put the information into the program that will then create a time-blocked schedule that shows you exactly when to complete each task and for how long in order to meet all of your deadlines and goals. When combining calendar tools and scheduling checks, this on average will take your VA 30 minutes a day!
3. **Speedy Data Entry and Organization:** Tools like Zapier or Integromat, integrated with your VA, can automate data entry tasks, ensuring accuracy and organization within a short timeframe. For example, an automation can log leads into a CRM. Connecting an automation with the oversight of your VA can be as quick as 30 minutes twice a week to ensure all is working properly and no missing fields are left blank.

4. **Quick Language Translation:** Google Translate API or Microsoft Translator API can be integrated with your VA to provide rapid and accurate language translations, overcoming language barriers in a matter of minutes.

5. **Research Support:** AI-powered research tools like IBM Watson or Google Scholar assist your VA in navigating through vast information databases, extracting key insights and summarizing research findings within 30 minutes. There are also AI tools like Rows, that can help sort and conduct research of data.

6. **Social Media Updates:** Social media management tools such as Hootsuite or Buffer, integrated with AI algorithms, can schedule, analyze, and suggest social media content efficiently, maintaining your online presence without consuming excessive time. Along with AI writing tools, your VA can create SEOed content that will reach your target audience in a matter of seconds. They will adjust the content as needed so it fits your company's tone and voice, then schedule and post, all under 30 minutes.

7. **Prompt Expense Tracking:** Apps like Expensify or Zoho Expense, integrated with your VA, can categorize and generate expense reports rapidly, facilitating quick decision-making based on financial insights.

8. **Effortless Meeting Transcriptions:** AI transcription services like Otter.ai or Rev can be employed by your VA to swiftly convert spoken words into written text, providing accessible records and with a human eye, checking for formatting and tech errors. It can be accomplished usually within 30 minutes, depending on the length of the meeting. These tools are great for creating transcripts for podcasts, YouTube videos, and even social media-posted videos as well. There are also AI integrations that will automatically add captions to your videos without you typing them in. Meaning, your VA can create a YouTube video with full captions in seconds.

9. **Instant Customer Support Responses:** AI-driven chatbots from platforms like Intercom or Chatbot.com, integrated with your VA, can address routine customer queries promptly, ensuring swift responses and enhanced customer service. These options are also available on some social media platforms. So your VA can set up automatic responses to customers that DM you, to help improve your social media interactions with no extra effort.

10. **Automated Task Execution:** Workflow automation platforms like Zapier or Microsoft Power Automate can be integrated into VAs to automate repetitive tasks, such as file organization and data backups, ensuring seamless operations within 30 minutes.

11. **Rapid Document Summarization:** Tools like Summarly or SMMRY use AI algorithms to analyze and summarize documents quickly, providing key insights in a concise format within the allocated time.

12. **Efficient Workflow Optimization:** Process optimization platforms like Kissflow or Trello, coupled with AI analytics, can assess and optimize workflows, identifying areas for improvement and implementing changes swiftly for enhanced efficiency.

13. **Professional Video Editing:** AI tools like Pictory and VideoBolt have made it so even those without video editing experience can create high-quality videos. With these tools

your VA you can create eye-catching videos with custom brands from your webinars, recordings, or even text on the topic you want to share. All in a half an hour.

By integrating AI-driven tools and platforms into Virtual Assistants, these digital aides can tackle a variety of tasks within 30 minutes, making them indispensable for time-sensitive responsibilities. The examples provided offer a glimpse into the vast ecosystem of AI-powered tools that can enhance your Virtual Assistant's capabilities, making it a time-saving ally in both personal and professional spheres. Remember, these are suggestions and independent assessment of the tasks at hand is important. Your VA can help with analyzing which tools will be most beneficial to your business and effective for your individual needs.

Why You Should Embrace (and Not Retreat From) the Tech Change

Technology has improved quicker than most businesses expected and is projected to continue to evolve at an exponential rate. Recognizing and harnessing these changes can offer numerous benefits crucial for sustained success and growth. But there is a scary component to it. There seems to be a fear factor concerning what happens if we don't evolve with technology on some scale. Will your business still succeed? Will your competition get there faster? In a highly competitive market, how can you be sure?

But staying technologically relevant is vital for meeting customer expectations. In an era where consumers are increasingly tech-savvy, businesses need to adapt to emerging trends to deliver seamless and enhanced customer experiences. Technologies such as artificial intelligence, data analytics, and digital communication platforms enable businesses to understand and cater to customer needs more effectively, thereby building stronger relationships and fostering customer loyalty. Customers can simply be turned off if you do not have a well-functioning and user-friendly website. They make decisions within seconds to use your service or turn to a competitor.

Embracing technology is synonymous with maintaining a competitive edge. Businesses that leverage innovative technologies gain an advantage by differentiating themselves from competitors, offering novel products or services, and responding more swiftly to market changes. In industries where disruption is common, being adaptive to tech changes is not just an advantage but a necessity for survival. Not only for the customer, but technology can provide valuable insights through data analytics, enabling informed decision-making. Business intelligence tools allow executives to make strategic decisions based on real-time data, market trends, and customer behavior. This data-driven approach enhances decision-making precision, reduces risks, and increases the likelihood of successful outcomes.

Adapting to technology is crucial for future-proofing businesses. All industries will continue to witness ongoing technological advancements. Business owners and executives who proactively embrace change position their organizations to navigate future disruptions, ensuring long-term sustainability and relevance. Again, approach with caution and do not use every software tool in the book. Pick and choose strategically for those that economically make sense for your business.

Business owners and executives must adapt and embrace technological change that rests on the pillars of efficiency, customer satisfaction, competitiveness, data-driven decision-making, and future-proofing. By incorporating and leveraging the latest technologies with your team and customers in mind, businesses will survive in the dynamic market and thrive, positioning themselves as industry leaders poised for sustained success.

CHAPTER FOUR

Marketing Metamorphosis: AI-Powered Strategies Today

MARKETING TRIUMPHS
Strategies Designed for Today and the Future

Today's marketing strategies are more data-driven than ever before, owing much of their success to a blend of innovative technologies, traditional techniques, and a profound understanding of human psychology. This chapter embarks on a journey through the multifaceted world of contemporary marketing, exploring the pivotal factors that shape and drive success in this digital age.

We will delve into the remarkable impact of Artificial Intelligence (AI) on marketing strategies, where machines and algorithms are not only streamlining operations but also enhancing the customer experience. We'll examine the transformative role of email marketing, a channel that has stood the test of time by adapting to changing consumer preferences and behaviors.

Throughout this chapter, we'll emphasize the importance of a brand in today's marketing landscape, delving into the value of a consistent and compelling brand identity that resonates with the target audience. Networking, both online and offline, will be explored as a critical element in expanding reach and forging valuable connections in a competitive market.

No discussion of modern marketing would be complete without a deep dive into the power of social media, its impact on brand perception, and the art of crafting successful campaigns that resonate with audiences. We will also explore the world of digital advertising, dissecting the role of ads in an age where attention is a valuable commodity, and optimizing for a higher ROI is the name of the game.

Lastly, we'll unravel the mysteries of Search Engine Optimization (SEO) and its continued importance in the digital realm. As search engines evolve, mastering SEO remains central to achieving visibility and, ultimately, business success.

So, fasten your seatbelts as we embark on a journey through the intricate web of contemporary marketing, where technology, creativity, and strategy converge to redefine the way businesses connect with their audience and thrive in a rapidly changing world.

"You can't buy a community, so how do we win the trust of our customers? Especially now when people aren't spending the same as they used to and you have to remember that there's always going to be another product or service out there that's competing up against you. It is important to understand that, and you can't throw money at things to fix things all the time. Organic

marketing and building community is super important. And it is a slow build so do not get discouraged."

Erica Rankin, CEO

Your Brand

Your brand acts as the most direct pathway to generating revenue. Within 30 seconds of engagement, the initial interaction sets the immediate tone and strikes a decision for the user to move forward or move on. Whether it is a visitor who lands on your website's front page, a prospect who scrolls past your social media, or someone you meet at an event, these are the pivotal moments where you must effectively convey essential pieces of information: your business's core function (mission), its ability to address the audience's needs (pain points), and what sets it apart from competitors (why you).

These fundamental components are what potential customers and prospects seek to understand to feel driven toward taking the next vital step in making a purchase. In branding and messaging, the notion of conversations that convert leads to clients, revolves around the strategic arrangement of these three vital elements. Presenting them in a specific order can be remarkably effective.

The first element is a concise tagline articulating your business's primary function and purpose. The key here is clear. It must be immediately recognizable to what your business is. It must convey your mission.

The second component is a compelling value proposition statement that emphasizes how your products or services provide solutions to your audience's most pressing needs and concerns—their pain points.

Finally, the third element encompasses differentiator statements. Differentiator statements are concise expressions that highlight the unique qualities, features, or advantages that set a product, service, or business apart from competitors. These statements aim to communicate a distinctive value proposition and create a memorable impression on customers. They often focus on the specific strengths, innovations, or characteristics that make a brand or offering stand out in the market. Differentiator statements play a crucial role in marketing and branding strategies, helping businesses differentiate themselves and attract target audiences based on what makes them special or superior. These statements convey what distinguishes your business and what makes it superior to competitors. This answers the question asked by many prospects or potential customers: "Why should I go with you?"

When these points are delivered in a deliberate sequence, they align with the psychology of potential buyers. The result is consistently captivating and guiding prospects toward the pivotal conversion point. This strategic messaging approach captures and maintains your audience's attention, propelling them to delve deeper into your offerings and ultimately make a purchase decision.

Understanding Brand Beyond the Logo: *"Initially, I had a misconception that branding was just about the logo, especially coming from a graphic design background. However, I've learned that branding, whether personal or for business, is much more. It's about understanding and articulating what we stand for and what we oppose. These core values are the foundation of effective branding, and everything else, including the logo, stems from these fundamental principles."*

Aligning Brand Values with Messaging and Design: *"Effective branding aligns your core values with both messaging and visual elements. This alignment ensures that every piece of communication, whether it's a website, flier, or brochure, resonates with your audience. Similarly, visual elements like fonts, colors, and graphics should reflect these values, creating a cohesive and impactful brand identity."*

The Concept of Brand Equity: *"Brand equity might sound complex, but it's essentially about the value your brand holds. It's developed gradually, influencing how your brand is perceived in the market and by your community. This perception is shaped by every interaction with your brand, from the logo to events and conferences."*

Target Audience and Brand Positioning: *"To effectively position your brand, start by asking two critical questions: What do you stand for, and what are you against? This clarity helps in identifying your target audience. Remember, trying to appeal to everyone means you resonate with no one. Focus on those who align with your values and will benefit from collaborating with your brand."*

Ari Krzyzek, CEO and Head of Strategy

Identifying and Engaging Your Audience

Do you really know your audience?

Do you know how they respond to your emails, social media posts, website call-to-actions, and other engagement touch points? What emotions are invoked? How long is it taking them to "convert"? How many touch points are necessary? And how many are wasted?

What subject lines capture their attention the most? What types of social media posts are they more likely to engage with? What gets you the best results?

You can begin to answer and analyze these questions by:

1. Identifying your email open rates
2. Reviewing what website pages they utilize the most
3. Analyzing your social media post engagement
4. Customer journey - what call to action buttons are the most appealing and where?
5. Conducting a dive into your clients pain points and what else that is attributed to
6. Collecting data from all sources and evaluating it as a whole

Now, this is only the tip of the iceberg when it comes to identifying your audience and predicting their behavior. Regular research and feedback from your audience will improve your knowledge, retention, and customer satisfaction.

"If you can educate or entertain your target audience, they'll always come back for more."

Adam Kirk, CEO, Oostas Marketing

Email Audience Analysis

Understanding your audience on a deeper level is fundamental to the success of your email marketing campaigns. You can employ various tactics, listed below, to gain valuable insights into who your audience is and how to engage them effectively.

Demographic Analysis

Start by collecting basic demographic data such as age, gender, location, and occupation. This information provides a foundational understanding of your audience's characteristics, enabling you to create content that resonates with their unique backgrounds.

When it comes to demographics, what separates an average versus a Not Your Average CEO is the true understanding of your audience that goes beneath the surface. Not only understanding their pain points in relation to your service, but understanding your audience's interests and hobbies, shopping habits, the products they are interested in buying, their purchase history, and most importantly, where they consume content.

Behavioral Tracking

Utilize available analytics tools to monitor how your audience interacts with your emails. Track which links they click, their time on your content, and which emails they open. This data can help you tailor your messages to align with their interests and behaviors. You are missing opportunities if you are not paying close attention to this data.

Surveys and Feedback

Periodically, you may send out surveys or feedback requests to your subscribers. Ask about their preferences, pain points, and what kind of content they'd like to see. This direct feedback can be invaluable in refining your email content and strategy. But, tread carefully with this. Avoid "survey fatigue" by following best practices. As it relates to time, for a B2B audience, consider sending surveys quarterly, while for B2C, tailor the survey frequency to reflect customer interaction frequency, multiplying it by two for an optimal approach. In terms of content, limit the number of open text fields and only ask one question at a time.

A/B Testing

Experiment with different email subject lines, content formats, and calls to action. A/B testing allows you to gauge which variations resonate most with your audience, ultimately optimizing your campaigns for better results. Beyond tweaking visuals or text, explore variables like color schemes, fonts, or even the placement of elements. Subtle changes in these aspects can sometimes lead to unexpected improvements. Recognize the impact of seasonality on user behavior. Preferences and engagement patterns can vary during different times of the year. Conducting A/B tests that account for seasonality can provide more accurate and actionable results.

Segmentation

In the quest to be a Not Your Average CEO, divide your email list into smaller, more targeted segments based on shared characteristics. You can enhance relevance and engagement by sending tailored content to each group. Beyond the typical behavioral segmentation factors like purchasing history, consider factors like brand interactions, product usage frequency, or response to promotions. This can provide more granular insights into customer behavior. Psychographic segmentation involves understanding customers' values, attitudes, and lifestyles. Consider factors such as personality traits, interests, and hobbies to create more personalized and resonant marketing messages. Tailor marketing strategies based on occasions and events. Understand how consumer needs and behaviors change during holidays, seasons, or specific life events, and adjust your segmentation accordingly.

Personalization

Leverage personalization techniques to address subscribers by name and recommend products or content based on their previous interactions. Personalized emails perform better in terms of open rates and conversions.

Monitoring Social Media

Monitor your audience's social media activity and engagement. This can offer valuable insights into their interests and trending topics, helping you align your email content with current conversations.

By actively employing these tactics, you can comprehensively understand your audience. This knowledge will empower you to craft emails that are clear, concise, highly relevant, and appealing to your subscribers. Remember, as Adam Kirk wisely suggests, educating and entertaining your target audience can be a powerful driver of customer loyalty. When you consistently deliver value and resonate with their needs and interests, they'll be more inclined to keep returning for more.

Email Alchemy

Email marketing comes in many sizes There are different formats of emailing, campaigns, messaging, automation, and promotional materials. Finding out what type of emailing works for which aspects of your business is vital in developing a method that connects you and your target market in the proper way. Email has become overused, and spam filters are becoming more advanced. Therefore emailing with a clear purpose is a necessity.

For every aspect of your business, you should have a process down for the next step, and email marketing is no different.

Knowing the right way to email is key. Develop a strategy as to when you will send an email and why. There are many different platforms and ways to capture email marketing. Getting started from scratch can often be easier than trying to repurpose. Your brain may get stuck with the old and not encounter the new.

Why are you sending this email?

Think about the purpose of this email. Know the origin and the end goal. This should be a strategy and not done on a whim. Ensure they signed up to be on your email list if it is a mass email. Ensure your email is well-structured with a clear introduction, body, and conclusion. Use bullet points or numbered lists to break up long paragraphs and make the content more digestible. Another key factor to consider is the tone of your email. Depending on the audience and purpose of your email, you should adopt a formal or informal tone. Be mindful of cultural differences and avoid using language that may be offensive or inappropriate. Finally, always proofread your emails before sending them out. Check for spelling and grammar errors, as well as any formatting issues. Make sure all links are working properly and that any attachments are included. By considering these factors when crafting your emails, you can ensure that they effectively communicate your message to your audience and achieve your desired outcomes.

What is your automation path?

When someone enters their email on your website or sends you their email and it goes into your CRM, there should be a trigger automation that sends an email after. One that you do not have to send.

Here is an example of automation as it relates to email marketing:

User Action: A visitor to your website enters their email address in a sign-up form or contacts you via email, expressing interest in your products, services, or content. You set up an automation trigger within your CRM. This trigger is configured to activate whenever a new email address is added to the system, either through a form submission on your website or direct communication.

Automated Email Content: You design an email template that serves as the automated response. This email can include a welcome message, a thank-you note, or additional information about your products/services. It's crafted in a way that aligns with your marketing goals.

Personalization: To make the automated email more engaging, consider personalizing it based on the user's input. Use their name, refer to the specific page they visited on your website, or tailor the content to match their expressed interests.

Timely Delivery: The automated email is sent promptly after the user's email is added to your CRM. This ensures a timely and relevant response, increasing the chances of capturing the user's attention while their interest is still fresh.

Monitoring and Optimization: Regularly monitor the performance of your automated emails. Track open rates, click-through rates, and conversion rates. Use this data to optimize and refine your automated email sequences for better engagement and effectiveness.

Automated email triggers like this not only save you time but also help in establishing immediate and personalized communication with your audience, enhancing the overall user experience and potentially converting leads into customers.

Have purposeful and meaningful content

Invite your audience to something, give a promotion, write a personalized email, send a newsletter, or follow up from an interaction.

Know when to email

Be exact and timely. Know your audience and optimal times to send emails. Most importantly, analyze and use data to evaluate and improve on your performance. Timing your emails strategically helps you stand out in the recipient's inbox. Avoid sending emails during peak times when the competition for attention is high. Instead, aim for times when your message is more likely to be noticed. But again, this relates to knowing your audience and when the optimal time is for them to be focused on their emails.

Make sure your emails are mobile-friendly

Ensuring that your emails are mobile-friendly is crucial, as a significant portion of email opens occurs on mobile devices. Use a responsive email design that adapts to different screen sizes. This ensures that your email looks good and functions well on various devices, including smartphones and tablets. Consider a single column layout for your emails. This simplifies the design and makes it easier for users to scroll through the content on smaller screens. Use a font size that is easy to read on smaller screens. Aim for a minimum font size of 14 for body text and ensure that headlines are larger for emphasis. Ensure that your call-to-action buttons are easily tappable and are not too small. Use a size that allows users to click without accidentally tapping neighboring elements. If you include phone numbers or addresses in your email, make sure they are clickable for easy dialing or mapping on mobile devices.

By following these practices, you can create emails that provide a positive experience for mobile users, increasing the likelihood of engagement and conversions. Regularly testing and optimizing your email templates for mobile responsiveness will contribute to the overall success of your email marketing campaigns.

Paid Ads - Is It the Way To Go?

Using ads rather than organic reach is surprisingly controversial. You either find value in using ads or you feel like you are driving down the street, winding down your window and tossing out a few wads of cash. Where do you start using ads or how can you audit the ones you currently have running?

The first step is to start with a clear understanding of your goals and target audience. Once you have this in mind, you can begin to audit your current ads to see if they effectively reach your intended audience. This may involve analyzing metrics such as click-through and conversion rates, as well as looking at your ads' overall design and messaging. From there, you can make informed decisions about how to optimize your ad campaigns moving forward. Whether you are just starting out with ads or looking to improve your existing campaigns, taking a strategic approach can help ensure that you get the most out of your advertising budget.

What can you do to be above average in this area? Implement dynamic ad content that automatically adjusts based on user interactions or preferences. This keeps your ads fresh and tailored to individual user experiences. Incorporate storytelling into your ad campaigns. Create narratives that resonate with your audience, making your brand more memorable and forging a deeper connection with potential customers. Experiment with interactive ad formats such as polls, quizzes, or interactive videos. Engaging users actively can boost interaction rates and create a more immersive experience.

Paid ads are always a topic for business owners.

"Companies don't have a lot of money sometimes when they start their businesses, and I think we're also led to believe that it can't work, and that you can't scale it. I think there's a big misconception around it. But time and time again, especially now with the tools that we have available to us like Instagram and LinkedIn, and social media is so powerful, even organically, when you're not putting tons of money into it. So I think it's very undervalued by a lot of companies or founders, they don't really see that it's a channel that they can grow on their own personally, using their personal brand. So I would say that's one of the reasons why I think having paid advertising is really great - I can definitely help but it shouldn't be like the whole cake. But I think organic should be the cake, and then the sprinkles and icing can be paid marketing. I think a lot of companies have it backwards."

Erica Rankin, CEO

Those who heavily rely on Pay-Per-Click (PPC) advertising should be particularly concerned about recent developments in the digital marketing landscape. The core consideration in organic search has always been reach and how effectively your content can be found by potential customers. PPC, on the other hand, is all about obsessively optimizing for return on investment (ROI). In the PPC world, ROI is intrinsically tied to being present when today's shoppers are actively looking for products or services. The catch is that you pay for the click, not necessarily the conversion itself. Even if your website's traffic decreases as a result of successful SEO efforts, your business can still thrive. What you lose is reach – reach that doesn't come with daily maintenance fees attached. A substantial part of this reach is derived from informational content that may not immediately convert but serves the crucial purpose of raising brand visibility.

In terms of revenue, not much is likely to change due to SEO-focused efforts alone. However, if Google decides to alter the appearance of online advertisements, you could expect a seismic shift in the volume of new business you receive. The rationale here is straightforward: PPC advertising primarily serves to display links to customers ready to make a purchase. They click, convert, and generate ROI. With Google's modification of search results layouts, your opportunities for clicks may dwindle, and you may need to invest more to access those opportunities. Google's revenue isn't likely to suffer significantly as they won't stop the competitive bidding process.

For those heavily reliant on PPC, there's a high likelihood of facing either substantial price hikes or negative impacts on business performance. However, for SEO specialists, there's no immediate cause for concern. Organic search results are not poised to disappear anytime soon. Organic search will continue to connect with as many users as possible. The real challenge lies ahead for businesses that have placed most of their marketing eggs in the PPC basket, as their income may experience a significant downturn in the wake of these developments.

Beyond Keywords: Crafting a Comprehensive SEO Strategy

Traditional SEO tactics are not enough anymore. We've all seen it - the countless tips and tricks for 'mastering' search engine optimization. But guess what? The game is changing. Thanks to AI-driven algorithms and user behavior patterns, the old-school SEO approach just won't cut it. Traditional SEO tactics, while still important, may not be sufficient on their own,

Here are some reasons why traditional SEO tactics may fall short and why businesses need to adapt their strategies:

1) **Changing search engine algorithms:** Search engines, particularly Google, regularly update their algorithms to provide more relevant and valuable search results to users. These updates can impact traditional SEO tactics and require businesses to stay informed and adapt their strategies accordingly. Factors such as user experience, mobile-friendliness, site speed, and content quality are now critical considerations in SEO.

2) **Increased competition:** As more businesses recognize the value of SEO, the competition for organic rankings has intensified. It's no longer enough to focus solely on optimizing on-page elements and building backlinks. To stand out, businesses need to invest in

comprehensive SEO strategies that encompass content marketing, user experience optimization, social media integration, and more.

3) **Evolving user behavior:** User behavior and search patterns are constantly changing. With the rise of mobile devices, voice search, and AI-powered assistants, users are seeking more personalized and conversational search experiences. Businesses need to adapt their SEO strategies to cater to these evolving user preferences and incorporate tactics such as optimizing for voice search and featured snippets.

4) **Multi-channel optimization:** Traditional SEO tactics often focus on optimizing for search engine results pages (SERPs). However, consumers now engage with brands across various channels, including social media platforms, video-sharing sites, and e-commerce marketplaces. Businesses need to adopt a holistic approach to SEO that encompasses optimization for multiple channels and platforms to maximize their online visibility.

5) **User intent and content relevance:** Search engines are increasingly prioritizing user intent and content relevance. Simply optimizing for keywords may not be enough to rank well. Businesses need to create high-quality, informative, and relevant content that satisfies user search intent and provides value. Understanding the target audience and delivering tailored content experiences is crucial for SEO success.

6) **Integration of other digital marketing disciplines:** SEO is no longer a standalone strategy. It needs to be integrated with other digital marketing disciplines such as content marketing, social media marketing, and online PR. Collaboration and synergy between these disciplines can enhance overall online visibility and improve SEO performance.

To address these challenges, businesses should embrace a modern and comprehensive approach to SEO that encompasses technical optimization, content marketing, user experience optimization, multi-channel optimization, and current industry trends. It's important to continually monitor and adapt strategies to align with search engine updates and evolving user behaviors. By embracing a holistic approach and staying ahead of the curve, businesses can maximize their chances of success in the competitive digital landscape.

The three key takeaways are:

1. Keywords alone don't ensure success. Know your audience and their questions to create value-based content. For example, a blog post on 'Top 10 SEO Tips' may not resonate with businesses looking for specific solutions. Follow the E-A-T (Expertise, Authoritativeness, Trustworthiness) method: demonstrate expertise in your field through authoritative and trustworthy content and build credibility by showcasing author bios, credentials, and industry affiliations.

2. Highly specific, less competitive phrases have higher conversion rates. Think outside the box and use long-tail keywords. For instance, instead of 'Digital Marketing Agency,' use 'Affordable Content Marketing Services for Small Businesses.' Use tools like Google Keyword Planner, SEMrush, or Ahrefs for keyword research.

3. Google loves diversified content! Mix and match infographics, articles, videos, and podcasts. For example, create a video tutorial on SEO techniques and turn it into a podcast episode for easy consumption. When you use video content, optimize it by providing detailed descriptions, relevant tags, and transcripts. Video content can enhance user engagement and time spent on your site.

When was the last time you had a check-up?

Regularly audit your website for technical SEO issues, such as broken links, crawl errors, and duplicate content. You can easily delegate this to a Virtual Assistant and ask that they bring you a report of any errors, duplicate content, or other items that need updating. This is a good time also to optimize meta titles, descriptions, and headers. There are now numerous tools and platforms you can use to analyze and optimize your SEO. This should be all encompassing and be a collection and a human interpretation of the data. For example, it should include information from your website, Google analytics, SEMrush, AI, and more.

Understanding Algorithms and Why They Are the Backbone

Algorithms are the unseen architects that shape our online experiences. Algorithms can make or break your social media marketing goals. These intricate systems wield immense power and determine which posts, videos, and updates appear on our feeds. As users, we might take these algorithms for granted. We need to fully comprehend the sophisticated mechanisms behind the content we see before we scroll through our favorite platforms. In this section, we dive into social media algorithms, shedding light on their significance, and unraveling the mystery behind their functionality.

Social media algorithms are the backbone of platforms like Facebook, Instagram, X, TikTok, and LinkedIn. These algorithms are designed to enhance user experiences by showcasing content that is most relevant, engaging, and valuable to each individual user. While each platform has its own unique algorithm, there are common principles that govern their operation.

1) **User engagement:** At the heart of social media algorithms lies user engagement. Platforms strive to display content that users are most likely to interact with, such as liking, sharing, commenting, or saving. Frequent updates help retain your existing

followers. A lack of fresh content may lead to a decline in interest, and followers may disengage or unfollow your profiles.

2) **Personalization:** Social media algorithms are tailored to each user's preferences, interests, and online behavior. The more a user engages with specific content or users, the more similar content they are likely to see.

3) **Timeliness:** Freshness matters! Algorithms prioritize recent content to keep users updated with the latest trends and news. By updating your content regularly, you increase the likelihood of your posts appearing in the feeds of your followers. This can (and will) enhance visibility and reach a larger audience.

4) **Network Effects:** Interactions between users are also taken into account. Viral or highly discussed content can receive a significant boost in visibility, fostering a network effect.

Battling the Echo Chamber: Diversifying Content Exposure

As algorithms aim to offer personalized content, they inadvertently create echo chambers, limiting exposure to diverse perspectives and ideas. This phenomenon can lead to polarization and reinforce pre-existing beliefs. Social media platforms are aware of this challenge and have taken steps to address it.

1. **Exploring New Interests:** Platforms encourage users to explore content outside their usual preferences by promoting a diverse range of posts. The concept of exploring new interests promotes serendipitous content discovery. Users are encouraged to encounter posts that may fall outside their habitual content consumption, leading to unexpected and enjoyable discoveries.

2. **Mixing Content Formats:** Algorithms may vary the type of content shown, such as images, videos, and articles, to keep users engaged and informed. Leverage platform-specific features to diversify content. For example, Instagram offers features like Reels, IGTV, and Stories for different types of video content. Facebook supports various multimedia formats, and Twitter has options for text, images, and short videos.

3. **Encouraging User Interaction:** Engaging with content from different viewpoints signals the algorithm to diversify content in the user's feed.

Content Creators' Dilemma: Navigating the Algorithmic Landscape

By focusing on these aspects and continually refining your approach, you can elevate yourself beyond the average and establish a lasting and impactful presence in the world of content creation. Here are essential strategies to navigate the algorithmic landscape:

1. **Consistency and Quality:** Regularly posting high-quality content that aligns with the interests of your target audience can increase engagement and visibility. Consistency is key. While it is a difficult task, it is a must.
2. **Authenticity:** Authenticity resonates with users. Authenticity encourages user-generated content. When your audience sees your brand as authentic, they are more likely to share their experiences and create content related to your products or services. This user-generated content can be a powerful marketing asset.
3. **Engage and Respond:** Responding to comments and engaging with your audience signals the algorithm that your content is valuable.

Social media algorithms are the invisible forces shaping our social media experiences. While their complexity might seem daunting, understanding the underlying principles can empower content creators and users alike. Embracing authenticity, valuing engagement, and diversifying content consumption are key to thriving in the algorithmic landscape. As social media continues to evolve, knowledge of these algorithms will be an invaluable tool in navigating the ever-changing digital landscape. Keeping a close eye on how AI and algorithms begin to meld together will be crucial to the success of your content. Continued understanding and adjustments to your strategy will lead to high achieving results for your social media marketing.

Have you ever come across the term Organic Search Optimization (OSO)?

It's high time we move beyond our fixation on Google and start dominating the entire search ecosystem. Why limit ourselves to a single platform when there's a vast universe of new possibilities waiting to be explored? Expanding our reach, reaching a broader audience, and becoming more effective marketers are all within our grasp.

SEO is in a constant state of evolution, and search platforms are no exception. Bing, DuckDuckGo, Apple Search, Google, and others are all changing the game's rules. Holding on to old habits won't cut it anymore—it's time to adapt to multiple search channels and elevate our skill sets. By doing so, we can uncover untapped opportunities, master crucial strategies, and optimize our content for all search engines. Embracing this change will result in exponential growth in our website traffic.

Education is a cornerstone of success in this dynamic landscape. Staying updated with the latest trends, statistics, and best practices is essential. OSO is the future of search, and those who embrace it will be the ones who define it. Learn to connect business metrics with organic search efforts, transforming your actions into measurable results that create real value for your clients, and your own business.

Diversifying your approach is key. Platforms like Google, TikTok, YouTube, Facebook, LinkedIn, and Pinterest are all essential. Limiting yourself to a single platform is no longer an option. To stay ahead of the curve and conquer new frontiers, expand your keyword research, monitor multiple platforms, and adjust your content strategy accordingly.

Furthermore, OSO is not just about keywords and links anymore. It's about embracing new technologies such as AI-powered tools, voice search, and wearable tech. These innovations can significantly bolster your OSO efforts and set you apart from the competition.

Remember, organic search is an ever-evolving landscape. To thrive in this environment, you must commit to continuous learning, adaptability, and pushing the boundaries of what's possible. Make OSO an integral part of your growth strategy, and you'll witness unparalleled success.

Separating Average from Not Your Average

"One of the most overlooked factors that the brightest minds talk about affirm dedication to reading books and industry articles. This is so underrated but so essential that it separates the good from the best."

Jeff Lizik, CEO, Redshift DM

Going from average to above average does not typically happen overnight. It is something that builds from experience, research, and ability. It also involves the willingness to make change and be flexible. One of these key aspects is the digital space, and in particular, digital marketing. Here are some reasons why digital marketing is most important to the CEOs who are elevating to Not Your Average status:

1) **Wide reach:** Digital marketing provides access to a global audience, enabling businesses to reach a large number of potential customers across geographical boundaries. With the growing number of internet users worldwide, businesses can expand their reach and tap into new markets more easily.

2) **Cost-effective:** Compared to traditional marketing methods, digital marketing is often more cost-effective, especially for small and medium-sized businesses with limited budgets. Online advertising, social media marketing, and email marketing campaigns can be tailored to fit various budget levels while still delivering measurable results.

3) **Measurable results:** One of the significant advantages of digital marketing is its ability to provide measurable and trackable results. With analytics tools and platforms, businesses can gather data on website traffic, conversions, engagement, and other key performance indicators. This data allows for insights and informed decision-making to optimize marketing strategies for better results.

4) **Personalization and customization:** Digital marketing enables businesses to personalize marketing messages and content based on customer preferences and behavior. This personalized approach enhances customer experience, builds customer loyalty, and increases the chance of conversions.

"Color psychology plays a crucial role in branding. The colors you choose must align with your brand values and resonate with your target audience. For instance, red can signify passion or danger, depending on the context. Every aspect of your brand's visual identity, including color choices, needs to be intentional and reflective of your brand's core values."

Ari Krzyzek, CEO & Head of Strategy, on "The Importance of Color Psychology and Intentionality"

5) **Interactivity and engagement:** Digital marketing offers various channels and formats that facilitate two-way communication and engagement with customers. Social media platforms, blogs, forums, and live chats allow businesses to interact with customers, address inquiries, provide support, and build relationships, fostering brand loyalty and customer satisfaction.

6) **Flexibility and agility:** Digital marketing allows for quick adjustments and modifications to campaigns in response to market trends, customer feedback, or changes in business goals. This flexibility enables businesses to stay agile and adapt their marketing strategies in real-time to maximize effectiveness and capitalize on opportunities.

7) **Integration with other channels:** Digital marketing can seamlessly integrate with other marketing channels and tactics. For example, offline advertising campaigns can be complemented with online elements, such as QR codes or social media promotions, to drive online engagement and conversions.

The main takeaway is that digital marketing plays a crucial role in running a business by offering a wide reach, targeting specific audiences, being cost-effective, providing measurable results, enabling personalization and customization, facilitating engagement, offering flexibility, and integrating with other marketing channels. Embracing digital marketing strategies can significantly enhance a business's visibility, growth, and overall success in today's digital-driven marketplace.

When mapping out your digital marketing strategy, keep the following key factors in mind:

1. **The importance of being consistent:** Make sure that the content you offer on a regular basis is of a high quality. Use consistent messaging and branding across all of your channels. Consistency in your content, your timing, and execution will solidify your audience engagement and fulfillment. Consistent keywords throughout your descriptions, hashtags, meta tags, titles, and other elements will enhance the algorithms' ability to understand your content, improving its visibility and relevance to your target audience.

"Start brainstorming content and find your niche. Start adding value and tap into being consistent and authentic."

Erica Rankin, CEO

2. **Tailor your method:** Understand where your audience is viewing the most content, and what that content is.
3. **Engage, engage, engage:** Quickly responding to people's comments and messages is important. Aim to always continue the dialogue. You may want to delegate this to a Virtual Assistant to ensure that it gets done quickly.
4. **Take masterful cues:** Have a specific goal in mind by finding the right people to look up to. It is not just one resource that makes a Not Your Average CEO, it is a conjunction. Networking and collaboration should not be underestimated.
5. **Invest in high-quality content creation to attract and engage your audience:** This can include blog posts, videos, podcasts, social media posts, and more.
6. **Finally, track your progress and adjust your strategy as needed:** Use analytics tools to measure the success of your marketing efforts and make data-driven decisions about where to focus your resources moving forward. With these tips in mind, you can create a comprehensive marketing plan that helps you.

AI Strategies in Digital Marketing

"AI will change marketing, but not replace it. Generative AI will push us all to be even more in tune with our customers and what they need. You need to embrace it. As a starting point, as a way to speed up the process, as a tool to do tasks that are repetitive. But never forget to infuse it with what you are best at. Being human. When a company truly understands its customer and offers value to them, that's when marketing magic happens."

Xand Griffin, Marketing Leader and Speaker

One of the key ways AI assists with marketing is through the use of chatbots and conversational AI. These technologies enable businesses to engage with customers in real-time, answer queries, and even complete transactions, all while providing a personalized experience. Chatbots can be deployed on various platforms, including websites, social media, and messaging apps, allowing businesses to reach customers where they are most active. Moreover, AI-driven chatbots can analyze customer interactions and collect valuable data that can inform marketing strategies, such as identifying common pain points, frequently asked questions, and customer preferences.

AI also plays a pivotal role in personalization, tailoring marketing content and recommendations to individual consumers. By analyzing user behavior and preferences, AI-powered recommendation engines can suggest products or content that are highly relevant to each user, increasing the likelihood of conversion. This personalization extends beyond e-commerce and is also utilized in email marketing, where AI can help craft customized email campaigns, subject lines, and delivery times based on recipient behavior and engagement history.

Furthermore, AI-driven predictive analytics can assist in segmenting and targeting the right audience. Platforms such as Google Ads and Facebook Ads employ machine learning algorithms to identify potential customers who are more likely to engage with your advertisements. These platforms also allow you to optimize your ad spend by automatically adjusting bidding strategies and placements to maximize ROI. In essence, AI can help marketers make data-driven decisions that improve campaign performance and reduce wasteful spending.

In the age of content marketing, AI can also play a significant role. AI-generated content, from product descriptions to blog posts, can help scale content production and maintain consistency, while human writers focus on more creative and strategic aspects. Additionally, AI can help identify trends and topics that are gaining traction on various platforms, providing insights for content creation and curation.

AI's ability to analyze and make sense of data from different platforms, be it social media, website traffic, or customer databases, is invaluable for marketers. AI-driven analytics tools can uncover patterns, trends, and customer behavior, helping marketers refine their strategies and make informed decisions. In summary, AI is a versatile and indispensable tool for modern marketing, offering the potential to automate tasks, optimize campaigns, and deliver a more personalized and effective customer experience.

Understanding AI-Generated Output

AI systems are built to learn from vast amounts of data and adapt their algorithms to produce outputs without explicit human intervention. These outputs may include creative works, such as art, music, and literature, as well as functional outputs like automated reports, code, and design solutions. As AI becomes more capable of producing innovative and valuable content, the question of ownership becomes crucial in determining the rights and responsibilities of those involved in the AI's development and deployment.

So what are the current legal issues that circle this output?

Current Legal Framework

The issue of IP ownership in AI-generated output is multifaceted and varies depending on the legal jurisdiction. In many countries, existing IP laws primarily recognize humans as creators and owners of intellectual property. Consequently, AI-generated works may not be eligible for copyright protection because they lack a human author.

For example, in the United States, the Copyright Act requires "human authorship" for a work to be eligible for copyright protection. Since AI lacks a human author, the AI-generated output would not be granted traditional copyright protection. Similar challenges exist in other jurisdictions with similar legal frameworks.

Terms and Services of these platforms play a role as well. Many of us sign up for software without reading the fine print. Some of the platforms state that the output is the intellectual property of the company and not the customer.

Content Creation and AI - AI as an Autonomous Creator

Artificial Intelligence is all over the business space at the moment, and content is being pumped out in massive amounts. You may not have given thought to who owns this content output, and have just been excited that you have a tool at your hand to create thousands of words in a click of a button.

But this raises questions. Who owns the intellectual property of the output and what are the terms of service agreements for these rapidly growing platforms? Yes, AI has revolutionized industries and transformed the way we interact with technology but to what extent should we be worried? With these advances, there are significant questions about the ownership of the intellectual property (IP) rights associated with AI-generated outputs. In this chapter, we dive into the complexities surrounding AI and the contentious issue of who rightfully owns the products of these intelligent systems.

On the opposite end of the spectrum, some argue that AI systems, as autonomous entities, should be recognized as legal persons with their own rights, including the right to own intellectual property. This perspective acknowledges AI's ability to generate original and creative works independently, without the need for human intervention.

In this scenario, AI-generated outputs could be treated akin to works created by humans, granting the AI system the legal ownership of its creations. The responsibility to protect and enforce these rights would then fall upon the entity or organization that operates and maintains the AI. Ensuring that you read all terms of service agreements is crucial to protecting yourself and your business.

One school of thought argues that AI should be seen as a tool or a tool extension, just like a computer or a paintbrush. In this context, the user who operates the AI system would be considered the actual creator and owner of the output. This viewpoint aligns with existing IP laws, where the user or operator takes on the role of the traditional creator. For instance, if an artist uses AI software to assist in creating a painting, the artist would be recognized as the owner of the artwork.

However, this approach may not be universally accepted, especially in cases where AI systems demonstrate a high degree of autonomy, generating outputs without direct human input or manipulation.

Given the complexities and diverse opinions surrounding AI ownership, some experts propose hybrid solutions or industry standards that can balance the interests of different stakeholders. These approaches may involve granting limited rights to AI systems while still acknowledging the role of human users as co-creators.

For instance, licensing agreements could be established, allowing AI systems to own the IP rights for their creations while granting users a non-exclusive, royalty-free license to use and commercialize the outputs. This approach could incentivize innovation while ensuring that human users can still benefit from AI technology. As AI continues to advance, the debate over the ownership of AI-generated output will persist. There are no clear regulations at this time, which always makes things dangerous. Proceeding with caution seems to be the overall consensus when it comes to AI and should definitely be the standard for what is considered your intellectual property. Balancing the interests of AI systems, their operators and human users is a complex challenge. Striking the right balance between recognizing AI's creative potential and upholding traditional notions of intellectual property will be crucial for fostering innovation and ensuring fairness in the AI-driven world. It is inevitable that the legal landscape will likely continue to evolve, navigating the intricate web of AI and intellectual property rights.

Overall, this chapter has illuminated the multifaceted world of modern marketing, where traditional principles merge seamlessly with cutting-edge technologies to create a dynamic and ever-evolving landscape.

We've delved into the pivotal role of Search Engine Optimization (SEO), the cornerstone of online visibility. By understanding the algorithms governing search engines and tailoring content accordingly, businesses can ensure that their voices are heard amidst the digital noise.

AI has emerged as a central figure in the marketing narrative, transforming the way businesses interact with their audiences. AI's ability to process data, automate tasks, and offer personalization has redefined the customer experience. It empowers businesses to make data-driven decisions, optimize campaigns, and engage with customers in more meaningful ways, ultimately fostering brand loyalty.

Digital marketing, encompassing a broad spectrum of channels and strategies, has provided businesses with unparalleled opportunities for reaching and engaging their target audience. From social media to paid advertising, the digital landscape is where brands can build their presence and convey their messages effectively. AI-driven analytics and advertising platforms have taken digital marketing to new heights, delivering measurable results, and enhancing ROI.

Email marketing, a timeless method, remains as potent as ever when approached with sophistication. With the aid of AI, marketers can craft personalized and relevant campaigns, ensuring that their emails land in inboxes, engage readers, and prompt action. Networking, both in the real world and the digital sphere, proves to be an invaluable asset for expanding one's reach, building partnerships, and fostering collaborations that drive growth.

"There's this belief that a marketing plan has to be complicated. The truth: if you do one thing well, you will be more successful than if you do ten things poorly. How do you know if you are doing your one thing well? Consistency and results. Make marketing an intentional part of how you are doing business everyday and make sure to look at your metrics. When you do this, you get valuable information on what to do next."

Xand Griffin, Marketing Leader and Speaker

Success lies in the synergy of these various elements. SEO guides your brand's visibility, AI optimizes your strategies, digital marketing broadens your horizons, email marketing connects intimately with your audience, and networking opens doors to opportunities. In this rapidly changing landscape, adaptability, and innovation are the keys to staying ahead. As marketing continues to evolve, those who harness the power of these tools and techniques will find themselves best equipped to navigate the dynamic waters of the marketing world, forging lasting connections with customers, and driving their businesses to new heights.

CHAPTER
FIVE

Mastering Time:
Gain Back Control of
Your Day

TAKE BACK YOUR TIME
Time Never Stops, Make it Work in Your Favor

Do you want your time back? Sure you do! Who doesn't?

Time never stops, and as CEOs and executives, it can feel like time is running fast both in our professional and personal lives. If you have even the slightest ability to take back a nugget of time, shouldn't you?

Imagine what you could do with just one hour a day back of your time. That turns into seven hours a week, 365 hours a year, and it equates to just over 15 days a year. Now what could you do with an extra two weeks a year?

There is a lot of information out there, circling daily along with the constant need to check off to-do lists and complete as much as we can in one day. One crucial piece when talking about time, especially in an executive role, is the average amount of information a person absorbs throughout the day. In recent years, the average amount of scrolling on their phone that one person does is about five hours per day. *But in reality, what are you actually absorbing? What are you engaging with? What do you see or hear that is bettering your life within that time frame?* Imagine what you can do to achieve your goals if you stop scrolling or completing monotonous tasks all day long and put that energy back into something important. Imagine if it was organized, calculated, and processed with a purpose. You would not only gain time back, but you would also stop the pointless and mindless activities. There is a time and place for technology, automations, AI, social media, and streaming, but it needs to be balanced and harmonized with your life and work style.

Differentiator of Time

Later in this chapter, we will go through steps that you can take overall as an executive to put action into play and begin moving pieces around to gain back time in your day. Earlier in the book, we spoke about self-awareness and the perspective of time. But right now we are going to talk about how to think of time itself and how to differentiate how we spend our time throughout the day.

A revolutionary part as a business owner is knowing what is essential that you need to handle versus what can be handed to someone else. One piece of this puzzle is knowing the difference between urgent and important.

"Important moves your business forward. Urgent is about getting things done. Urgent makes you feel good because you believe that you are getting stuff done. This thought process holds us back because we're always focusing on the urgency of getting stuff done, not on the important things that grow our organization. Since we are stuck in this urgency trap, it ends up slowly killing our business because all we focus on is getting stuff done. When you are focused on the urgent, you're not focusing on the important things like bringing in new business or on the right structure to support that. How do you get out of the Urgency Trap? At the start of each quarter, pick three to five things that are important that you need to work on to move your business forward. Work on those three to five important things over the next 90 days by making action steps that you can do each week to get these three to five things accomplished. If you keep doing this process, you will find that you are not focused on the urgent, you are focusing on the important things which will make you more successful in your business. Constantly working in urgency doesn't allow for us to focus on the growth of the organization. Urgency is short-term thinking. Importance is long-term thinking. When we are just working on all of the urgent needs of our companies, we aren't focused on the long-term important items that will make our company more successful. Think of it this way... you're building a house and you want to have a party at that house. What do you want to focus on... having a good foundation, electrical system, and plumbing, or are you focused on making sure you have good looking furniture and lighting? The challenge is if you are only focused on the furniture and lighting and not the foundation, the electricity and plumbing, you may have a great house but it will be falling down around you, you won't have water, and your electricity will be spotty. That's the difference between urgency and importance. Urgency in businesses tends to be well, what came up today? What do we need to solve today? What do we need to solve at the moment? All of these things make us feel good because we accomplished something but it doesn't help the long-term health and success of our company. The fact is that a lot of things that come up that are urgent. We think, Oh my God, if we don't get this done, something terrible is gonna happen to us. The reality is that organizations that work on the important things, which take time and are not necessarily fun, not always rewarding, as opposed to check, check, check, check, check, are the ones that tend to be way more successful than the ones that are running on urgent. The question you need to ask yourself, as a business owner, am I focused on the urgent or the important? The next question is: am I spending enough time focusing on the important things to make your business more successful? The answer to those two questions is what will make your business more successful or not."

Dr. Jean Oursler, CEO & Speaker, The Results Queen, Ph.D

Applying this philosophy of differentiating time allows us to make strategic decisions about the tasks at hand. Some tasks may not be practical to address immediately and can be slated for reassessment in the future, whether in three months, six months, or even earmarked for a future opportunity. It also empowers us to recognize which tasks should be delegated, whether they pertain to routine administrative duties or specialized functions like bookkeeping and sales. The urgency to tackle everything all at once can lead to burnout and, ultimately, hinder rather than propel personal and business agendas forward.

You can implement several practical practices to enact these valuable insights and regain control of your daily schedule as a business executive.

Here are some actionable steps to help you determine where your time is going:

1) **Learning to Say "No":** Recognize that saying "no" to certain tasks or commitments is essential to protect your time and focus on what truly matters. Before you agree to an activity, ask yourself "Does this align with my strategic objectives? How will this move me, my company, or my team forward?" There are ways to professionally and politely say "no" and take your own accountability of your time into your hands. In the long run, this is better than making excuses or pushing people off.

   For example, you can say: *"I appreciate the invitation to the meeting. However, I have prior commitments during that time and won't be able to attend. Thank you for understanding, and I hope the meeting goes well."* or *"I'm grateful for the collaboration proposal. Considering my current focus on other projects, I won't be able to commit to this at the moment. I value the opportunity and hope we can explore collaboration in the future."*

2) **Quarterly Priority Setting:** At the start of each quarter, identify key priorities that are critical for moving your business forward. These should be long-term, strategically significant objectives that require sustained attention. This should be automatically set on your calendar.

3) **Weekly Action Planning:** Break down those quarterly priorities into weekly action steps. This translates your long-term goals into manageable tasks that you can tackle incrementally. Setting specific, achievable weekly objectives keeps you on track and ensures steady progress. Remind yourself who needs to be a part of your weekly action plan.

4) **Effective Time Management:** Employ time management techniques, such as the Eisenhower Matrix with its distinct four quadrants, to categorize tasks as urgent, important, neither, or both. Prioritize important, non-urgent tasks, as these have the most substantial long-term impact. Allocate your time accordingly.

5) **Content Calendar Review:** Evaluate your calendar or planner to identify where your time is currently being allocated and where it could be better spent. Identify any inefficiencies or areas where your expertise is not needed, or where you are spending too much time that could be an easy email or be streamlined. Consider reallocating time from lower-impact activities to higher-impact ones to maximize the effectiveness of your day.

Executive Tip: Conduct a deep dive into where your **energy** is being spent.

- Are you using your time wisely?
- Where are you wasting time?
  - Is it in meetings? Could that meeting have been an email?
  - Is it scrolling on your phone?
  - Is it watching TV? Or doing other mindless activities?
  - Doing monotonous tasks that could be delegated to someone else on your team or your Virtual Assistant?

These questions are really important to maximizing your efficiency as a CEO or executive. *Making sure you have enough time to think at a high level and expand is imperative.*

Think about how much it costs you to conduct the tasks you are doing. How much could you be profiting from someone else handling them?

Delegate and Outsource: Recognize that not every task requires your personal, undivided attention. Delegate lower-level administrative tasks to capable team members or consider outsourcing specific functions, such as bookkeeping or sales. This frees up your time to focus on high-impact, strategic activities.

Strategic Planning: Reserve time for strategic planning and reflection. Regularly evaluate your progress on important long-term objectives and adjust your strategies as needed. This helps maintain a clear focus on the bigger picture. Make sure these are written down and exist in a living document. Google Sheets or Google Docs are perfect in this scenario as they can be shared across a leadership board.

Time Blocking: Implement time-blocking strategies to allocate specific time slots for various tasks. Designate time for meetings, email correspondence, deep work, and personal activities. Consistency in these routines enhances efficiency.

Executive Tip: Use your calendar in time blocking segments. Color-coordinate that calendar into categories that work for you. For example, red are meetings that cannot be moved. Gray are tasks to complete. Blue are personal time blocks. Use this daily to understand where your time is being allocated. Move tasks when need be. This should be a living calendar and flexible process. It is important to remain flexible but accountable here. Place your goals on there and reminders when goal limits are nearing.

Technology and Tools: Utilize productivity tools and technology to streamline tasks and automate routine processes. This can include project management software, email filters, and virtual assistants to enhance efficiency.

Remember not to overcrowd and overspend here. It is important to hone in on what is necessary. Use this appropriately to gain back your time in areas that can be outsourced to technology and automation tools.

Continuous Learning: Invest time in continuous learning to stay updated on industry trends and acquire new skills. While this may seem like a non-urgent task, it's crucial for long-term growth and adaptability.

Executive Tip: Choose several times a year to do continuous learning. Schedule learning opportunities into your weekly routine. This could be simply spending ten minutes a week reading a few articles, or it could be as detailed as attending industry conferences and classes four times a year.

Personal Well-Being: Prioritize self-care and well-being. Regular exercise, a healthy diet, and sufficient rest contribute to your overall effectiveness and ability to focus on important tasks. While you're thinking of your own personal well-being, think about building a support system, too. Cultivate a network of friends, mentors, or fellow CEOs who can provide support and advice. Sharing experiences with others in similar roles can be both reassuring and insightful.

Use your calendar to your advantage here. Set reminders and time blocks to add in your personal well-being tasks and time. Stick to it! It can be very quick and simple to skim over this. Make the time, it is just as important. If you are not healthy, your team is not healthy. Burnout is a very quick way to lose your time.

These practices can be instrumental in helping business executives reclaim their time, shift their focus from urgent to important matters, and ultimately drive their organizations to greater success. By balancing the demands of the present with a keen eye on the future, you'll find yourself in a better position to meet both short-term and long-term objectives.

Taking Your Time Back With Project Management

It's only recently become a part of the vernacular. It's easy to see why: project management is a way for organizations to streamline their workflow and ensure every employee is working on projects that are important to the company's success. This essentially flows into how your company operates. Its processes, data, and resources are managed and utilized effectively. Companies can streamline their operations and increase productivity by utilizing project management techniques. This can lead to greater profitability and a more efficient use of resources. Additionally, project management allows for better communication between team members, reducing the risk of misunderstandings or miscommunications. By breaking down tasks into smaller pieces, executives can ensure that each team member clearly understands their responsibilities and can work more efficiently towards achieving the project's goals. Ultimately, effective project management can help businesses stay competitive in today's fast-paced marketplace by enabling them to adapt quickly to changing circumstances and deliver high-quality products and services on time and within budget.

Executives use project management to keep their businesses on track and make sure they're getting the most out of their resources. The ability to prioritize and organize tasks, manage multiple projects at once, and ensure that all parties involved in a project know what needs to be done and when, is essential for any executive who wants to keep their company running smoothly. Project management helps executives monitor the progress of their team members' work, identify problems before they escalate into a full-blown crisis, and ensure that projects are completed on time (or ahead of schedule!). This also allows executives to delegate tasks more effectively by breaking them down into smaller chunks, ultimately giving executives more time in their day to focus on other areas of concern within the company.

Take Your Time Back With Operations

Second to none, operations must run seamlessly to gain back your time. Procedures, processes, and systems are the backbone of any successful business. To ensure that operations run like a well-oiled machine, it's imperative to document and optimize your workflows. Start by mapping out your business processes from start to finish. This not only provides clarity on how tasks are completed but also reveals potential bottlenecks and areas for improvement.

Once you have a clear process map, focus on standardizing and simplifying procedures wherever possible. Remove unnecessary steps, reduce paperwork, and automate routine tasks. By doing so, you not only save time but also minimize the risk of errors that can result from manual processes.

Implementing efficient systems, such as inventory management software or project management tools, can further enhance the smooth operation of your business.

Regularly review and update your procedures to ensure they remain efficient and aligned with your business goals. Involve your team in this process, as they often have valuable insights and suggestions for improvements. Continuous refinement of your operations ensures that you're always optimizing for time and efficiency.

Moreover, don't underestimate the power of metrics and key performance indicators (KPIs) in gauging the effectiveness of your operations. Track relevant data points to monitor the performance of your processes and systems. This data-driven approach allows you to identify areas that require attention and make informed decisions to further streamline your operations. By keeping a vigilant eye on your KPIs, you can proactively address issues and continuously enhance your operational efficiency.

The pursuit of regaining time in your business necessitates a comprehensive approach to operations. Documenting, standardizing, and optimizing your procedures and processes, along with the strategic use of technology, will undoubtedly lead to smoother operations and more reclaimed hours in your day. Regular reviews and data-driven insights ensure that your operations remain finely tuned, enabling you to focus on the strategic growth and success of your business. Ultimately, seamless operations are the linchpin to unlocking the potential of time in your entrepreneurial journey.

Don't Shy Away From Your Data

In order to gain back time, you need to know exactly where your money and energy is being spent. In the modern world of business, data mining has become an important tool for making sense of all the information that is available. Similar to how the average person spends a lot of time every day looking through the internet, businesses often find themselves buried in a flood of data. Data mining is a way to find your way through this confusing digital landscape. It gives companies the ability to find useful information in the seemingly endless sea of data. Instead of idly taking in information, data mining lets people get involved, make better decisions, and push businesses to greater heights.

"Give your data a seat at the table, and it will help you grow your profitability. As a CEO, it's important to do this, as data should be part of every conversation and every decision, and it should be considered just as important as any other input. Don't think of data as something scary and daunting. Start with one simple thing and let your mind guide you to the next steps. The more visual your data is, the easier it is to understand and the more impactful it is. Data is not

just for big corporations with huge teams and budgets. It can be leveraged by small businesses too, and it can make a huge impact on their profitability and growth."

Jack Tompkins, Owner and Founder, Pineapple Consulting Firm

It is often hard for executives to start working with their data instead of on their data. Excel, spreadsheets, formulas - they all can be triggering for those who do not like math or feel they do not thrive in this area. Implementing a process and using technology can make this venture to data review less painful.

Think about the untapped potential in your business data that is just ready to be used in a methodical way. Data mining is a skillful way to find patterns, trends, and hidden connections in a business's operational data. It changes raw data into information that can be used to make good decisions. In the field of supply chain management, for example, data mining can be used to find bottlenecks, improve inventory levels, and speed up logistical processes. In this case, it means that hours that were previously wasted on aimless scrolling have been turned into a methodical, organized system that increases output and makes the best use of resources.

Also, data mining shows a powerful way to make customer relations more personal. In the same way that people look for material that makes their lives better within the limits of their daily screen time, businesses can give their customers tailored experiences. By digging deep into customer data, you can figure out what they like and how they tend to act. This, in turn, makes it easier to give people offerings that are perfectly timed and exactly what they need. A smart method like this not only makes customers happier but it also makes them more engaged and loyal. In essence, data mining changes the shape of business operations into a well-tuned tool, with data serving as the compass that points the way to growth, efficiency, and success. All the while, it makes sure that technology and each business's unique way of doing things work well together.

Your Time Is Important

In the world of entrepreneurship, where demands are constant and opportunities abound, being cautious with time is paramount. Business owners must recognize that their time is a finite and precious resource that should be invested strategically to align with their overarching goals. First and foremost, a clear focus on larger goals necessitates the ability to discern between tasks and opportunities that contribute directly to these objectives and those that do not.

You are worthy of being in control of your time. Adapting practices that make your day the most efficient and productive towards your professional and personal goals.

Business owners often find themselves inundated with requests, collaborations, and commitments. Learning to decline opportunities that do not align with overarching goals allows for the preservation of personal time and well-being. It also prevents burnout and fosters a sustainable work-life balance, which is essential for long-term success.

Learn to Say No

As business owners and executives, we have an inherent need to say 'yes' to everything as we feel that the more we take on, the bigger our business and goals will become. But saying no enables business owners to maintain a level of control over their schedules. Without proper time management and the ability to decline non-essential commitments, entrepreneurs risk becoming reactive rather than proactive in their approach. By being selective about the opportunities they pursue, owners can proactively shape their businesses and respond strategically to challenges and changes in the market.

This concept is difficult to grasp or adapt to in your daily work. You may find having your goals written in front of you all day helpful. When considering what to take on your plate, look and see if it will allow you to reach your goals.

- Does this make sense for me?
- Does it make sense for my team?
- Does this align with our mission and vision?
- Is it a 'no' altogether?
- Can I send this to someone else, such as an affiliate partner?

An Example of a 'Yes' That Should Be a 'No'

Imagine a small graphic design agency that specializes in creating branding materials for various businesses. The agency has a set of core services, including logo design, business card creation, and marketing collateral development. A client, who has been a regular customer for basic design services, approaches the agency with a request to build a complex e-commerce website.

In this scenario, the client strongly desires to have the agency handle the entire development of the e-commerce site, including product listings, payment gateways, and order fulfillment. The business owner, eager to maintain a positive relationship with the client and increase revenue, might be tempted to say yes without thoroughly assessing the situation or consulting with the team.

However, upon closer examination, the business owner should recognize that building an e-commerce website falls outside the agency's core competencies. It requires specialized skills in web development, security, and e-commerce platforms that the graphic design team might not possess. Taking on this project could lead to subpar results, potential delays, and a strain on resources that could be better allocated to the agency's primary strengths. It could lead to a loss in revenue, a loss of team members, a dip in profits, etc.

In this case, saying yes to the client's request may result in the agency overextending itself and risking the quality of its deliverables. Instead, the business owner should diplomatically communicate the agency's expertise and limitations, recommending that the client seek a specialized web development service for the e-commerce project. This approach ensures that the agency focuses on its core competencies, delivers high-quality work, and avoids potential pitfalls associated with taking on projects outside its expertise. There could have been a possible referral or affiliate partnership opportunity here as well that would have been a better option for revenue and the client.

Caution with time and the ability to say no are integral to the success of business owners. These practices ensure that energy and resources are directed toward activities that align with broader goals, enhance productivity, preserve work-life balance, facilitate strategic decision-making, and maintain a sense of control over the business trajectory. As stewards of their enterprises, business owners must recognize the value of their time and wield the power of saying no judiciously to propel their businesses toward sustained success.

CHAPTER SIX

Thriving Through Growth: Adapt or Become Obsolete

GROW OR GET LEFT BEHIND
Learning the Balance

The world is developing in ways that we have never seen before. Growth is a nonnegotiable requirement for success today. Staying stagnant may work for today but in the next few years, it will start to decline the business. If you want to grow within your company without getting left behind, you need to make sure that your growth is sustainable.

This means making sure that the skills and knowledge you gain are relevant to your current role as well as future roles. It also means ensuring that the way you grow aligns with the company's goals. You may find yourself considering a new role or responsibility in order to grow, but if it isn't going to help you reach those goals or make an impact on the team, it's not worth taking on.

In order to stay current with the times, companies need to be able to grow their business without getting left behind. This will also fall over into team members because as the company grows, the team must as well or they will be left behind.

In a world characterized by rapid change and fierce competition, businesses and individuals must strike a delicate balance between growth and sustainability. While the pursuit of expansion is a natural inclination, it should be accompanied by a commitment to sustainability. This ensures that growth is not just about achieving immediate gains but about building a foundation for long-term success. Let's explore the nuances of this balance further.

Balancing the Growth

Sustainable growth, at its core, is about ensuring that the steps taken today contribute positively to both your present circumstances and your future prospects. It's not merely about expanding the scale of operations but about developing resilience and adaptability. Consider the following facets of sustainable growth:

1. Initiative: One of the best ways to get ahead is by taking initiative. When you see a problem, opportunity, or place for growth, don't wait around for someone else to take care of it – take action yourself! If you're not sure how to go about something, ask for help from your team or your Virtual Assistant. It's better to ask for help than to sit around and wait for someone else to figure out what needs doing.

2. Social Impact: Sustainable growth encompasses a commitment to making a positive social impact. It entails corporate social responsibility, community engagement, and a dedication to giving back. Businesses that prioritize social impact build strong relationships with their communities and stakeholders, enhancing their long-term sustainability.

3. Learning and Development: The kind of growth that lasts involves a continuous commitment to learning and development. It's about acquiring new skills, staying updated on industry trends, and adapting to changing circumstances. Lifelong learning is not just a personal pursuit but a critical component of organizational sustainability.

4. Agility and Adaptation: Sustainable growth requires agility. This means not only seizing opportunities but also being prepared to pivot when circumstances change. A growing company needs to respond quickly to changes in the market. Agility allows the organization to identify market shifts, emerging trends, and customer preferences promptly. The ability to adapt to market changes ensures that the company's products or services remain relevant and aligned with evolving customer needs.

Another way to grow within a company is by paying attention. Pay attention to what other people are doing, what they're saying, and how they're behaving. That way, when opportunities arise or problems arise, you'll be able to jump right in and solve them! Paying attention also helps with networking and relationship-building – two things that are very important for career success down the road.

Strategic Planning for Sustainable Growth

To achieve sustainable growth, strategic planning is necessary. It's not enough to simply chase after every available opportunity. Each move must be deliberate and calculated. Consider these strategies:

1. Set Clear Objectives: Start by defining your growth objectives. What do you want to achieve, both personally and for your organization? Having clear, measurable goals provides a roadmap for your growth journey.

2. Assess Resources: Sustainable growth should be supported by the necessary resources, whether that's financial capital, skilled personnel, or technological infrastructure. Assess what resources are available and what may be required to facilitate your growth plans.

3. Risk Management: Growth involves taking calculated risks. Identify potential risks and devise mitigation strategies to minimize their impact on your sustainability. This may include financial risk management, contingency planning, or market analysis.

4. Align With Values: Ensure that your growth plans align with your values and the values of your organization. Ethical alignment is crucial for long-term sustainability, as it makes sure that there is a sense of purpose and integrity in your actions.

5. Stay Humble: It's easy to think that because you have your own ideas, experience, and opinions, that everyone else should just listen when you speak up – but that's not true at all! Remember that everyone has something valuable to contribute. Never become so confident in your own skills that you shut down other competent voices.

6. Monitor and Adjust: Sustainable growth is an ongoing process. Continuously monitor your progress, assess the effectiveness of your strategies, and be prepared to make adjustments as needed. Flexibility is key to maintaining momentum in the face of changing circumstances.

Collaboration and Innovation

Collaboration and innovation play pivotal roles. Collaborating with other individuals and organizations can lead to new opportunities and perspectives. It can also help spread the responsibility for sustainability, as collective efforts often have a more significant impact.

Innovation, on the other hand, is the engine that drives sustainable growth. It involves finding creative solutions to challenges, exploring new markets, and developing novel products or services. Innovation keeps you ahead of the curve and allows you to adapt to emerging trends and technologies.

We can't overstate how collaboration and innovation stand out as indispensable pillars, propelling businesses towards enduring success. By fostering partnerships with diverse individuals and organizations, a business can unlock new dimensions of opportunity and gain fresh perspectives. Not only does collaboration broaden the scope of possibilities, but it also shares the responsibility for sustainability, harnessing collective efforts for a more profound and lasting impact.

Collaborative Initiatives: A compelling example of effective collaboration is the partnership between multinational corporations and local communities. This collaboration aims not only to drive economic growth but also to address environmental and social concerns. Initiatives that promote shared value, such as sustainable supply chain practices, not only enhance the brand image but also contribute to the overall well-being of the communities involved. At Virtual Assist USA, for example, we collaborate with partners such as vendors who use platforms that our clients can find value in. We continue to expand on this collaboration year over year, bringing in new trusted partners which in turn expands our own center of influence.

Moreover, collaborative efforts within industries can lead to the establishment of standards and best practices for sustainable operations. Industry-wide initiatives, like sustainability certifications or alliances for ethical business practices, provide businesses with a roadmap for integrating sustainability into their core operations.

Social Collaboration: Social collaboration is a known strategy, but not a commonly used one. Authentic connections to influencers can lead to immense traction for your business. This dynamic approach to marketing allows you to leverage the influence of individuals your audience already trusts. Add this tactic on to your road map to growth.

Leveraging Trust through Influencer Collaborations: In the white noise time of ad-blockers and information overload, trust is a valuable currency. Audiences are becoming increasingly discerning, seeking authenticity in the brands they support. This is where influencer collaborations come into play. By partnering with influencers who share a genuine connection with your target audience, you can tap into the trust they've already established. This trust provides a solid foundation on which your business can build a meaningful relationship with potential customers.

The Path to Growth through Personal Connections: Why? Personal connections through organic SEO is a path to growth. Personal connections are at the heart of successful marketing. When your brand aligns with the values and interests of your target audience, you're better positioned for growth. Building these connections organically is often a long and arduous journey. However, when you collaborate with influencers, you're taking a shortcut to establishing personal connections. Influencers have spent years nurturing relationships with their followers. By partnering with them, you're essentially piggybacking on these genuine, personal connections.

How to Harness the Power of Influencer Collaborations

1. **Identify Relevant Influencers:** The first step in this powerful strategy is to find the right influencers who resonate with your brand and target audience. Look for individuals who share the same values and cater to a similar demographic. Tools like influencer marketing platforms (such as AspireIQ and Inzpire.me that connect companies with influencers) and social media analytics can help you identify these influencers.
2. **Build Authentic Partnerships:** Once you've identified potential collaborators, it's time to build authentic partnerships. Authenticity is key in influencer marketing. Approach influencers with a sincere desire to create a mutually beneficial relationship. Discuss how your products or services align with their interests and how your collaboration can provide value to their own followers as well.

3. **Let Them Amplify Your Message:** The magic of influencer collaborations lies in their ability to amplify your message. Influencers have a dedicated following that trusts their recommendations. When they endorse your product or service, it's like a friend recommending something to another friend. Ensure that the content they create for your brand is aligned with their style and voice, as authenticity is the key to success.

Don't miss out on the opportunity to partner with influencers who share your brand's values. Now is the time to team up with influencers and unlock the full potential of your marketing strategy. Your business's growth depends on your adaptability, likability, and flexibility in an ever changing landscape.

Innovation as the Driving Force

Innovation emerges as the force that propels growth into the future. Consider the renewable energy sector, where continual innovation has not only made clean energy more accessible but has also driven down costs. Breakthroughs in solar technology, energy storage, and grid management showcase how innovation can reshape entire industries, aligning economic growth with environmental sustainability.

Innovation isn't limited to technological advancements; it extends to business models and processes. Companies that embrace circular economy principles, like recycling and repurposing materials, exemplify innovative approaches that minimize waste and environmental impact. Beyond environmental considerations, such practices often lead to cost savings and increased operational efficiency.

The Synergy of Collaboration and Innovation: The synergy between collaboration and innovation becomes especially potent in incubators and accelerators that bring together startups, established businesses, and experts. These ecosystems facilitate cross-pollination of ideas and resources, fostering an environment where innovative solutions to sustainability challenges can flourish. An example is the collaboration between tech startups and traditional manufacturing industries, leading to the development of sustainable technologies for production processes.

The integration of collaboration and innovation into the fabric of a business is not just a strategy but a mindset. It's a recognition that the challenges of sustainability are best met collectively and that innovation is the compass guiding businesses towards a future where growth is not just sustainable but transformative. By forging strategic alliances and embracing creative solutions, businesses can navigate the complexities of sustainable growth with resilience and foresight.

The Long-Term Perspective

Sustainable growth is, by definition, a long-term endeavor. It requires patience, perseverance, and a commitment to the bigger picture. While immediate gains can be enticing, they should always be evaluated within the context of their long-term impact.

The quest for growth must be accompanied by a dedication to sustainability. Sustainable growth encompasses environmental and economic changes, continuous learning, agility, and more. Strategic planning, alignment with values, risk management, and a commitment to monitoring progress are essential components of this journey. Collaboration and innovation further fuel sustainable growth, ensuring that your path forward is not just enduring but also adaptable to the ever-changing world. Remember that the balance between growth and sustainability is not a static point but an ongoing process, and it's this ongoing commitment that leads to lasting success.

It is often easy to push these ideologies to the side when we get caught up in our day to day fires or strategic goals. Setting specific times on the calendar to reassess these goals will be helpful. Here are some tasks to place on your calendar now:

- **Platform Reassessment and Evaluation** – Once every two years, research competitors' pricing, abilities, new automations, and compare to your current setup. For example, perhaps a new system came about that now encompasses two of your platforms and combines them into one. This would streamline internal operations and bring costs down.
- **New Technologies** – Annually, spend half a day diving into the new technologies that are available or that will be coming available in the next year. If you see something interesting, place a reminder in your task management system.
- **Competitive Analysis** – The consensus among the experts is this should be rolling. You should always have a firm understanding of your direct and indirect competitors. However, setting it periodically on your calendar to ensure it is completed is important..
- **Growth Networking** – Expanding, rather than simply maintaining, your networking abilities is critical. Place time two times a year on your calendar to build upon your networking items. Plan to attend a conference, join a new group, and reassess your networking goals. Developing a hand-in-hand network in an ever-growing tech economy is your direct way to success. AI cannot replicate personal recommendations and trust. See Chapter 4 for more.
- **New Risk Assessment** – Annually, set half a day to review your company's risks and risk management. This ties in to our 'what if' plan we discussed in earlier chapters. However, assessing what new risks are applicable to the company can be a lifesaver.

Chasing sustainable growth is like committing to the long game. Quick wins might feel good at the moment, but real success comes from finding that sweet spot between growth and sustainability. Getting there involves some savvy planning, staying true to your values, managing risks, and keeping an eye on your progress. Collaboration and thinking outside the box are key to rolling with the punches in our ever-changing world. Don't let these principles slip away in the midst of everyday challenges or big-picture goals. Regular check-ins, like looking at your platforms, trying out new tech, sizing up the competition, networking for growth, and keeping an eye on risks, are smart moves to make sure your organization stays on track and tough in the face of change. Build these habits into your schedule, and you'll set the stage for long-lasting success – a journey where growth isn't just a one-time thing but a steady, sustainable ride.

CHAPTER SEVEN

Strategic Investments: Navigating Smart Risks

CALCULATED RISKS
The Art of Making Smart Choices

It is a fine line to walk between smart and risky decisions in business, especially when discussing growth. Is it time to be safe and hunker down, or is it time to reach out and take a chance?

It is incredibly nerve-wracking to take a risk because the return on investment can be detrimental or exponentially profitable. Risk-taking is where the magic happens. It's the space where out-of-the-box ideas mingle, sparking the kind of innovation that doesn't just push boundaries but obliterates them.

Embracing Calculated Risks

The ability to make smart choices – even when they're risky – is often the differentiating factor between stagnant companies and those that soar to new heights. Or, more plainly, the difference between average and Not-Your-Average when it comes to executives.

As a CEO, you are tasked with navigating uncharted territories, identifying growth opportunities, and embracing innovation. It is crucial to strike a balance between calculated risks and conservative decision-making. This chapter will explore the art of making intelligent choices and why calculated risks can lead to remarkable success.

1. Analyze the Potential Upside

When faced with a risky decision, first evaluate the potential upside. Identify the opportunities beyond the comfort zone and consider the rewards of taking a calculated leap. By carefully assessing the potential gains, you can weigh them against the risks and make an informed choice. Remember, stagnation seldom leads to breakthroughs, and the boldest decisions often yield the most significant rewards. What is the "best thing" that could happen? How would your company or its growth trajectory be impacted if this decision delivers the anticipated rewards?

2. Conduct Thorough Research

Before embarking on a risky endeavor, arm yourself with knowledge. Conduct comprehensive research, gather market insights, and analyze relevant data. Informed decision-making requires a deep understanding of the industry landscape, market trends, and competitive dynamics. By staying abreast of the latest developments and gathering relevant information, you can mitigate uncertainties and make more intelligent choices. As the saying goes, "Knowledge is power." If this is another task that you just don't have the time for, do not go in blind, rather, have your Virtual Assistant spend a few hours of cost-effective research so that you have all of the information needed.

3. Embrace Thinking Outside the Box

A company that has a culture of innovation is more likely to succeed in making smart but risky choices. Encourage yourself – and your team – to think outside the box, challenge the status quo, and explore unconventional ideas. Are you providing a working environment where calculated risks are celebrated, and mistakes are viewed as valuable learning opportunities? By nurturing an innovative mindset, you create a foundation for making bold decisions that have the potential to transform your organization. What can you do that no one else has dared to do yet?

In a world where complacency reigns – and safe bets are sure bets – innovation and improvement become distant ideals. Take Thomas Edison as an example. Had he been content with the status quo of gas lamps, the groundbreaking developments of light bulbs and electricity might never have materialized. It underscores the significance of thinking beyond accepted norms. An illustrious case in point is the tech giant Apple, renowned for crafting its success around a pivotal mantra: "Innovate uniquely."

4. Look for the Differences

For example, in our company, Virtual Assist USA, we practice this. Our CEO Danielle Cuomo noted, "As the CEO, I work closely with Nicole as our COO on daily decisions. When Nicole believes in a particular decision, idea or initiative, she is not afraid to say it and provide backup for why. Nicole and I have sometimes thought differently about decisions, yet her points have always been backed up with reason, logic, and research. More than once, I was convinced that Nicole was right and she changed my decision. If the reason was on my side, Nicole happily accepted the decision, without any ego issues. Having this alternate viewpoint and being able to have honest, open and respectful discussions has made all the difference."

5. Test the Waters with Pilot Projects

Before committing to a high-risk initiative, consider testing the waters through a small pilot project. This approach allows you to gather real-world feedback, validate assumptions, and assess the viability of your chosen path. By conducting smaller-scale experiments, you can reduce potential risks and adjust your strategies based on tangible results. Piloting enables you to refine your approach and make more informed decisions when scaling up. What can you do on a smaller scale to develop proof of concept? How can you test the waters without taking the full-on risk?

6. Develop Contingency Plans

When embracing risks, it's crucial to develop contingency plans to mitigate potential downsides. Instead of idly anticipating the worst-case scenario, make a plan. Identify alternative paths and develop backup strategies that can be activated if needed. By planning for potential setbacks, you can minimize the negative impact of unexpected challenges and maintain business continuity. Flexibility and adaptability are essential when it comes to navigating risky waters. What will you do if it doesn't work out the way that you planned? What changes can be made so that all is not lost? Do you have a Plan B (and Plan C and Plan D)?

Know that the days are bound to bring unforeseen events, some of which may be unprecedented in your organization. Remember the months-long pandemic shutdowns? Consider this assessment as a tool to uncover elements you can proactively prepare for and to stimulate everyone's creativity regarding potential challenges and outcomes. This approach sets the stage for heightened awareness, a flexible mindset, and a proactive orientation toward finding solutions.

7. Learn from Both Successes and Failures

Each and every decision, whether successful or not, offers valuable lessons. Embrace both your successes and failures as opportunities for growth and learning. Celebrate achievements and conduct post-mortems for initiatives that did not yield the desired outcomes. Reflecting on past experiences allows you to refine your decision-making processes, improve risk assessment, and refine your ability to make smarter choices in the future.

Of course, it's easy to focus on the times when you've made poor calls or hedged risk. Decisions have generally been viewed as the prerogative of individuals – usually the CEO and COO. The process employed, the information used, and the logic relied on have been left up to them in something of a black box. Data goes in, decisions come out – and who knows what happens in between? Second, unlike other business processes, decision-making has rarely been the focus of systematic analysis inside the firm. Very few organizations have "reengineered" their decisions. Yet, there are just as many opportunities to improve decision-making as any other process. Valuable insights have been available for a long time. For example, academics defined "groupthink," the forced manufacture of consent, more than half a century ago.

The consequences of this inattention are becoming ever more severe. It is time to take decision-making out of the realm of the purely individual and idiosyncratic. As a CEO, you must lead by example by being able to employ better decision-making processes. Better processes won't guarantee better decisions but can make them more likely.

A Framework for Improving Decisions

Focusing on decisions doesn't necessarily require a strict focus on the mental processes of CEOs. It can mean examining the accessible components of decision-making – which decisions must be made, what information is supplied, the critical roles in the process, and so forth. Intelligent organizations make multifaceted interventions by addressing technology, data, organizational structure, methods, and personnel. They can improve decision-making in several steps.

The Three I's of Decision-Making

1. Identification

CEOs should begin by listing the decisions that must be made and deciding which are most important – for example, "the top 10 decisions required to execute our strategy" or "the top 10 decisions that have to go well if we are to meet our financial goals." Some decisions will be rare and highly strategic ("What acquisitions will allow us to gain the necessary market share?"), while others will be frequent and on the front lines ("How should we decide how much to charge this client?"). Without some prioritization, all decisions will be treated equally – which probably means that the important ones won't be analyzed with sufficient care.

2. Inventory

In addition to identifying critical decisions, you should assess the factors that go into each. Who plays what role in the decision? How often does it occur? What information is available to support it? How well is the decision typically made? Such an examination helps an organization understand which decisions need improvement and what processes might make them more effective while establishing a common language for discussing decision-making.

3. Intervention

Having narrowed down your list of decisions and examined what's involved in making each, you can design the roles, processes, systems, and behaviors your organization should use to make them. The key to effective decision interventions is a broad, inclusive approach that considers all improvement methods and addresses all aspects of the decision process – including the execution of the decision, which is often overlooked.

We've worked hard at Virtual Assist USA over the years to improve our decision-making. And in doing so, we've found a few fundamentals in our process:

1. Decision-makers often needed more information about the intellectual property, competitors, analytics, cycle times, and likely market for new offerings. There is no such thing as too much information.
2. Clarity is needed on who plays what roles when making a decision, and who is responsible for the final decision. Note that in our company, it is not always the CEO as it is in many organizations. This gives a greater autonomy to your highest level leaders and shows that you trust them.
3. The structure of the process could have been more specific. There is always room for improvement in the clarity and detail of the decision-making process. Set a timeframe for the decision-making and don't let the process be drawn out forever. You can only "circle back" so many times!

Multiple Perspectives Yield Better Results

Analytics, and decision automation are among the most powerful tools for improving decision-making. Many firms embrace the former strategically and tactically, building competitive strategies around their analytical capabilities and making decisions based on data and analytics. Analytics are even more effective when embedded in automated systems, which can cause many decisions virtually in real-time. But if one of these approaches goes awry, it can seriously damage your business. For example, if you need to make better decisions on pricing or operations, you can lose money in a torrent. Therefore, balancing and augmenting these decision tools with human intuition and judgment is critical. Organizations should ensure that they are very literate with analytics. You have to be a quantitative person when you're managing a company because those details matter.

It's also important to know when a particular decision approach doesn't apply. For example, analytics isn't a good fit when you have to make a fast decision. And almost all quantitative models – even predictive ones – are based on past data, so if your experience or intuition tells you that the past is no longer an excellent guide to the present and future, you'll want to employ other decision tools, or at least to create some new data and analyses.

Like any other business activity, decisions will improve with systematic review. You need to know which of your choices are most important to be able to prioritize improvements. If you don't understand how decisions are made in your company, you can't change the process for making them. You need to assess the results of your changes to make better decisions. The way to begin is to give decisions the attention they deserve. Without it, your organization's decision-making success will be primarily a matter of luck. While everyone could benefit from a bit of luck, it will not be the reason your business succeeds.

Tech in Emotional Decision-Making

Not your Average CEOs and executives can harness the vast potential of big data analytics to inform strategic decisions. Investing in advanced analytics tools and data-driven insights empowers leaders to identify patterns, trends, and opportunities with unprecedented precision. This is a tool that was not an option before, and while we always advise to use AI with caution, there are useful tactics to incorporate into your decision-making process that can lead to prosperous outcomes.

AI and Predictive Analytics

Utilizing predictive analytics models to forecast future trends and potential outcomes is done faster now than ever before with the use of AI tools. By analyzing historical data and market trends, CEOs can proactively position their organizations for success.

This innovative methodology enables CEOs to simulate potential outcomes and adapt strategies accordingly. For example, predictive models can analyze historical data and market trends to forecast future demand for products or services. This information is crucial for developing strategic plans, optimizing inventory, and staying ahead of market fluctuations.

CEOs can also use predictive models to forecast future revenue based on historical financial data, market conditions, and other relevant factors. This aids in budgeting, resource allocation, and overall financial planning. From a human resources perspective, a CEO can use predictive models for workforce planning by analyzing historical employee data to predict future staffing needs, turnover rates, and skills gaps. This aids in strategic talent acquisition and retention efforts.

Here are some popular data analytics tools that you can consider:

1. Tableau: Tableau enables users to create visually appealing and interactive dashboards, charts, graphs, and maps. This graphical representation makes it easier for decision-makers to comprehend complex data sets at a glance.

2. Power BI (Microsoft Power BI): Power BI supports self-service analytics, allowing decision-makers to perform ad-hoc analyses without extensive technical expertise. Users can explore data, create reports, and derive insights independently, promoting agility in decision-making.

3. QlikView: The associative data model enables exploration and discovery, aiding in decision-making.

4. Google Analytics: Google Analytics offers insights into website performance, user behavior, and online marketing effectiveness. CEOs can use this data to make informed decisions about digital strategies and customer engagement.

5. Semrush: Semrush is a valuable tool for competitive analysis in the digital space. CEOs can gain insights into competitors' online strategies, keyword performance, and market trends, aiding strategic decision-making.

6. Looker: Looker serves as a platform for collaborative exploration of real-time data, allowing CEOs to gain insights and share them with stakeholders.

7. Domo: Domo's cloud-based BI platform integrates data from various sources, empowering CEOs with real-time analytics and collaboration tools for decision-making. Domo is the first cloud platform in this space and they've been perfecting their tools ever since.

8. Sisense: Sisense leverages the power of AI to assist users in uncovering valuable insights from their data. From anomaly detection to predictive analytics, the platform empowers users to make data-driven decisions based on accurate forecasts and trends.

9. IBM Cognos Analytics: IBM Cognos Analytics offers enterprise-grade analytics and reporting tools, enabling CEOs to conduct comprehensive data analysis and forecasting.

10. Databricks: Databricks provides a unified analytics platform for large-scale data processing, supporting CEOs in data engineering, collaborative analytics, and machine learning.

11. RapidMiner: RapidMiner focuses on predictive analytics and data science, assisting CEOs in predictive modeling and deriving actionable insights from data. It's important to note that this is a no-code platform so it is one of the most user-friendly and popular.

12. Yellowfin BI: Yellowfin BI provides an environment conducive to shared business insights, incorporating visualizations and analytics tools that CEOs can leverage for well-informed decision-making.

When selecting a data analytics tool, CEOs and executives should consider factors such as ease of use, scalability, integration capabilities, and the specific needs of their organization. Additionally, cloud-based solutions offer flexibility and accessibility, allowing CEOs to make data-driven decisions from anywhere.

Remember that it is only helpful to invest in a platform if you're actually going to use it. Don't collect subscriptions! A platform is the most impactful when accompanied by a commitment to its active utilization.

Decision Diagramming

Decision diagramming is a visual representation of the decision-making process, involving the creation of a structured diagram outlining choices, factors, and potential outcomes associated with a decision.

CEOs can utilize decision maps to create a visual landscape of decision factors, aiding in understanding relationships between variables, uncertainties, and possible paths, fostering clarity and strategic foresight.

When building a decision map, consider the following:

1) **Decision Factors:** Identify the key factors influencing the decision at hand, including market conditions, financial considerations, internal capabilities, and external influences. Other factors may include ethical or legal considerations. In this step, also be sure that you're identifying the key stakeholders involved in the decision – this doesn't have to only be the executive team. What other groups or individuals may be impacted by the decision or have a vested interest in its outcome?
2) **Decision Criteria:** Establishing clear decision criteria ensures the map aligns with organizational goals, encompassing feasibility, profitability, risk mitigation, and strategic alignment. Ideally, decision criteria should be quantifiable or qualifiable, allowing for a clear assessment of how well each alternative meets the specified standards. This facilitates a more objective evaluation process. Decision criteria are not all equal in significance. Some may carry more weight or be more critical in influencing the final decision. It's important to prioritize and assign relative importance to each criterion.
3) **Map Outcomes and Scenarios:** Decision maps incorporate various outcomes and scenarios, allowing CEOs to analyze best-case, worst-case, and most likely scenarios for comprehensive risk assessment and strategic planning.

Decision diagramming has many benefits, not the least of which is increased clarity. Decision diagramming in a visual way offers CEOs a clear visual representation of the decision landscape, facilitating communication and ensuring all stakeholders share a common understanding of the decision context.

You can also identify dependencies between decision factors, revealing potential ripple effects and interconnected relationships, crucial for anticipating the impact of decisions across the organization.

Decision diagrams aid in risk assessment by highlighting uncertainties and potential pitfalls. You can proactively address risks and develop contingency plans, promoting resilience in the face of unexpected challenges.

As a real-world application, think of using decision mapping when you go about strategic planning. This is something that we do at Virtual Assist USA when we need to assess various strategic options. The visual representation in particular allows us to align decisions with long-term goals, and ensure the chosen path is congruent with the organization's vision. It's important to encourage collaborative decision-making in this process, so be sure to involve key stakeholders in the mapping process to ensure a diversity of perspectives.

When you do this, it makes the right decision obvious.

Making decisions is a daily occurrence, and it involves a complex process influenced by personal experience, biases, intuition, and critical thinking. Some decisions are almost automatic, rooted in familiar experiences, like approving a promotion for a strong employee.

However, in unfamiliar situations, decisions require careful consideration of benefits and potential risks. Decision mapping documents and organizes all options, ensuring that no important information is overlooked, even if it falls in the middle of a discussion.

By providing an objective perspective, decision mapping helps avoid giving disproportionate weight to recent or sensational events, mitigating the impact of availability bias.

What are the other benefits?

- **Reduces stress:** When you're trying to manage people, projects and time, adding decision-making to the mix can just increase the stress. And of course, making a decision while you're experiencing stress is almost always a mistake. However, by using decision mapping, you're able to think more clearly and concisely.
- **Team focus:** When you're working with others on your leadership team, it's easy to go off on tangents and lose focus of what you are trying to accomplish. The map helps to keep the team on the same page and remain focused on various ideas and suggestions. When all points of view are recorded graphically, it's easier to weigh the pros and cons on each as you work together to find the best solution.
- **Conflict resolution:** Decision diagramming is a recommended approach to conflict resolution because of its visual charting processes. It helps teams to stay focused so they can tackle problems that can affect stakeholders. For example, decision diagramming with web-based applications makes it easy for hybrid and remote teams to collaborate together in real time no matter where they are located. Teams have better focus as they work together to address and solve complex problems.

Now, let's explore the steps for creating a decision diagram. Although there isn't a strict standard, here are some steps we find effective:

1. Illustrate the problem and proposed resolutions using shapes.
2. Establish connecting lines between the problem and resolutions.
3. Evaluate the pros and cons associated with each resolution shape.
4. Record arguments and sub-arguments for thorough documentation.
5. Make decisions to accept or reject propositions based on the presented arguments.

Keep in mind that the goal of this process is to streamline the decision-making process. Therefore, strive to maintain clarity, avoid unnecessary complexity, and ensure that team members can swiftly interpret the information presented.

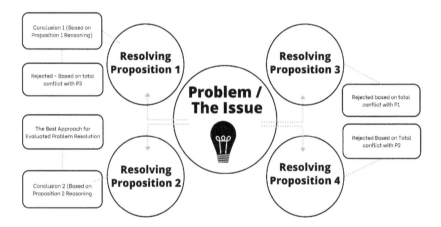

As you can see from the above example, there can be lots of options to choose from and the hierarchical grouping of the options are particularly useful. Most interestingly, when done correctly, *the decision diagram reveals the answer*.

CHAPTER EIGHT

Revamping Your
Revenue Strategies

ASSESS YOUR PROFITS
Configuring Your Revenue for Sustainability

The overall necessities to running a business have shifted. For a long time, rent, utilities, expensive leases, paper items, phones, desktops, file cabinets, electric bills, business cards, letterhead, and more were necessary expenses for any business owner. It truly seems so foreign now.

Even though computers and internet technology have been around for decades, it wasn't until the 2010s that it became a true advantage to business owners and not an added expense, in terms of equipment and daily running costs.

And, it has only been in the past few years that the concept of a virtual workspace has become more accepted. While the technology has been around for more than a decade, it was seen as an added burden rather than a strength. How does this tie into revenue generating strategies and profit reassessments? We will dive into that throughout this chapter.

Reassess Your Profits: Expense Reassessment

The first step in profit reassessment is evaluating where your expenses are coming from. This means reviewing your software and spreadsheets by going line item by line item. For ease, you will want to break it down into columns to assess individually what is a necessity. For example, a column or bucket on the spreadsheet, for independent contractors such as accountants, bookkeepers, attorneys, or marketing specialists is prudent. Another column could be used for platforms and softwares. You likely already have something similar in your bookkeeping system, if you use a platform like Quickbooks or Freshbooks. However, we found using an Excel spreadsheet with columns more simple and visually appealing. This way, you're not looking at repetitive monthly or weekly charges but rather an annual overall cost per platform. Think of it this way: $5/month per user doesn't sound as impactful as $60/year per user. A good task for your Virtual Assistant is to take all of your expenses and put them in a spreadsheet for this exercise.

Software Platforms

It is important to speak with your team to understand what software is being utilized, how often it is being accessed, and how imperative it is to their working day. If you are a solo-entrepreneur, this would be applied to what you are currently utilizing. If you are working with a team, ask them to write a list. Most platforms, software, and services are monthly and recurring. When looking at the subscriptions you are paying for, research if there are cheaper alternatives. These charges can add up quickly and without notice because they are small monthly payments that fall under the radar. These should be the first to go, especially ones that are not used or have other alternatives that can be free or less expensive. Additionally, identify any redundancies. Chances are, you have several! Other questions to ask yourself or your team could be:

- What is the ROI compared to the cost incurred?
- Are there any pain points with this platform?
- Is there a free version that would handle the same tasks?
- How well does this platform integrate with the other tools and systems in our organization?
- What is the scalability of this platform – how will it work with us in the future? As our users increase, will our cost increase as well or is it a per-company license?
- Is this platform meeting the security requirements that exist today for our organization as well as our clients and other stakeholders?

Payment Processing Fees

Payment processing fees hover around 3 to 4%, an astronomical cost for any business that is responsible for lowering actual profit numbers. When was the last time you looked into your payment processing fees? Did you know that there are other options available? Every few years, exploring new payment processing solutions might reveal cost-effective alternatives that can significantly enhance your bottom line. It's an essential task for a CEO to regularly reassess your payment processing setup to ensure you're not leaving money on the table. So, take the time to evaluate your options and find the most efficient, cost-friendly solution that suits your business needs.

Office Operations

If you're not already working remotely, can you explore options to reduce the need for large office spaces? If in-person work is necessary in your industry, think outside the box by considering shared workspaces or flexible office arrangements. If none of these are possible, just about every business can save money by implementing energy-efficient practices to lower facility and operational costs, such as going paperless.

If the COVID pandemic taught us anything, it is that virtual meetings and conferences are suitable and certainly reduce travel expenses. Regularly monitor and analyze the cost savings achieved by reducing travel expenses. This data can inform future budgeting decisions and highlight the financial benefits of virtual practices.

Pipeline Journey

Take a thorough journey through your entire pipeline, covering the entire process from initiation to completion. This may even entail going through the entire customer experience, including making a purchase from your own company. This means receiving the invoice, making the payment, and receiving the product. In the case of an intangible product or service, consider incognito evaluation of its operation. If it involves tangible goods, scrutinize how the product is delivered and assess the quality of the packaging and the final product.

During this journey, it is also time to begin assessing who your target market is. Do you have a clear niche for your target audience?

If you are targeting everyone, you will attract no one.

Let's break it down further.

Before you can effectively market a product or service, it's crucial to identify who your potential customers are. This involves analyzing demographics, psychographics, and other relevant factors. You've heard before that you need to know their age, gender, location, income level, interests, values, and pain points. This information helps you create a comprehensive profile of your ideal customer. Trying to target everyone or a very broad audience can be counterproductive and can tank profits.

Yet here's why this marketing principle matters when it comes to revenue:

Message Dilution: When your message is too generic, it doesn't resonate strongly with anyone. People need to feel a personal connection to your brand or product, which is hard to achieve when your messaging is too broad.

Resource Wastage: Marketing resources, including time and money, are finite. Targeting everyone means spreading your resources too thin. You won't get a good return on investment because you're not effectively reaching the people who are most likely to buy from you.

Competition: In a crowded marketplace, targeting everyone means you're competing with numerous other businesses for the same customers. It's challenging to stand out and establish a unique value proposition.

Understanding your target market and having a clear niche allows you to concentrate your efforts where they are most likely to yield results. By doing so, you can build a stronger brand, connect with your audience on a deeper level, and ultimately drive greater business success

"I always ask every individual, especially the owner, what their Joy & Genius Zone™ is. Most people know that a genius zone is what you're best at in all the land. Your joy zone is what you do that actually gives you energy. It's critical that the work we do combines them. What are the things you do that you're both amazing at and that energize you? That's what you should be doing, and you should delegate everything else."

Samantha Hartley, President, Enlightened Marketing

A well-structured pipeline journey can significantly contribute to increasing revenue for a business. A pipeline journey refers to the stages that a customer goes through from initial awareness to final conversion. Depending on your industry, the length of time for this journey will differ. A streamlined pipeline helps the sales team efficiently manage opportunities, reducing the sales cycle and increasing the chances of successful conversions.

Don't sleep on the post-purchase! Post-purchase stages in the pipeline journey allow for identifying opportunities for upselling or cross-selling based on the customer's needs and preferences. Successfully delivering additional value through upselling or cross-selling contributes to customer satisfaction and loyalty, increasing the lifetime value of each customer, and thus increasing your revenue as well.

In summary, a carefully designed and managed pipeline journey ensures that each stage in the customer's interaction with the business contributes to revenue growth. By understanding customer needs, providing valuable content, building relationships, and leveraging data-driven insights, businesses can optimize their pipeline journey to maximize revenue potential.

How Much Do You Know About Your Profit Margin?

What is your profit margin?

Can you rattle the number off on demand?

You should know this off the top of your head at all times, the actual number after everything is all said and done and paid for. Understanding this key financial metric will help you make informed decisions about pricing, cost management, and overall business sustainability. It's a critical aspect of maintaining a successful and profitable operation.

Where to begin?

Start with a breakdown of how much it costs you for one item within your business. Make sure to take into account how much it costs to maintain an employee, platforms, and any other overhead. Don't forget to consider taxes and other government fees for states and localities here. It is often easier depending on your service or product to look at this in a per item or per month scenario to obtain the actual number. This detailed cost analysis will enable you to identify areas where expenses can be optimized and efficiencies can be enhanced. By having a comprehensive understanding of your cost structure, you can make strategic pricing and operational adjustments that will positively impact your bottom line and ensure the long-term viability of your business.

Once you know your profit, are you comfortable with this number?

There are ways to change your profit assessment and pricing. Keep in mind that reassessing your pricing does not always mean increasing your prices. Assess whether or not your purchase options make sense. If your business offers a service, do you offer bundle options? Do these options work with the service you offer? If your business provides a product, do you have options that make the profit margin expand if someone buys in bulk? How does that relate to services?

Here are some other revenue-generating actionable ideas to consider when assessing profits:

1. **Engage.** Set a goal to engage with just three new people each week. Truly connect with them. Don't just like their social posts. Read the post and make a thoughtful comment, and message them with intent. Schedule a "get to know you" call. Maybe even refer someone to their business. This will exponentially grow your network and in turn, you will see new business drum up. Put this networking and engagement on your calendar and stick to it.
2. **Increase your stickiness and likability.** What added value do you bring to your customers? This can be something incredibly small that has a minimal cost to you. For example, have you ever made a purchase and it comes incredibly well packaged, with a nice handwritten thank you note and a 10% discount code for a next purchase? Go the extra mile for your customer, and you will stand out from other businesses.
3. **Trim the excess fat.** When was the last time you walked through all the platforms and services you are paying for? Have you calculated and compared all the expenses your business goes through? Weigh what is necessary versus what is unnecessary. Platforms can help with automation, but you need to make sure you are using everything to the fullest. There are so many options out there now that one will make sense for you. This is something that our CEO and COO do together on a quarterly basis so that there are two sets of eyes on this.

4. **Team and automation.** Spend some time looking at what can be automated within your business. This will take tedious tasks off yours or your team's plate and free up time to do more higher level work. Make way for advancements and opportunities to shine in other aspects of the business. Ask your team for advice or what their input is in next steps with growing the business.

5. **Understand pricing and profits.** Have confidence in the value of you and your products or services. People will pay you what they think you're worth. But remember, you are the one controlling their thoughts. Their interaction with you and their perception all stem from your own energy. Keep an eye on your competitors' pricing strategies. If they have successfully implemented price increases, it may indicate that the market is receptive, making it easier for you to justify similar changes.

Ask yourself:

- What value are you bringing to your clients that no one else has?
- What problems are you solving for your clients and how much money does it save them?
- Who else can solve this problem for them? Is it another company, or even a software program?
- What small value-add can you do to stand out?

Doing the math here will make a difference in your approach as to why someone should pay you the price you place on what you are selling. Knowing the breakdown of your deliverable outline for the client places confidence in an upfront breakdown.

It's not just your price that affects your profitability. It's also who you are marketing to and what you are marketing. Consider the Pareto principle (often known as the 80/20 rule) and how it could apply to your business. In simple terms, applying the Pareto principle suggests that around 80 percent of your profit is gained from 20 percent of your products or services. The same percentage of profit is often also gained from the same percentage of customers.

Focusing on your most profitable customers – even if it means letting the less profitable ones go – could boost your profitability, so long as it is handled carefully. You may also be able to trim down your packages and service offerings to focus only on the most profitable ones in your niche.

"Most people are doing too many things. And when you do too many things, it's not profitable, because you don't get efficiency and traction around any single offer. So instead of doing and offering all kinds of things, find the two or three that resonate most with your clients. It is okay to explore and offer different things in the first two or three years of your business, but after you start to learn what attracts your audience and where you get the best results, focus on that.

Instead of doing multiple quick-fix, one-off projects, take that one main thing and put it into a long-term program, something I call a "transformational engagement." It's a program that solves a major problem for your client – something you can't do in a few weeks or months. And because it's a major problem, they're willing to invest significant money to solve it.

For example, if an organization is losing good people, that is an expensive problem and usually an urgent one. When you come in to help, you can get some quick wins in the beginning. But for the change to really sustain, it takes a longer time horizon. That may be a year or three to five years. Massive change that lasts can only happen with a transformational engagement. It's better for the client, it's better for those they serve, and it will keep you off the Revenue Roller Coaster."

Samantha Hartley, President, Enlightened Marketing

Growing a successful, profitable business is hard work, and the hard truth is that not everyone succeeds at it. On average, about 25% of new businesses fail during their first year, a shocking 50% of businesses fail during the first five years, and over 60% fail during the first 10 years. To be considered one of the successes, pay attention to what Samantha Hartley says above. Paying attention to your offerings is a good start but also remember that it's not exhaustive. To own and run a successful business, be in a constant state of learning and adapting.

The Story You Tell and How it Impacts Revenue

How often have you thought about the stories that you tell in a professional setting? I bet you do not think about it in this context, but you are always telling stories. Bringing this ideology to life and front of mind can change your revenue strategy greatly.

"The word 'story' brings up all sorts of ideas for different people, from a watercooler conversation to an epic movie series to the progression of our business or individual lives. Story is all that and more, but it can actually be defined very simply: A story is where a character wants something, overcomes obstacles to get it, and experiences transformation as a result."

Jeff Bartsch, Storyteller and Communication Strategist, Story Greenlight

This is essential to human interaction, connection, and ultimately revenue success within your business. To begin your journey into incorporating story into your business, we implore you to start with just today.

1. Did you talk to someone and tell them a story about something from the past?
2. What is the story of your business?

3. What are your customers' stories?
4. What are your employee stories as it relates to client success?
5. How often are you incorporating stories into your everyday conversations?

"When we focus our thinking of the story down to ideas of character, desire, obstacles, and finding change, we find that the story exists at the tactical level where individual stories are told and messages are shared. Most people stop right there at the idea of tactical storytelling. Here's what most people don't know: that same story definition operates at the strategic, big picture scale too. This is where the true power of story comes into play, because it attaches the ideas of identity, desire, obstacles, and change to literally any interaction any human being has with another human being. So if our business deals in any way with people – spoiler alert, there is no business that doesn't – story affects what we do, and it definitely affects whether our business reaches its goals or not."

Jeff Bartsch, Storyteller and Communication Strategist, Story Greenlight

When we marry story and business, we can increase our revenue by using story to connect with our target audience and clients.

"In business, we all interact with stakeholders with their own unfolding storylines: ourselves, our team, our vendors, our investors, etc. But if we want to drive revenue in our business, the first story to examine is our customer, our client. When we understand who they are, what they want, what's getting in their way, and how our product or service can help them, it affects everything we do. It affects the way we market to them, it affects the sales process, it affects customer service, and it affects how we operate our business. And when the people we serve know that our product or service is here to help them get what they want, they happily give us money to make that happen."

Jeff Bartsch, Storyteller and Communication Strategist, Story Greenlight

Finally, ask yourself:

1. What are my customers main pain points?
2. What does our service or product do to relieve their pain?
3. Can we market our product or service in a different way to better tell the story of success our offering brings to our customers?
4. Do I incorporate story into my sales calls, or our customer journey?

Taking a fresh approach and perspective to how story ties into your business will stir up new avenues for revenue growth and strategy.

The Interplay Between Profitability and Growth

Let's delve into the nuanced distinctions between these two dimensions, exploring how businesses can strike a harmonious balance that propels them toward sustainable success.

Profitability is the measure of a company's ability to generate a profit, typically expressed as a percentage of revenue. It reflects the efficiency of operations in converting sales into earnings.

Profitability emphasizes operational efficiency, cost control, and maximizing the bottom line. It is essential for sustaining a healthy business that can weather economic fluctuations.

Growth, on the other hand, signifies the expansion of a business, often measured by increases in revenue, market share, or the scale of operations. It can involve entering new markets, introducing new products, or acquiring competitors. Key metrics here involve revenue growth rate (the percentage increase in revenue over a specified period) and customer acquisition rate (the pace at which a company gains new customers). Growth-centric strategies prioritize market expansion, innovation, and strategic investments to capitalize on emerging opportunities.

Successful businesses recognize the symbiotic relationship between profitability and growth. While profitability ensures financial stability, growth fuels the engine of innovation and market presence.

CEOs often face dilemmas when deciding where to allocate resources. A focus on immediate profitability may lead to missed growth opportunities, while excessive investments in growth can strain profitability in the short term.

Short-Term Gains vs. Long-Term Sustainability:

Short-Term Profitability: Prioritizing short-term profitability may involve cost-cutting measures, optimizing existing processes, and streamlining operations. This approach is strategic during economic uncertainties.

Long-Term Growth: Investing in long-term growth requires a forward-looking mindset. Businesses may incur initial costs for research and development, market expansion, and talent acquisition to fuel sustained growth.

The decision for a CEO to focus on profit or growth depends on various factors, including the company's current stage, industry dynamics, and long-term strategic objectives. Striking the right balance between profit and growth is often crucial for sustainable success. Here are considerations for CEOs:

What is the current company stage?

Startups often prioritize growth over immediate profits. The focus is on gaining market share, attracting customers, and establishing a strong presence. Established companies may prioritize profitability, especially if they have already captured a significant market share. This allows for reinvestment in the business or returning value to shareholders.

What about industry dynamics?

Industries with rapid technological advancements or changing consumer preferences may require a focus on growth to stay competitive. In more stable industries, where market share is not easily gained or lost, a focus on profitability may be more appropriate.

What is your risk tolerance?

Companies with a higher risk appetite or companies in industries that demand constant innovation may lean towards growth strategies, even if they come with short-term losses. Some companies prioritize profitability as a risk mitigation strategy, ensuring financial stability in uncertain economic conditions. A growth-focused strategy may be necessary to achieve or maintain market leadership. Prioritizing profitability can contribute to financial stability, enabling the company to weather economic downturns and make strategic investments when opportunities arise.

What is more important – customer acquisition or retention?

Growth strategies often involve aggressive customer acquisition efforts, even if initial profits are lower. Profitability-focused strategies may prioritize customer satisfaction and retention, ensuring a stable revenue stream from existing clients.

What about resource allocation?

The availability of financial resources influences the CEO's decision. Limited resources may require a more balanced approach, while abundant resources may allow for simultaneous profit and growth initiatives. CEOs can enhance profitability through operational efficiency measures, which can provide a solid foundation for growth.

Balancing profit and growth is a nuanced art for CEOs. The ideal strategy often involves a dynamic approach that adapts to the company's specific circumstances, industry dynamics, and the broader economic environment. CEOs may find that a thoughtful integration of both profit and growth strategies aligns with the long-term vision and sustainability of the organization.

In the intricate dance between profitability and growth, successful businesses recognize that neither dimension exists in isolation. The art lies in finding the optimal equilibrium – a delicate balance that ensures financial stability, fosters innovation, and propels the organization toward sustained success. As CEOs navigate this interplay, they sculpt a path that leads not only to immediate prosperity but also to enduring resilience and relevance in a dynamic business landscape.

This chapter has navigated the transformative shift in the essential components of running a business. Now you can see how many strategic advantages there are to discover as you embark on profit reassessments. One immediate action step that you can take after reading this chapter is to trim the excess expenses, automate tedious tasks, and seek input from a team of experts. The journey of reassessment, optimization, and strategic focus is a pathway to sustained success, steering businesses away from the fluctuations of the Revenue Roller Coaster and towards a future of efficiency, profitability, and enduring client satisfaction.

Yet there's a piece that we haven't addressed. To be successful and remain in business, both profitability and growth are important and necessary for a company to survive. Profitability is, of course, critical to a company's existence, but growth is crucial to long-term survival. There is a distinct difference between the two. In future chapters, we will talk about tips for growth. Determining and focusing on profitability is essential. On the other hand, growth of market and sales is the means to achieving that initial profitability. Identifying growth opportunities should become the next important item on any company's goal list after the company moves beyond the profit reassessment stage.

CHAPTER NINE

Elevating Your Sales Conversations: The Neuro Emotional Approach

SALES CONVERSATION
Rewire Your Thought Patterns on Sales

What do your consumers want? What are their pain points? How do you capture their attention and turn that into a sale? These questions have not changed, and will likely never change. But, the execution or the connections to the final point of sale have certainly changed. It actually requires science.

The ability to engage and connect with potential customers is key. Elevating your sales conversations beyond the ordinary requires a strategic approach that goes beyond simply pitching your product or service.

Understanding Neuro-Emotional Technique in Sales

Neuro-emotional sales techniques go beyond traditional sales pitches and the old "Dale Carnegie" model of selling. Neuro-emotional sales, also known as neuroselling, is a sales approach that integrates principles from neuroscience and emotional intelligence to understand and influence customer behavior. The basic idea is to leverage insights from the field of neuroscience to comprehend better how the brain processes information and makes decisions and then use this knowledge to create emotionally resonant and persuasive sales strategies. Most sales professionals immediately trigger sales resistance by asking the questions they've been trained to ask. Neuroscience helps sales professionals understand the cognitive processes and emotional triggers that influence decision-making. This includes how the brain responds to different stimuli, the role of emotions, and the interplay between rational and emotional decision pathways. Alternatively, you build credibility and trust by approaching the conversation as an interested party. These are the two ingredients necessary for a successful sale. Approaching the conversation collaboratively with a goal of problem-solving is the key to success.

Gathering, Analyzing, and Diagnosing

Questions serve as your investigative tools. They help unearth your prospect's issues, if any exist, and gauge their readiness for change. These questions not only unveil problems but also delve into their root causes and their impact on your prospects. Before you even enter into the conversation with the prospect, make sure that you've spent time in research. Review their website, LinkedIn page, social media, and industry publications. This doesn't have to take hours of research but even 20 to 30 minutes can improve your understanding. If you can't squeeze the time out of your schedule, this is a perfect task to outsource to your Virtual Assistant and request they provide a summary.

When you speak to prospects, find a way to mention your research early on in the conversation. An example would be to bring up a recent LinkedIn post or mention an industry trend. This simple but powerful tactic will let their guard down and begin to build trust. If you can make an authentic connection whether it be similar interests, groups, or a personal mention, it will elevate and enhance your conversation significantly. The few minutes of research will shine light on any possibility of this.

It's also important to use sales mirroring (or mimicking) to mirror their language and nonverbal cues. This is an important rapport-building strategy. The goal is to put the person at ease by using these strategies. In most cases, mirroring or mimicking is nonverbal.

When done correctly, the idea is that mirroring in conversations will increase trust and credibility. You've heard that people buy from those that they "know, like, and trust." But they're also more willing to compromise and move forward with people that they know, like, and trust.

The first step is to stay focused. You can't be distracted because it requires 100% of your attention to do this authentically and effectively.

Keep in mind that this is a small, subtle act. Obvious mirroring is off-putting. If you don't master this technique, it can give prospects the incorrect impression that you're mocking them or insulting their behaviors.

Here are some tips to be sure that you're being subtle yet effective with mirroring:

1) **Sit in the same way that your prospect is.** If they cross their legs, do the same. If they lean forward, do this in a subtle way. Are they using their hands to speak? Notice what the prospect is communicating with their body – are they relaxed or serious? Mirroring involves matching the tone and pitch of the prospect's voice. If the prospect speaks in a measured tone, adjust your own tone to match. Similarly, if the prospect is enthusiastic and energetic, mirror that energy. Matching the pace and speed of the prospect's speech is another element of mirroring. The purpose of mirroring language in sales is not to mimic or imitate the prospect in a way that feels artificial or insincere. Instead, it is about subtly aligning with the prospect's communication style to create a more comfortable and positive interaction. This may be nodding when they nod, or clasping their hands when they do. When done effectively, mirroring can help establish rapport, build trust, and make the prospect feel more understood.

123

2) **Complement their behavioral style.** Sales professionals have a stereotype of being congenial, outgoing, and gregarious. If your prospect is more reserved, this will be very off-putting. Take the time to match your prospect's tone of voice, energy level, and cadence of speaking. Take the time to learn behavioral styles and how to pinpoint your prospects' style and adapt your style accordingly.
3) **Meet them where they are.** Do they seem most interested in the contract specifics like payments and milestones? Or are they more focused on the outcome? Are they looking for the nitty gritty details or do they just want to hear about the results? Don't be afraid to veer away from familiar sales pitch frameworks if it means that you are giving them exactly what they want – whether they're saying it verbally or nonverbally. This shows that you're paying attention.
4) **Don't fake authenticity.** The "old model"of selling tells you to find their interests and discuss common experiences. Example, if they're a golf enthusiast then the advice is that you talk about the best golf courses. But truly, don't pretend or feign interest in something you know nothing about. When it's clear that you're bluffing, you lose all trust. This doesn't mean that you have to avoid small talk and bonding over shared interests. If you truly can't find something in common, ask about their family.

Internally Persuading Your Prospect

Skillful questions internalize motivation within your customers. As they respond to your questions, they experience a powerful internal drive, making them inclined to take immediate action rather than procrastinating. You no longer need to exert external persuasion. Instead, you can guide them by asking the right questions.

Taking Control of the Conversation

Using neuro-emotional programming is able to put you in command of the conversation, not for the sake of dominance, but to steer the sales discussion in the right direction. In this case, you are not necessarily needing to be dominant but rather inquisitive and curious. Your tonality, pitch, and choice of words are important in this case to show that you are truly listening.

Priming and Persuasion

Trust is a critical factor in sales. Understanding the neurobiology of trust can guide sales strategies. Factors such as authenticity, consistency, and empathy play a role in building trust, and sales professionals can use this knowledge to establish and maintain positive relationships with clients. Neuroscience studies the concept of priming, where exposure to certain stimuli influences subsequent behavior. Sales strategies can leverage priming techniques to influence customer perceptions and preferences, making them more receptive to specific messages or offers.

Revealing Consequences

These questions compel your prospects to contemplate the consequences of maintaining the status quo. They start thinking about how their situation may deteriorate if they don't address their problems promptly. However, creating a sense of scarcity or urgency can backfire because this is such a tried and true technique. Most savvy prospects can see through the threats that your product or service is in such high demand that it won't remain accessible after a period of time. Instead, highlight the distinctive benefits of prompt action. Focus on what might happen if there are delays or that they might otherwise overlook an opportunity.

Creating Value in You and Your Product or Service

By posing the right questions at strategic moments, you automatically establish your value in your prospects' eyes. They buy into you as someone who genuinely comprehends their needs, thanks to your diligent listening and relevant questioning.

The Role of Questions in Overcoming Concerns

Questions become your allies when prospects raise concerns. Instead of handling objections conventionally, ask questions to uncover the root of the concern, allowing prospects to devise solutions themselves.

Consider a simple yet effective technique. Transform your statements into questions. Instead of presenting your solution outright, begin by asking questions to uncover what your prospects already know about the subject. This approach makes your prospects feel more involved in the decision-making process and take ownership of their issues.

By adopting a neurosales approach, you position yourself as a "trusted authority" or "trusted advisor" in your prospects' eyes. They see you as genuinely interested in their needs, differentiating you from traditional salespeople who push solutions without taking the time to understand. This newfound status makes prospects more receptive, even proactive, in seeking your guidance and ultimately purchasing from you.

Using neuroscience to develop your questions is your key to unlocking a more persuasive and effective sales journey, one that empowers your prospects to recognize the need for change and guides them towards action on their terms.

The neuroscience sales approach is built upon the idea that successful sales conversations should revolve around four core elements: the customer's needs, emotions, problems, and questions. By addressing these elements deliberately and empathetically, you can significantly enhance your sales effectiveness.

1) **Needs:** Understanding and addressing your customer's needs should be at the core of your sales strategy. To do this effectively, start by listening actively. What are their pain points? What goals are they trying to achieve? What is motivating the change? The art of listening involves learning how to ask open-ended questions and actively listen to your customer's responses. This not only helps you uncover their needs but also shows that you genuinely care about their concerns.

2) **Emotions:** Decision-making is heavily influenced by emotions, particularly in the realm of purchasing. The way individuals feel emotionally about a product or brand often guides their choices.

3) **Communication:** Connect with your prospect on a personal level. Understand their emotional state and acknowledge their feelings. Share stories and examples that resonate emotionally with them to build a stronger connection.

4) **Problems:** Most customers approach a sales conversation with a problem they want to solve or a challenge they need to overcome. Your job is to identify and empathize with these problems. When you position your product or service as the solution to their specific challenges, you become a problem solver, not just a salesperson.

5) **Problem-Centric Approach:** Tailor your pitch to address the specific problems your customer is facing. Highlight the benefits and features of your offering that directly alleviate these issues.

6) **Questions:** Encourage a two-way dialogue by asking thoughtful and relevant questions. Engage your customer's curiosity and invite them to actively participate in the conversation. By doing so, you empower them to take ownership of the decision-making process.

7) **Open Dialogue:** Foster an environment where your customer feels comfortable asking questions and expressing concerns. Be prepared to provide clear and informative answers that guide them toward a confident decision.

Putting Neuro-Emotional Sales into Practice

Injecting this cutting-edge knowledge of neuroscience into your sales practice is a powerful way to elevate your sales conversations to a new level of effectiveness and authenticity. By prioritizing the customer's needs, emotions, problems, and questions, you can create meaningful connections, build trust, and ultimately drive more successful sales outcomes.

Skillfully crafted questions have an internal persuasive effect on your prospects. Responding to these thoughtful questions triggers a potent internal motivation for your customers, prompting them to feel compelled to take action immediately rather than postponing it to an indefinite "someday."

Here are some examples of actual questions that you can use in an outline on a sales conversation:

Build Connections

- What are you using now to perform this service for you?
- How long have you been using that service or product?
- What is and isn't working for you with your current solution to the problem?
- How long have you been associated with your current company? How has your role evolved?
- What aspects of your work do you enjoy, and are there any challenges?
- What do you believe distinguishes your company in the eyes of your customers and employees?

Uncover the Problems

- From what you told me, things are going okay for you now, but considering your current situation, is there anything you would change?
- Why would you consider making that change?
- What makes it important for you *now?*

Solution Awareness

- In addressing this issue, how would your approach differ from the current situation?
- If you were to take steps to resolve this, how do you envision the outcome?
- Can you share previous attempts to address this? How effective were they?
- What has prevented you from making changes in the past?

Consequential

It's important to ask these in the normal cadence of the conversation; be casual and intentional in your tone. Show that you're serious and curious about their answers. You can also do this by pausing and asking with intent.

- Have you considered the potential consequences if no action is taken to address this problem?
- What if the product or service you're contemplating doesn't deliver the expected results?
- Have you thought about the implications of maintaining the status quo for the next few years?

Transition

This is where you transition from developing rapport and gathering information to beginning to make the sale.

- Based on our conversation, our offerings might align with your needs. For example, you mentioned [state their problem], and our solution addresses that by [briefly describing benefits]. Does this resonate with what you're looking for?
- Why do you feel our solution might be suitable for you?

Committing

Committing questions in sales are inquiries strategically designed to guide potential customers towards making a commitment or expressing a positive inclination towards a product or service. These questions are crafted to elicit responses that signal a readiness to move forward in the sales process.

- Can you see our solution as a means to reach your goals? Why or why not?
- Given our discussion, the next step would be to finalize arrangements. Does that make sense?
- How would you like to proceed from here?

Past Situation

Questions related to past situations can be seamlessly integrated at any stage of the conversation, offering versatility and adaptability to various selling scenarios based on your specific product or service.

- Can you share your thoughts on your current provider, including likes and dislikes?
- What hurdles have you faced in the past while addressing this issue?
- How has your company evolved since you started, and have these changes impacted you?

Current Questions

- How does your ideal situation compare with your current arrangement with your current vendor?
- Looking ahead, where do you envision improvements for your [specific area]? What are you most looking forward to?
- When you initially choose your current vendor, what criteria did you consider? How have these criteria changed?

Probing

These questions are extremely persuasive and based in neuroscience. The idea is that you are working to pull out your prospect's emotions which helps them to understand why they need to change their situation and instills a sense of urgency. These are persuasive questions and the tone that you use is very important here. Be sure to be curious, insightful, and genuine.

- In your vast experience, what is causing this particular issue?
- Can you provide an example so I can really understand from your perspective?
- What prompted you to explore changes in this area? Was it just one thing or a series?
- Let me know what qualities you're looking for in a [product/service/vendor.] How does that compare with what your [boss] looks for?
- I know that you recognize that this is a major [problem/challenge] in your company. We've talked about that, but are you aware of anyone else who feels the same?

Budgeting

- Just so that I can see if it could even be of help to you, could you walk me through your budgetary process for addressing this issue?
- What budgetary constraints are you currently working within?
- Who, besides yourself, would be involved in approving the budget for this initiative? Are there any obstacles that may happen?

Neuroscience explains prospects' unconscious buying behavior and helps identify the ideal path forward. It's truly a powerful framework that combines elements of neuroscience, emotional intelligence, and language patterns to enhance sales effectiveness. In the context of sales, neuroscience leverages the understanding of how the brain processes information and emotions to influence and connect with potential clients on a deeper level.

At its core, neuroscience in sales recognizes that purchasing decisions are often emotionally driven. By employing language patterns that resonate with the emotional aspects of a buyer's decision-making process, sales professionals can establish stronger connections and increase the likelihood of closing deals.

The methodology involves carefully crafting language to evoke specific emotional responses, fostering trust, and building rapport. This extends to understanding and mirroring the emotional states of potential clients, creating a sense of empathy and understanding. These techniques also emphasize the importance of nonverbal communication, including body language and tonality, to complement the chosen language patterns.

Using neuroscience in sales is not manipulative but rather aims to align the sales message with the buyer's values and motivations. By addressing both the logical and emotional aspects of a purchasing decision, this methodology enables sales professionals to create a more compelling narrative that resonates with the individual buyer.

Ultimately, the application of neuro-emotional language programming in sales is a nuanced and strategic approach, leveraging the principles of neuroscience and emotional intelligence to optimize communication, build trust, and enhance the overall sales experience for both the seller and the buyer.

CHAPTER TEN

The Power of Nudge Theory: Influencing Positive Behaviors

NUDGE THEORY
The Science of Decision-Making

Achieving desired outcomes and fostering positive behaviors within your organization is a constant challenge. As a Not Your Average CEO, you understand the importance of not just setting the right goals but also ensuring that your employees and stakeholders are aligned with your vision. This chapter explores the principles of behavioral economics and "nudge theory" as powerful tools for achieving this alignment and promoting positive behaviors within your organization.

Human decision-making is a complex interplay of cognitive biases, emotions, and environmental factors. Often, people make choices that may not align with their long-term goals or the best interests of the organization. This is where behavioral economics and nudge theory come into play.

Behavioral Economics: This field combines insights from psychology and economics to understand how people make decisions. It recognizes that individuals do not always act rationally, as traditional economic models suggest. Instead, people are influenced by emotions, social norms, and cognitive shortcuts, leading to systematic biases in their choices.

Nudge Theory: Nudge theory, popularized by Nobel laureate Richard Thaler and legal scholar Cass Sunstein, builds upon behavioral economics. It proposes that small, subtle changes in the way choices are presented can "nudge" people toward making better decisions without restricting their freedom of choice. These nudges can lead to significant shifts in behavior by making the desired option more salient, attractive, or convenient.

Nudging for Positive Behaviors

Now, let's explore how you can apply nudge theory within your organization to encourage positive behaviors among your employees, stakeholders, and customers.

1. Choice Architecture: Carefully design the choices people encounter within your organization. For example, when presenting health insurance options to employees, place the most cost-effective and comprehensive plan as the default choice. This simple change can lead to higher enrollment in the preferred plan. The concept of choice architecture is rooted in behavioral economics and psychology, recognizing that the way choices are presented can have a significant impact on decision-making.

2. Defaults: Leverage the power of defaults. Make the desired behavior the default option unless individuals actively opt out. For instance, set automatic enrollment in retirement savings plans with an option for employees to adjust their contributions. This encourages retirement savings without coercion.

3. Feedback and Social Norms: Provide individuals with feedback on their behavior and compare it to social norms. If you want to reduce energy consumption in your office, share monthly reports on energy use and highlight how it compares to similar organizations. This taps into people's desire to conform to societal expectations. Presenting choices in a way that highlights social norms or the behavior of others can influence decisions. People often look to others for cues on what is considered normal or acceptable.

4. Framing and Messaging: Pay attention to how information is framed and messaged. Positive framing emphasizes the gains or benefits of a behavior, while negative framing highlights the losses. Depending on your objectives, choose the framing that aligns with your goals. For example, when promoting workplace safety, focus on the potential benefits of following safety protocols. How information is presented, including the framing of choices and the order in which they are presented, can impact decision outcomes. For example, the same information framed positively may yield different results than when framed negatively.

5. Simplicity and Convenience: Simplify processes and make desired behaviors more convenient. If you want employees to use public transportation, provide easy access to transit passes, shuttle services, or bike-sharing programs. Reduce friction in the desired behavior.

6. Gamification: Incorporate gamification elements into workplace tasks and processes. Create challenges, leaderboards, and rewards systems that make achieving objectives engaging and fun. This approach can boost motivation and participation.

7. Feedback Loops: Implement feedback loops that provide immediate information about the consequences of actions. In sales, for instance, real-time notifications about successful deals can motivate sales teams to achieve more.

8. Personalization: Tailor nudges to individuals' preferences and behavior. Use data analytics to understand their past choices and customize nudges accordingly. This makes the nudges more relevant and effective.

9. Temporal Framing: This scientific-approach suggests that individuals perceive and evaluate information differently based on the temporal context in which it is presented. Temporal framing has implications for decision-making, risk perception, and goal-setting. Presenting choices in a way that emphasizes immediate benefits or long-term gains can influence preferences. Temporal framing is closely linked to the concept of time discounting, where the perceived value of rewards or costs diminishes as they move further into the future. Individuals may prefer immediate gratification over delayed rewards.

Ethical Considerations

While nudge theory can be a powerful tool for influencing positive behaviors, it's crucial to approach it with ethics and transparency in mind. Here are some ethical considerations:

1. **Transparency:** Ensure that the nudges are transparent and that individuals are aware of the choices presented to them. Avoid hidden or manipulative tactics. There is an ethical imperative for nudges to be transparent and not manipulate individuals without their awareness.
2. **Choice:** Respect individuals' autonomy and freedom of choice. Nudges should not restrict options but guide individuals toward better decisions. Ethical nudging seeks to guide choices without coercing individuals, allowing them to maintain control over their decisions.
3. **Beneficence:** Use nudges for the benefit of individuals and the organization, promoting their well-being and aligning with ethical principles. Ethical nudges prioritize promoting individual and societal well-being. Nudges that encourage healthier lifestyles, environmental responsibility, or financial prudence align with ethical considerations.
4. **Respecting Cultural Differences:** Ethical nudging respects cultural differences and values. Strategies should be culturally sensitive to ensure that nudges are appropriate and well-received in diverse communities.

Case Studies: Real-World Applications

To illustrate the effectiveness of nudge theory in promoting positive behaviors, we will explore examples of real-world case studies from organizations that have successfully implemented nudge-based interventions. These examples are easily replicable within your organization in different facets.

Case Study 1: The Cafeteria or Lunch Nudges

A tech company revamped its cafeteria layout to encourage healthier eating choices. They placed water in more prominent locations, made salad bars more appealing, and positioned unhealthy snacks less conspicuously. This simple redesign led to a 30% increase in salad consumption and a corresponding decrease in the consumption of sugary drinks and snacks.

Case Study 2: The Future Well-Being Study

A Virtual Assistant Company provided its employees with options on benefits, both long term and short term. The short term benefit options included medical, dental, or vision, and the long term ones included 401K, wellness programs, continued education courses, and tuition reimbursements. The employees unanimously chose the long term benefits and invested in their future well-being, both personally and professionally.

Case Study 3: Smarter Energy Decisions

A software company used behavioral science to help utility companies encourage energy conservation among their customers. By providing households with personalized energy reports and comparing their usage to that of their neighbors, they nudged customers to reduce their energy consumption, resulting in substantial energy savings.

But How Does It Apply to a Remote Environment?

Implementing nudge theory in a remote work environment requires thoughtful consideration and creative strategies. Here are some practical things that a CEO can do to apply nudge theory in a remote setting:

Digital Communication Nudges:

- **Automated Reminders:** Use automated reminders for important tasks, deadlines, or virtual meetings. Timely reminders can nudge employees to stay on track with their responsibilities. Tailor digital communications, such as emails or messages, to provide personalized feedback. Use data analytics to understand individual preferences, behaviors, and performance, and deliver messages that resonate with each team member.
- **Positive Language:** Encourage the use of positive and inclusive language in digital communications. Tone and wording can subtly influence the emotional tone of remote interactions. Providing and leading by example can make a world of difference when it comes to improving upon positive language within your organization.
- **Default Settings:** Set default options in project management tools or communication platforms that align with desired behaviors. For example, default settings for project timelines can nudge teams toward efficient planning.
- **Optimize Digital Interfaces:** Design digital platforms with choice architecture principles in mind. Optimize the layout, options, and features to guide users toward preferred actions, making it easier for them to make positive choices.

Virtual Recognition and Rewards:

- **Digital Badges and Certificates:** Introduce digital badges or certificates for achievements and milestones. These virtual rewards serve as positive reinforcement and can be shared across remote teams, fostering a sense of accomplishment. This could also include recognition in virtual meetings, digital gift cards, or other online perks. In our company, we have previously implemented an Employee of the Month program that was well-received.
- **Digital Communities:** Create virtual communities or channels where employees can share their experiences with flexible work. Nudges can encourage employees to join or contribute to these communities, fostering a culture of flexibility.

Flexible Work Options:

- **Encourage Breaks:** Remind employees of the importance of taking breaks. Consider scheduling automated messages encouraging short breaks to enhance well-being and productivity.
- **Flexible Work Hours:** Provide flexibility in work hours to accommodate different working preferences. Nudging towards a culture of flexibility can enhance work-life balance. For instance, set the default start time a bit later to nudge employees towards considering a later start if it suits their preferences.

Collaborative Decision-Making Platforms:

- **Inclusive Decision-Making Tools:** Implement collaborative decision-making tools that allow team members to contribute ideas and feedback. This fosters inclusivity and nudges employees to actively participate in the decision-making process.

Training and Development Nudges:

- **Microlearning Modules:** Implement microlearning modules for continuous skill development. Sending periodic nudges with quick, engaging learning opportunities can encourage ongoing professional growth.

Well-Being Initiatives:

- **Virtual Wellness Challenges:** Organize virtual wellness challenges that encourage healthy habits. Nudges can be incorporated through regular updates, reminders, and positive reinforcement for participation.

Feedback and Recognition:

- **Regular Check-ins:** Schedule regular virtual check-ins to provide feedback and recognition for accomplishments. Positive reinforcement through virtual meetings can be a powerful nudge.

Digital Goal-Setting Platforms:

- **Goal-Setting Reminders:** Utilize digital platforms for goal-setting and send automated reminders. Nudges towards achieving personal and professional goals contribute to a sense of accomplishment.

Team-Building Initiatives:

- **Virtual Team-Building Activities:** Organize virtual team-building activities that encourage collaboration and camaraderie. Regular nudges about upcoming activities can boost participation.

Knowledge Sharing Platforms:

- **Highlighting Contributions:** Implement platforms that allow employees to share their knowledge and achievements. Regularly highlight and celebrate these contributions to nudge a culture of continuous learning.

Employee Surveys:

- **Pulse Surveys:** Conduct regular pulse surveys to gauge employee sentiment and preferences. This real-time feedback can guide nudges that address specific needs and concerns.

By incorporating these practical strategies, a CEO can effectively apply nudge theory in a remote work environment, influencing employee behavior in positive and subtle ways that align with organizational goals and values.

Nudge theory offers a compelling approach to influence positive behaviors within your organization without resorting to heavy-handed or coercive measures. By understanding the principles of behavioral economics and implementing carefully designed nudges, you can guide individuals toward choices that benefit both your organization and its stakeholders. This chapter has provided an introduction to nudge theory and its applications, but the potential for innovative and ethical nudging is vast. Embrace this powerful tool to create a more positive and productive organizational culture, fostering a climate where desired behaviors are not just encouraged but become the default choices for your employees and stakeholders.

CHAPTER ELEVEN

Mastering Leadership in a Remote World

VIRTUAL LEADERSHIP
An Integral Part of Our Organizations

The remote work culture has become an integral part of how organizations operate. As CEOs and executives, your leadership in this digital era requires more than a passive acceptance of remote work; it demands active engagement and a well-defined strategy to ensure your organization thrives in the virtual space. In this chapter, we will outline the essential action steps to help you navigate the challenges of remote CEO leadership.

For those who are opposed to the idea of remote work, we challenge you to be open to how this concept can save you time, money, and even liability. Now, embracing remote work as a strategic imperative requires a shift from traditional leadership paradigms. It involves recognizing that the virtual workspace demands a different set of skills, communication methods, and approaches to team collaboration. As a leader, actively engaging with the intricacies of remote work entails fostering a culture of trust, open communication, and accountability within the organization. Navigating the challenges of remote CEO and executive leadership requires a keen understanding of the unique dynamics at play. Issues such as team cohesion, motivation, and the potential for feelings of isolation among remote employees must be actively managed. This may involve the implementation of virtual team-building activities, regular check-ins, and fostering a sense of connection through digital channels.

In seizing the opportunities presented by the remote work culture, leaders must leverage technology to enhance organizational agility. This includes embracing data-driven decision-making, utilizing analytics to monitor team performance, and creating a culture of continuous learning. Remote executive leadership also involves capitalizing on the potential for a more diverse and globally distributed workforce, tapping into a wealth of talent irrespective of geographical boundaries.

Let's dive into some key points, action items, and ideologies to sharpen your leadership techniques.

1. Prioritize Asynchronous Communication:

Asynchronous communication in a remote work environment refers to interaction where team members do not need to be online or engaged in real-time exchanges to communicate effectively. Instead, messages, information, and updates are shared through channels that allow individuals to participate at their own convenience. Think of tools like Slack, Microsoft Teams, Trello,

Asana, or Jira which enable teams to collaborate on projects asynchronously. Users can update project status, assign tasks, and provide feedback at their own pace.

Asynchronous communication is a cornerstone of remote work success. Encouraging your team to communicate and collaborate without the constraints of real-time exchanges fosters an environment of flexibility and productivity. Different team members have varying preferences for when and how they work most effectively. Prioritizing asynchronous communication acknowledges and respects these individual differences, contributing to a more inclusive and adaptable work environment. By embracing asynchronous communication tools like email, messaging platforms, and project management systems, you empower your workforce to engage on their terms, transcending time zones and schedules.

2. Create Space for Virtual Collaboration:

Effective teamwork in a remote setting requires a conducive environment for collaboration. As a remote CEO, it's crucial to cultivate an atmosphere where virtual collaboration is welcomed and actively encouraged. Could you provide your teams with the necessary tools and platforms to facilitate seamless cooperation, from video conferencing to virtual whiteboards, to ensure that distance does not hinder their creative synergy?

Consider the case of a tech startup with a diverse team of software developers, designers, and project managers spread across different geographic locations. The company's remote CEO understood that collaboration is vital for innovation and project success. The company adopted a video conferencing platform that allowed team members to connect face-to-face virtually. Regular video meetings were scheduled to discuss project updates, share ideas, and facilitate real-time communication. This not only helped in building a sense of camaraderie but also ensured that nonverbal cues and expressions were not lost in the virtual space. Recognizing the importance of brainstorming and visual collaboration, the CEO introduced virtual whiteboard tools like Miro and Microsoft Whiteboard. These platforms enabled team members to ideate, sketch, and collectively work on visual concepts in real-time, simulating the collaborative experience of an in-person whiteboard session. This proved invaluable for the creative aspects of the company's projects, enhancing synergy among team members. Additionally, the CEO implemented project management and communication tools that centralize information, track tasks, and provide a transparent overview of project timelines. This ensured that everyone was on the same page regarding project progress, goals, and deadlines, mitigating the challenges of distance and time zone differences.

To further encourage informal interactions and team bonding, the CEO established virtual water cooler spaces. These are designated channels or platforms where team members can engage in casual conversations, share non-work-related updates, and build social connections. This helped recreate the spontaneous interactions that often occur in a physical office setting. As a result of these initiatives, the remote team experienced heightened collaboration and creativity. The virtual tools not only bridged the geographical gaps but also empowered team members to work cohesively, leveraging each other's strengths. The company's projects benefitted from a dynamic exchange of ideas, efficient communication, and a shared sense of purpose, ultimately contributing to the startup's success in the competitive tech landscape. In this example, the remote CEO's proactive approach to providing the right collaboration tools demonstrated a commitment to overcoming the challenges of distance and fostering an environment where effective teamwork thrives and employee engagement soars.

3. Encourage Employees to Set Boundaries:

Remote work can blur the lines between professional and personal life.

As a leader, you can support your employees' well-being by empowering them to establish clear boundaries.

Encourage them to define their work hours, take breaks, and create a designated workspace within their homes. You promote productivity, job satisfaction, and overall employee morale by encouraging a healthier work-life balance. Maintaining an open discussion about this will help remind employees that it is important to draw clear lines when it comes to working from home and their workspace. Reminding them in their training, employee handbook, daily communication about breaks, will all help bring this to the front of mind for your employees.

Dedicate a Work Space.

Remote work thrives when employees have a dedicated workspace within their homes. Encourage your team members to create a designated quiet work area. This physical separation helps improve focus, productivity, and the mental transition from personal to professional responsibilities. Again, when our work space collides with our personal space too much emotions between the two can significantly blur, causing confusion and potential turmoil.

Dedicate a Virtual Work Space.

It's imperative to have an accessible knowledge-sharing system in place. Ideally, this virtual workspace should function as a "self-serve" environment, allowing employees to access the information they need without relying on constant assistance. Transform your virtual workspace into an internal content management system (CMS) equipped with user-friendly templates that empower your staff to create, publish, update, share, and archive content effortlessly, regardless of their technical skills.

4. Promote Greater Communication:

Communication is a key pillar of remote leadership. Building trust and a sense of open-door policy within your organization necessitates open communication and the free flow of information. Ensure that your organization's decision-making processes are transparent and that communication channels are accessible to all team members. Transparency fosters trust and allows for more informed decision-making at all levels. The impact of these transparent communication practices becomes evident as trust among team members grows. Team members feel informed about the company's direction and are more engaged in their work. The open-door policy empowers individuals to contribute meaningfully to the organization's success.

5. Schedule In-Person Time:

It's important not to overlook the value of face-to-face interactions. Whether through a hybrid work model that combines remote and in-person work or regular face-to-face video conferencing, maintaining human connections is essential. These interactions solidify team bonds, enhance collaboration, and maintain a sense of belonging even in a virtual setting. While remote work offers flexibility, there's still value in in-person interactions. Arrange in-person meetings, team-building activities, or gatherings whenever it works best for you. These events strengthen team bonds, nurture relationships, and create a sense of belonging. No matter the size or the frequency, they are important.

6. Check-In with Employees Regularly:

As a remote CEO and executive, staying connected with your team members becomes even more crucial. Regular check-ins provide insight into their well-being, project progress, and any challenges they may face. These interactions go beyond task-related discussions. They show that you are committed to their growth and success within the organization. This is where the important conversations happen. Setting this up for the quarter or the year will turn it into actionable items and remove it from your brainspace. Make sure that you have an agenda set for the meetings in the calendar invite descriptions therefore the topic of discussion is already set. You can also schedule virtual coffee breaks or casual meetings where team members can engage in non-work-related conversations. This helps recreate the informal interactions that naturally occur in an office setting. One important activity that we do as a company is we have virtual town hall style meetings quarterly to communicate important company-wide updates, future plans, and address any questions or concerns from the entire team. This gives the team an opportunity to have a high level view, which is important when fostering a company culture and binding employees together.

7. Be Present:

Being present as a remote CEOand executive goes beyond mere attendance in virtual meetings. It entails active participation, engagement, and accessibility. How could you show your team members that their concerns and contributions matter? Could you do it by actively participating in discussions, providing feedback? What about being available for ad hoc conversations? Your presence reinforces your leadership and fosters a sense of unity among remote team members.

Executive Tip: Keep notes on an employee on things that are important to them. You can pick this up from simple conversations. For example, your employee may mention that they like working with a certain brand of office equipment. Making a note of this and sending it as a thank you gift will bring a sense of remembrance and importance to the employee. Perhaps they mention a favorite sports team, or TV show. Your brain is not the best way to take notes, so write it down in one place and keep it for a rainy day.

---

8. Be Forward-Looking:

The remote work landscape will evolve, and that change is driven by technological advancements and societal expectations. As forward-thinking CEOs, we must anticipate future trends and challenges in remote work. Position your organization to adapt and thrive by staying informed about emerging technologies, industry developments, and best practices for remote work.

Remaining informed about cutting-edge technologies is a strategic imperative. Whether it's the integration of artificial intelligence to enhance workflow automation, the utilization of advanced collaboration tools for virtual team engagement, or the adoption of augmented reality for immersive remote experiences, staying ahead of technological trends is key to unlocking new possibilities and maintaining a competitive edge. This is how you go from an average CEO to a Not Your Average CEO. This is done by prioritizing technological awareness and adoption within the organization. A forward-thinking CEO and executive can leverage the latest tools to enhance productivity, communication, and overall business efficiency.

Executive Tip: Develop a tech chat within your organization and the main form of communication. This tech channel should be infused with new technologies, articles, open-ended

148

discussions, brainstorming sessions, that are all fueled by the CEO or COO. This shows a commitment to fostering a culture of continuous learning and innovation. By actively participating and driving conversations on emerging technologies and industry trends, leadership sets a powerful example for the entire organization. This tech chat becomes a dynamic hub for knowledge sharing, idea generation, and collaborative problem-solving, creating a sense of excitement and engagement among team members. The executive leadership's active involvement not only instills a shared vision for technological advancement but also reinforces the organization's dedication to staying at the forefront of industry developments. As a result, this vibrant tech channel becomes a catalyst for innovation, propelling the company forward in the ever-evolving landscape of remote work and digital transformation.

---

9. Be Cautious, Assuring, and Precise:

Effective communication in a remote environment requires heightened caution, assurance, and precision. Misunderstandings can easily occur in written or virtual conversations. Please be sure to exercise care in your choice of words, provide clarity, and reassure your team members when addressing concerns or challenges. This approach builds trust and minimizes potential misinterpretations. Effective communication in a remote setting requires a deliberate and thoughtful approach.

It is important to remember that virtual communication is documented. Being cautious with your words and virtual etiquette is critical. The absence of face-to-face interactions amplifies the risk of misunderstandings, making it necessary for leaders to approach written or virtual conversations with care. The choice of words becomes a powerful tool in conveying intentions. Where nuances of tone and body language are absent, the potential for misinterpretation is significant. Leaders must exercise care in articulating messages, providing explicit clarity, and employing reassurance when addressing concerns or challenges. By acknowledging potential points of confusion and proactively addressing them, leaders build trust within the team, via a culture where open communication is valued and misunderstandings are minimized.

10. Practice Email Etiquette:

To continue the last point, email remains a primary mode of communication in the remote workplace. Set clear expectations for email communication within your organization, emphasizing brevity, clarity, and professionalism. Encourage using informative subject lines, concise messages, and proper formatting to enhance efficiency and effectiveness in email exchanges.

Executive Tip: Encourage your team to adopt practices that enhance the efficiency and effectiveness of email communication. Start by emphasizing the importance of informative subject lines. A well-crafted subject line provides recipients with a quick understanding of the email's purpose, enabling them to prioritize and respond more efficiently. This practice contributes to a culture of respect for others' time. Providing examples and templates that are available to all employees will help set the tone, expectations, and boundaries.

In addition, promote the use of concise messages. Encourage team members to convey information succinctly, avoiding unnecessary details that may contribute to confusion. Clear and to-the-point communication not only saves time but also reduces the likelihood of misinterpretations.

11. Use an Online Project Management Tool:

Efficient project management is the backbone of remote work success. Implementing a robust online project management system like Teamwork Project Management or Asana streamlines tasks, tracks progress, and enhances collaboration among remote teams. These tools provide a centralized hub for project-related information, ensuring that everyone is on the same page, regardless of their physical location.

Let's look at an example. Consider a scenario where a marketing agency with a dispersed team of graphic designers, content creators, and project managers embraces the significance of efficient project management in the realm of remote work. The agency recognizes the need for a streamlined approach to handle diverse projects, from designing marketing collateral to creating digital content. In response, the team decides to implement a robust online project management system. After careful evaluation, they opt for a comprehensive tool that offers task-tracking, collaborative features, and centralized project information. With the new project management system in place, the agency experiences a transformative shift in how they approach and execute projects. Team members can now access a centralized hub that houses all project-related information, including timelines, task assignments, and important documents. This ensures that regardless of their physical location – whether working from different cities or time zones – everyone is on the same page regarding project progress and goals.

The task-tracking feature proves instrumental in keeping projects organized and on schedule. Each team member can update task statuses, upload deliverables, and communicate progress within the project management platform. This real-time visibility not only reduces the need for

150

constant status update meetings but also fosters a sense of accountability among team members. Collaboration among remote teams sees a significant improvement. The platform facilitates seamless communication through integrated messaging and commenting features. Team members can share feedback, brainstorm ideas, and discuss project details within the project management system, eliminating the need for scattered email threads and ensuring that crucial information is stored within the project's context. The system's document-sharing capabilities contribute to a more efficient workflow. Design files, content drafts, and project guidelines are stored and accessible within the platform, eliminating the challenges associated with version control and ensuring that the latest iterations are readily available to all team members.

12. Create Signals for "At Work" or "At Home":

Establishing clear signals indicating whether a team member is "at work" or "home" can help maintain work-life balance. These signals can be as simple as setting a status on communication platforms or using physical cues like closing a home office door. Consistently implementing these signals fosters respect for individual boundaries.

13. Virtual Open-Door Sessions

Maintain an open-door policy, virtually. Let employees know they can reach out at any time to discuss concerns, ask questions, or seek guidance. Choose a virtual meeting platform that accommodates the size of the team. Popular choices include Zoom, Microsoft Teams, or Google Meet. Schedule regular open-door sessions, making the timing convenient for different time zones if applicable.

Actively invite team members to participate. Send out calendar invites, reminders, or even personalized messages encouraging employees to join the virtual open-door sessions. Make it clear that all topics and questions are welcome.

Document key points discussed during the virtual open-door sessions and follow up on action items. This demonstrates that the leader values the input and is committed to addressing concerns or implementing suggestions.

14. Our Last Tip: Get Dressed.

Yes, really!

Don't underestimate the power of appearance and routine. Encourage your remote team members to dress professionally, even when working from home. This simple act helps maintain a sense of professionalism and structure, supporting their overall productivity and mindset. As the CEO or executive, set the tone and lead by example. The act of dressing professionally helps create a mental shift, signaling the transition from personal to professional responsibilities. This simple ritual contributes to a heightened sense of professionalism and structure, fostering a mindset that is conducive to focused and efficient work.

As a CEO or executive, you have the opportunity to set the tone for the entire organization. Leading by example in this regard involves consistently presenting yourself in a professional manner during virtual meetings, whether through video conferencing or other communication channels. Your commitment to maintaining a polished appearance reinforces the organizational culture and underscores the importance of professionalism in the remote work context.

Establishing a routine is equally vital.

Remote work provides flexibility, but a well-defined routine contributes to stability and productivity. Encourage your team members to establish a daily schedule that aligns with their natural rhythm and includes designated work hours, breaks, and moments for personal well-being. This routine serves as a framework for organizing tasks, managing time effectively, and maintaining a healthy work-life balance.

The power of appearance and routine extends beyond individual benefits to fostering a cohesive team culture. When team members share a commitment to professionalism and structured routines, it creates a sense of unity and shared values. This can be particularly important in a remote setting where physical distance might otherwise hinder the development of a strong team identity.

By embracing these action steps and continuously adapting to the evolving landscape of remote work, CEOs can lead their organizations to a future where geographical boundaries are no longer barriers to success. CEOs and executives must navigate the uncharted territories of remote leadership. From cultivating a culture of trust and open communication to implementing robust technology infrastructure, the actions outlined herein are designed to equip leaders with the tools and insights necessary to thrive in the virtual realm. By actively engaging with the challenges and opportunities of remote work, leaders can steer their organizations toward sustained success in the digital era.

CHAPTER TWELVE

A Deeper Dive into
Embracing Remote
Leadership

VIRTUAL COMMUNICATION
Building a Solid Foundation

"If you've never met your co-workers in person, do you even work there?"

That was the question posed by a recent New York Times article. This touches upon the fact that companies with remote workers are often mistakenly thought of as having no company culture.

The one element they have been missing? Building a remote-first culture.

A remote-first culture is a company culture built on the concept that everyone is remote. The building blocks of company culture like communication, team building activities, company events, values and ethics are all created with remote workers in mind. In typical workplace cultures, most company interactions are prioritized for in-person. Company events, communication, feedback, and team-building all happen from one central location.

Our Own Experience

As a remote-first culture company, we invested in Employee Engagement Directors to foster culture. Our handbooks and policies are all digital and everything that we do encourages interacting virtually.

Having a remote first workplace at Virtual Assist USA isn't only about the individuals being able to work when and where they're most productive. It's also beneficial to us as a company because we can hire more broadly, have a much wider access to different skill sets, and shrink and expand quickly according to our needs and economics.

We've been remote since our founding in 2008, so we have seen our share of mistakes when companies try to adapt to remote or hybrid work. Simply put, you can't take what you did in the office and easily translate it online. It just doesn't work that way. Building a remote-first culture isn't as easy as having virtual happy hours every other month. It requires intentionality.

Just like office culture, you build on pillars that range from how you communicate with each other to your values and the benefits you offer. So, what are some pillars that you can consider? The first place to start is by creating a company handbook or culture outline that everyone can look at as the one source of truth for the organization. You can then construct your pillars from there.

Here are some of the elements that remote experts recommend to include:

Communication

Communication guidelines set a standard for how your remote teams interact with each other. This framework helps prevent a culture of anxiety, the kind where people feel they need to be on call 24/7. It establishes a culture that sets healthy boundaries between work and personal life. It sets clear expectations and lets everyone work at their most productive hours without being interrupted. If you are a hybrid organization, have everyone take calls from their computer even if they are in the same room together. This sets a precedent for honest communication in meetings between people in the office and remote workers.

A formal internal communications guide ensures that everyone – regardless of location – has access to the ins and outs of where workplace communication flows and where informal bonding occurs.

The first step to getting teams on the same page is ensuring they're speaking in the same venue. In distributed teams, it's critical to document where communication happens, so there's no guesswork involved. A formal location creates a single source of truth where everyone can check-in and read the latest without needing a status meeting.

When assembling a remote team, or leading a team in general, communication is paramount.

"Integrity, honesty, leadership, having a servant heart, clear communication, looking out for others, and personalities that fill in all the gaps."

Adam Kirk, CEO, Oostas Marketing

Effective communication is the linchpin that holds a remote team together, creating a sense of unity and purpose among its members. It not only ensures that everyone is on the same page, but it also promotes trust and transparency within the team. Transparency in communication is essential, as it allows team members and leaders to openly share their ideas, concerns, and feedback, leading to a more collaborative and productive work environment.

Additionally, clear and consistent communication helps remote team members feel connected, despite physical distances, creating a cohesive and well-functioning team. As such, embracing these principles of integrity, honesty, leadership, and servant leadership, while fostering an environment of open and transparent communication, is key to the success of any remote team.

Inclusion with Your Mission

A problem in many company cultures that existed even before the world went remote was making each employee feel included in the mission. With the absence of in-person interaction, it is even easier for team members to slip through the cracks. By highlighting your team's diversity, you encourage all of your employees to be their true professional selves. It opens up dialogues about topics and creates stronger bonds across the team.

Start by creating an ethos statement and HR guidebook. Record and describe the elements of your own team culture that live in your organization or team. Every organization wants to ensure that team members with issues or challenges feel they can speak up, be heard, and get support. This happens mainly through small gestures every day, as well as within written policies. For example, leaders and supervisors can encourage collaboration by checking in on their reports, offering a mentoring system within your organization, and providing external counselors or support resources for your employees.

Many remote-first organizations have bolstered their initiatives with extra days off, organized additional online events and support where possible, and encouraged small in-person meetings with local team-mates. Perks can be facilitated through food or restaurant gift certificates.

Employee Engagement

Your plan for employee engagement and support should be more than meetings, one on ones, and the randomly scheduled virtual party. Informal communication is just as important to build connections across your organizations. The water cooler is not where culture is made, as many CEOs would like you to believe. However, it still plays an essential role in creativity and innovation.

Variety is the spice of life, as the old saying goes! So we recommend looking at all the various touch points where workers can chat informally, share photos, images, GIFs, and jokes. Most likely, this is on Slack and IM systems. Visual Collaboration boards and galleries could hold holiday or sports challenges images. Also, galleries can hold images to introduce individuals' families, personal interests, and their home or coworking setup. You can use software like Donut on Slack to introduce members casually for coffee calls and chats every week. You can have a trivia night, a monthly book club, or Fantasy Football sports events that you organize on Zoom.

Team building is aligning around a common purpose AND enjoying working together. We create camaraderie by understanding each other's intrinsic motivations.

1. Why do our colleagues and we come to work every day?

2. What drives us to do what we do?
3. What does success look like to our employees?
4. What benefits are important to our team members?
5. Do our team members align with our vision and mission?
6. Better yet, do our team members understand our organization's vision and mission?

Understanding each other's intrinsic motivations is key to humanizing our work relationships and ensuring that we see our colleagues as human beings. Learning what our colleagues need to feel connected, particularly on a team, allows us to create better relationships and increase cohesion. Connection happens when we pay attention to each other.

Non-Concurrent Work

This topic has been a bit overplayed post-pandemic, but it cannot be repeated enough because organizations are still struggling.

Asynchronous work means each team member balances having sprints and completing a portion of a project on their own time. In the end, they finish the project in increments.

By including asynchronous work as an element of your remote-first culture handbook, you encourage your employees to work flexibly. They can collaborate across time zones without physically having to be on calls together.

These methods are especially critical to the success of hybrid and flexible teams because they:

- Demonstrate respect for people's work and time
- Increase productivity due to more focused deep work
- Avoid loss of information as people switch their working locations
- Improve thoughtful decision-making regardless of where employees are working
- Promote equitable experiences between remote and in-office employees
- Save teams time and money due to fewer interruptions and more efficient meetings

Companies run the risk of increased employee burnout and higher turnover when they fail to learn and implement async-first behaviors and only think of a single time zone, nine to five work.

Every organization should routinely check in with their employees to ensure a good balance of async and sync. Without enough quality sync time, employees may feel detached and isolated. New employees and early career professionals may require additional synchronous interactions. But too much sync time and employees may feel micromanaged. The goal is to find a balance between autonomous work and rich communication.

Hiring and Onboarding Remote Workers

This process should be a documented part of your culture because it sets the first impression of your company brand to any prospective or new employee. Establishing a comprehensive onboarding process is not just a procedural formality. It serves as a foundational element and a documented part of your organizational culture. The onboarding process plays a role as it is often the first interaction a new employee has with your company, setting the initial impression, and shaping their perception of your brand.

Without a documented onboarding process, employees can disassociate from their new job. To avoid overwhelming – or even underwhelming – new hires, think about setting an itinerary for their first week, sending a welcome package and giving them an easy and not time-sensitive task to start.

Consider using a checklist for new team members to work their way through that includes the obvious things like setting up their technology and email access but also has things like reviewing your five most recent blog posts, examining brand guidelines, and spending time on your social media pages. You may even include booking a 15 minute "get to know you" meeting with other team members, just to say hi.

A documented onboarding process ensures consistency and clarity, offering a structured introduction to the company's values, mission, and work culture. This is particularly crucial in shaping the first impression that prospective or new employees form about your organization. It becomes a reflection of your company's commitment to professionalism and employee experience, contributing significantly to employer branding. In the absence of this, new hires feel adrift, leading to disengagement or a sense of detachment from their roles. To mitigate this, it is imperative to establish an onboarding itinerary that is carefully designed to provide a comprehensive and welcoming experience. This includes sending a thoughtful welcome package and assigning a manageable initial task to help new hires acclimate gradually to their roles.

Creating a detailed checklist for new team members further reinforces the importance of a systematic onboarding process. Beyond the basic logistical elements like setting up technology and email access, the checklist should encompass a broader spectrum of activities.

- Use technology to your advantage here to really brighten up a new hire's experience. This does not need to be a boring Word document checklist. You can consider using Canva to create graphics and slides that are more visually appealing. Other current platforms include JazzHR, Workday, or Namely which feature employee engagement opportunities.
- Place indicators in areas where you expect certain information to be, yet it is absent, to serve as an effective method to gauge the attentiveness of new hires. As an illustration, a

task on the checklist may involve accessing a particular webpage, but if the page is password-protected and the password hasn't been provided, it prompts the new hires to identify the right person to request it from. This approach allows you, as a leader, to assess whether they are actively engaged or merely going through the motions. Additionally, it serves as a signal to determine their level of attention to detail.

- Assessments during your hiring and onboarding process are a great way to start to know a candidate or employee. In our company, we use DISC assessments, a widely used behavioral assessment tool based on the DISC theory. The DISC model was developed by psychologist William Moulton Marston in the 1920s and later refined into a behavioral assessment system. The DISC model categorizes human behavior into four primary personality traits which helps us to understand team member's communication styles and adapt our leadership style to better engage and motivate our teams. Remember to obtain informed consent from employees before administering any assessment. Clearly communicate the purpose of the assessment and how the results will be used. Be transparent about the nature of the assessment. Clearly explain that it is a tool to understand communication and behavioral styles, and emphasize that it is not a measure of job performance, intelligence, or personal traits.
- Create videos that capitalize on bringing connection to new hires, such as team members describing their work day, or introducing themselves to help bridge the gap between in person and remote disconnects.
- An interactive training module for new hires is a great way to engage them from the start and set the tone that this is a collaborative environment.

Additionally, incorporating interpersonal elements into the onboarding checklist is equally vital. Encouraging new team members to schedule short introductory meetings with their colleagues fosters a sense of community and helps build interpersonal relationships. These meetings serve as a platform for casual introductions, creating a friendly and inclusive environment from the outset.

The onboarding process extends far beyond mere paperwork. It is a strategic tool for integrating new hires into the fabric of the organization. A strategic and documented onboarding process reinforces your company's commitment to employee success, enhances brand perception, and sets the stage for a positive and collaborative work environment.

How Leaders Can Embrace Remote-First Culture

How do employees stay connected when they don't see their leadership team day to day?

It's common in our business that employees may go their entire tenure without ever having met in person. We've made top-down transparency a foundational part of our culture. This includes having video meetings where our senior leadership team gives reports and operational initiatives to the entire company in real time.

One of the biggest worries for leaders is that remote work has failed to produce an engaging company culture. Time has shown that although the process is more complicated, creating a virtual culture is possible. It is possible to have engaged employees and robust support systems within corporations while working from home.

But if the leaders show doubt, that trickles down to the employees and everyone thinks returning to the office is the solution to their lack of culture. If there are no conscious efforts to shift mindsets, benefits, workflows, or activities to remote, then everyone will continue to suffer from endless zoom meetings, poor work-life balances, and burnout.

As a leader, you must show that you make remote-first a competitive advantage and a pillar of your company, instead of just something that you tolerate but don't take seriously.

Our remote work policy is a significant part of our interview process, starting at the very beginning. This includes asking candidates if they've considered their work-from-home set up. We are cognizant to remind candidates that not everybody thrives working from home. We are up front about the pitfalls. Questions we ask: How do you stay disciplined? Do you have a dedicated and quiet office space?

Remote-first is the future of work, and the more companies' mindset, the more they will be prepared in the coming years. A 2022 study in the Harvard Business Review found the following:

- **Productivity** — Remote workers are on average 35 to 40% more productive than their office counterparts. They have measured an output increase of at least 5%.
- **Quality** — With greater autonomy and a bias towards asynchronous communication, workers produce results with 40% fewer quality defects.
- **Engagement** — Higher productivity and performance combine to create stronger engagement, or in other words, 41% lower absenteeism.
- **Retention** — 54% of employees say they would change jobs for one that offered them more flexibility, which results in an average of 12% turnover reduction after a remote work agreement is offered.
- **Profitability** — Organizations save an average of $11,000 per year per part-time remote worker, or report 21% higher profitability.

Ideas for Remote Employee Engagement

1. Virtual Book Club: Create a virtual book club where team members can read and discuss a chosen book each month. This not only encourages reading but also provides an avenue for in-depth, intellectual discussions.

2. Random Pairing: Implement a random pairing system where employees are matched with a colleague for a virtual coffee chat or discussion. This can help team members connect with colleagues they might not interact with regularly.

3. Online Art or Cooking Classes: Offer online art or cooking classes where employees can learn a new skill together. It's a creative way to bond over shared interests and create something tangible.

4. Themed Virtual Meetings: Plan themed virtual meetings where team members can dress up according to a specific theme, such as '80s retro day or favorite movie character day. It adds an element of fun and creativity to meetings.

5. Mystery Gift Exchange: Organize a mystery gift exchange program. Employees are paired up, and they send each other surprise gifts based on a budget or a chosen theme. This develops relationships between team members who may not otherwise engage with one another.

6. Virtual Travel Experiences: Share virtual travel experiences like virtual museum tours, city tours, or cooking lessons from around the world. It allows employees to explore new cultures together.

7. Creative Competitions: Host creative competitions, such as a pumpkin carving contest, art contest, or photography competition, where employees can showcase their talents and vote for their favorites.

8. Collaborative Playlists: Create collaborative music playlists, such as on Spotify or Pandora, where employees can add their favorite songs. It's a simple way to connect over shared musical interests.

9. Virtual Office Tours: Have employees give virtual tours of their home offices, sharing insights into their workspace, personal touches, and organization tips. This is also a really great time to meet the four-legged coworkers!

10. Local Cuisine Exchange: Encourage employees to order and share local or regional cuisine with colleagues from different locations during a virtual lunch meeting. Danielle, CEO of Virtual Assist USA, said of another idea, "During the holiday season, one of our supervisors takes charge on organizing a cookbook of the team's favorite holiday recipes and family traditions. It's a favorite and one that our remote team members look forward to all year."

These unique ideas can inject variety and excitement into remote team interactions, helping to strengthen social bonds and create a vibrant virtual workplace culture. The key is to maintain a balance between work-related discussions and these social activities to keep employees engaged and connected.

Navigating Remote Work Realities - The Dance of Motivation and Discipline

CEOs find themselves at the intersection of motivation and discipline, navigating the delicate dance between inspiring their teams and ensuring the disciplined execution of strategic initiatives. But what are the nuances of motivation versus discipline?

For CEOs and leaders, the twin pillars of success are motivation and discipline, though these terms carry distinct meanings. When propelling yourself or your team toward a specific goal, the question arises: Should you rely more on motivation or discipline?

Motivation infuses your daily activities with passion, fostering a positive attitude and eagerness to work on your business.

There are two main types of motivation: extrinsic, meaning driven by external rewards or avoidance of punishment, and intrinsic, meaning stemming from internal enjoyment or fulfillment.

Stephen Covey, in "Principle-Centered Leadership," defines discipline as "the ability to make and keep promises and to honor commitments." Discipline ensures the execution of the right actions for long-term gain, even when alternatives seem more appealing.

Discipline is the commitment to fulfilling promises, even in the face of daily business challenges. The difference between motivation and discipline lies in the "why" behind your actions versus the actions themselves.

Motivation versus Discipline: A Dichotomy

Motivation initiates your journey, providing the impetus to start a company or make a difference. Discipline, on the other hand, sustains the effort required to build your business over the long term. While motivation represents the initial burst of inspiration, discipline is the force that propels you toward your goals when the initial fervor wanes.

In the context of running a business, motivation may drive you to work on your business every day, develop a robust go-to-market strategy, and understand your ideal customer thoroughly.

Discipline, however, is what keeps you committed to these actions day in and day out.

The CEO's Conundrum: What's More Important?

Motivation is foundational for embarking on an entrepreneurial journey. It acts as the fuel that propels you towards your dreams, instills hope during discouraging times, and inspires others to rally behind your mission.

Discipline, then, is the key to putting in extra hours, going the extra mile, and committing to wellness routines that prevent burnout. It helps you stay focused, fight procrastination, and progress steadily toward your goals.

For CEOs, tapping into both motivation and discipline is crucial. At Virtual Assist USA, we've found that each one is more important at various times. It flip flops, in other words. The way that we think of it is that motivation provides the extra push needed whenever you're fatigued or stressed, but discipline is what propels you through each challenge.

Cultivating discipline may not come naturally to many, but adopting certain strategies can enhance both motivation and discipline, ultimately boosting productivity:

Embrace Your Purpose: Remind yourself of your purpose, as it precedes passion. When motivation wanes, reflecting on the reasons behind your goals and the chosen professional path can reignite your drive. Focus on the "why" more than the "how."

Prioritize Preparation: Effective preparation involves not only organizing daily schedules but also aligning your heart and mind. Consider the tasks that truly enhance productivity and imbue your day with significance. Preparation is key to sustaining motivation and discipline.

Maintain Focus: Strive for progress over perfection. It is something that we say often in our organization. Concentrate on a select few tasks or habits initially, concentrating on refining one aspect at a time. Excellence emerges from consistent discipline, fostering a sense of accomplishment.

Engage in Reflective Practices: Allocate time each day, both morning and evening, for self-reflection. Assess your daily experiences, acknowledge your accomplishments, and draw upon past victories to bolster confidence. This reflective practice serves not only as a motivational tool but also as a reservoir of strength during personal or professional challenges.

By integrating these practices into your routine, you can cultivate a harmonious balance between motivation and discipline, amplifying your overall productivity and paving the way for sustained success.

CHAPTER THIRTEEN

Modern Workforce: Navigating the New Employee Culture

MODERN WORKFORCE
Understanding the Nuances of Today

It has become no secret that employees are vastly different today then they have ever been. Employee behavior, wants, and needs are always changing, but this shift is the biggest and most drastic yet. The generational behaviors and attributes have become such a large gap that it is hard for productivity, interactions, connections, and understanding. Understanding and managing this divide has become crucial for fostering productivity, positive interactions, meaningful connections, and overall harmony within the workplace.

One of the key factors contributing to this disparity is the emergence of a multigenerational workforce. With baby boomers, Generation X, millennials, and now Generation Z coexisting in the same workspace, each group brings its own set of values, communication styles, and work preferences. The clash of these different perspectives can lead to challenges in teamwork, communication, and overall synergy within the organization. Efforts and collective work are required to address the gap that has emerged. Recognizing the inevitability of change is paramount. Rather than resisting it, embracing and leveraging change can become a powerful advantage. Change can bring new opportunities, fresh perspectives, and innovative solutions.

It's about acknowledging that where there are humans involved, change is a constant, and adaptation is the key to success.

But what does the modern workforce require these days?

What are the expectations and key indicators for success? Several factors contribute to the ever-changing dynamics, and it's crucial to explore what the contemporary workforce requires and the key indicators of success in this context.

Investing in professional development opportunities that cater to different learning styles and preferences can enhance employee engagement and satisfaction. Recognizing and celebrating achievements across generations can also contribute to a positive workplace culture that values the contributions of every individual, regardless of age. Additionally, the modern employee embodies an entrepreneurial mindset, taking ownership of their work, seeking innovative solutions and driving positive change within their organization. They are driven, self-motivated, and capable of navigating the complexities of today's workplace with confidence and enthusiasm.

One of the key pillars of the modern workplace is the utilization of digital collaboration tools and platforms. These tools enable employees to connect, communicate, and collaborate irrespective of their physical location. With the rise of cloud computing and mobile technology, teams can collaborate in real-time, share documents, and co-edit projects, breaking down geographical barriers and enabling global teams to work together seamlessly.

Human Resource Management in the Modern Workplace

Many CEOs and executives think that you only need Human Resources when you have a team over 20 people, but the fact of the matter is that you even need HR with just one employee. It is important to note the difference between using an independent contractor, or assistant for hire through a service, versus hiring your own employee. When looking to build your team, considering all of your options and doing a cost analysis is foundational to your success and profit assessment.

This section below will discuss the needs for human resources if you have one or more employees.

HR is an indispensable aspect of any organization, and its dynamic nature requires constant attention. In the world of HR, routine tasks hardly exist because change is an inherent part of working with people. There's no such thing as an "average day" because the human element brings unpredictability. To navigate this effectively, it's essential to establish your HR processes and procedures early and maintain a commitment to their continual development and enhancement. Just as you wouldn't seek medical attention from a dentist for a broken arm, it's important to rely on specialists in HR to manage the intricacies of human resource management. Specialist HR professionals are valuable assets to both you and your organization.

Today's HR team juggles more than ever before. The modern HR team is tasked with a multifaceted role that extends beyond traditional administrative functions. This includes compliance, regulations, policies, culture, employee retention and engagement, lawsuits, federal and state laws, and the list is growing.

Talent Acquisition and Recruitment: HR teams are at the forefront of attracting and acquiring top talent for your organization. In addition to traditional recruitment methods for sourcing candidates, they leverage digital platforms, social media, and data analytics to identify and engage with potential candidates. The competition for skilled professionals has intensified, making effective recruitment strategies crucial for the success of the organization.

A strong HR professional or team must:

- Understand the workings of recruitment platforms. Current platforms such as Indeed, ZipRecruiter, and Linkedin are at the top of the list.
- Know when to use a Virtual Assistant service, such as Virtual Assist USA, or a freelance service such as Upwork or Fiverr. A strong HR professional will be able to outline the pros and cons of these services and how they impact your own business.
- Assess platforms and candidates in a compliant manner.
- Utilize Applicant Tracking Softwares (ATS) and understand their pros and cons.

Payroll onboarding and state registrations can be tricky to manage and should be completed by a trained professional or service. Each state and locality has different regulations such as for paid family leave, different ways of calculating unemployment insurance. and varied reporting requirements.

Employee Engagement and Retention: Retaining a talented workforce is just as important as attracting one. HR professionals are tasked with creating and implementing strategies to enhance employee engagement and satisfaction. This involves understanding the unique needs and expectations of employees, fostering a positive work culture, and developing retention programs that promote loyalty and commitment.

- Turnover can completely tank profitability. The average cost of employee turnover in 2023 was around 35% of an employees base salary.
  - Base Salary: Let's consider an employee with a base salary of $50,000 per year.
    Cost of Turnover: The cost of turnover, in this case, would be 35% of the base salary. Cost of Turnover = Base Salary × Turnover Percentage
    Cost of Turnover = $50,000 x 0.35 = $17,500
    So, in this example, the cost to the company of turnover for one employee would be $17,500.
  - Now, let's consider the impact on profitability when multiple employees leave the organization.
    Number of Employees Turned Over:
    Suppose 10 employees leave the organization in a given year.
    Total Cost of Turnover = Cost of Turnover per Employee × Number of Employees
    Total Cost of Turnover = $17,500 x 10 = $175,000
    In this scenario, the organization incurs a total cost of $175,000 due to employee turnover. This cost includes expenses related to recruitment, onboarding, training, and the temporary decrease in productivity as new employees get acclimated to their roles. This example illustrates how the financial impact of turnover, when

expressed as a percentage of an employee's base salary, can have substantial implications for a company's profitability. Managing turnover effectively becomes not just a human resources concern but a critical business strategy to maintain financial stability and ensure sustained growth.

Training and Development: Continuous learning is a key component of the modern workplace, and HR teams are responsible for designing and implementing training programs. This includes both onboarding initiatives for new hires and ongoing development opportunities for existing employees. The emphasis is on upskilling and reskilling to ensure that the workforce remains adaptable and equipped for evolving roles.

- Consider what your competition is providing to their staff. What do they have in place to offer training and development opportunities for their employees? Are they expanding upon their services and quality of work because they are training their employees?

Performance Management: HR professionals are involved in establishing and maintaining performance management systems. This includes setting performance goals, conducting regular evaluations, and providing constructive feedback. Performance management is not just about assessing individual contributions, but also aligning them with organizational objectives.

Employee Relations and Conflict Resolution: Handling employee relations and resolving conflicts is a delicate yet essential aspect of HR responsibilities. HR teams mediate disputes, address grievances, and create a conducive work environment that minimizes conflicts. Effective employee relations contribute to a positive workplace culture.

Compliance and Regulatory Adherence: Staying abreast of labor laws, regulations, and compliance standards is a critical responsibility for HR professionals. They ensure that the organization operates within legal frameworks, mitigating risks and potential legal issues. This includes managing issues related to employee rights, benefits, and workplace safety.
- Checking with your payroll provider to see if they offer assistance with this can save time and money for you and your team.
- Understanding all of your compliance and legal requirements should be at the top of your priority list. One lawsuit can completely bankrupt your company.
  - Consider this scenario and all that comes with it: Imagine a small company with 50 employees, operating in a highly competitive industry. One day, an employee files a lawsuit against the company, alleging workplace harassment and discrimination. The employee claims emotional distress and demands significant compensation.
  - Financial Impact: Hiring legal representation to defend against the lawsuit can be expensive. Legal fees can quickly accumulate, especially if the case becomes

protracted or goes to trial. The average hourly rate here is between $500 to 700 per hour.

- Even if the employee is completely making up the claim, the amount in fees to fight the claim is substantial. The internal work to find proof and documentation can take hours alone.

   - This is also assuming that the company has the proper practices in place to defend properly against a claim. For example, were proper measurements taken when the employee told the company about the harassment? Did the company have a written and signed no harassment policy with proper annual training and documentation?

- Settlement Costs: To avoid a potentially higher judgment in court, the company may decide to settle the case. Settlements often involve a substantial financial payout to the plaintiff, further straining the company's resources. This alone could bankrupt the company.

- Reputation Damage: The negative publicity associated with a lawsuit can damage the company's reputation, potentially leading to a loss of customers and business partners. This can be seen in negative reviews whether via Google or other platforms.

- Insurance Premiums: Depending on the outcome of the lawsuit, the company's insurance premiums may increase significantly. This can add an ongoing financial burden to the organization.

- Productivity Loss: Managing a lawsuit can divert management's attention from day-to-day operations. This distraction may result in decreased productivity and hinder the company's ability to generate revenue.

- Employee Morale and Turnover: Workplace lawsuits can negatively impact employee morale and trust in the company. This may lead to increased turnover, further disrupting the business and incurring recruitment and training costs.

- Regulatory Fines: If the lawsuit uncovers violations of labor laws or workplace regulations, the company may face additional fines and penalties imposed by regulatory authorities.

- Impact on Investors and Stock Value: If the company is publicly traded, the negative consequences of a lawsuit can lead to a decline in stock value. This, in turn, affects the company's market capitalization and attractiveness to investors.

- The cumulative financial strain from legal fees, settlements, reputation damage, increased insurance costs, productivity loss, employee turnover, regulatory fines, and stock devaluation could be overwhelming. In a worst-case scenario, these factors could push the company into financial distress, making it difficult to meet its financial obligations and potentially leading to bankruptcy.

It's important for companies to prioritize a proactive approach to prevent workplace issues, establish robust HR practices, and invest in legal compliance to mitigate the risk of employee lawsuits and their financial consequences.

Benefits Administration: HR teams oversee the design and administration of employee benefits packages. This involves managing health insurance, retirement plans, and other perks. The goal is to offer competitive benefits that contribute to employee satisfaction and well-being.

- If it is not within your wheelhouse to provide elaborate benefits, there are perks for employees that are not extremely costly but important for employees.
  - For example, signing up for different perks for employers such as Corporate Perks, or Perks at Work. These types of companies offer perks and discounts to employees. Oftentimes they even offer hundreds of training videos and live sessions in a multitude of areas such as customer service, wellness care, cooking and more.
  - If you are unsure, just ask your employees. Create an anonymous poll that asks them what benefits matter most to them. Maybe it is a hybrid work schedule or a flexible day, instead of the traditional benefits.

Adapting to Technological Advances: The integration of technology in HR processes has become increasingly prevalent. HR teams adopt and manage human resource information systems (HRIS), applicant tracking systems, and other digital tools to streamline processes, enhance data analysis, and improve overall efficiency.

- Do the math, and assess how many manual hours are being put into these areas, and what the cost would be to adapt one of these platforms to increase productivity.
  - Example: Using an applicant tracking system may cost several hundred dollars a year. However if you are manually searching for candidates, sorting them by hand, this could take hours. Cost of Applicant Tracking System:
    Assume the annual cost of an applicant tracking system is $500.
    Time Cost of Manual Processes:
    Suppose, without an ATS, manually searching for candidates and sorting applications takes 10 hours per week, and the average hourly wage for the personnel involved is $20. This is assuming you the CEO or executive are not doing this! Time Cost of Manual Processes = Hours Spent per Week × Hourly Wage
  - Time Cost of Manual Processes = 10 hours per week x $20 per hour = $200 per week
  - Over a year, the time cost of manual processes would be $200 per week x 52 weeks = $10,400.
  - In this example, using an ATS costs $500 per year, while the manual process incurs a time cost of $10,400 per year. While using an ATS still requires a human

component, it can likely be knocked down to one or two hours. **A total cost savings in this example is $8,320 per year.**
This example demonstrates how the initial investment in an applicant tracking system can result in significant time and cost savings over the long term. The efficiency gains and improved productivity from using an ATS can far outweigh the relatively modest upfront cost.

Crisis Management and Well-Being Support: In times of crisis, such as the global pandemic, HR teams play a crucial role in crisis management. They are involved in developing and implementing strategies to support employee well-being, ensuring effective communication, and managing the organizational response to unforeseen challenges. An HR team is the front line of questioning and panic control for your employees. This is an invaluable resource for your employees to have comfort in their work environment.

The modern workforce requires a human resource management component in a big way. It is an area that cannot be overlooked for the consequence can be detrimental to your company.

Creating a Culture

It takes a Not Your Average CEO to drive the workforce and company culture today.

"'Not Your Average CEO' is someone who has boots on the ground and has their sleeves rolled up working with their team members directly, rather than it being a hierarchy. Everyone is at the same level, doing the same things and figuring things out together."

Erica Rankin, CEO

The modern employee is looking to relate with their company culture that is directly related to the ethics of the CEO. The term "modern workplace" is used to describe organizations that have embraced the reality of digital collaboration, solutions, and integration as the way of the future. This new way of defining the workplace has paved the way for technologies supporting automation, digital workspaces, and hybrid work. In the modern workplace, traditional office boundaries are expanding, and technology plays a central role in facilitating seamless communication, efficient workflows, and enhanced productivity.

Taking a step back and assessing the current culture of your organization is the first step. Writing down your assessment first is the perfect step to properly assessing the current state of the culture. This introspective evaluation allows leadership to identify strengths and weaknesses within the organizational culture. By understanding the current dynamics, decision-makers can implement targeted strategies to enhance teamwork, communication, and overall employee satisfaction. The second step is crucial and it is to involve employees in this process, encouraging open and honest feedback to gain diverse perspectives. The use of HR here, or simple anonymous forms can be helpful. Looking at your turnover rate and employee retention can give insight into the current culture. In the last stage, reflect on the kind of employee culture you aspire to cultivate. Consider the values you wish your company to embody and project outward. Again, write them down and set achievable goals to maintain a specific employee culture. Seeking help from HR professionals is always an option here as well. Additionally, fostering a culture of continuous improvement ensures that the organization remains adaptive to changing trends and challenges. Through this ongoing assessment and commitment to positive cultural development, the organization can cultivate a thriving and inclusive atmosphere that not only attracts top talent but also sustains long-term success.

What Do Employees Look For?

In today's atmosphere employees are looking for multiple opportunities within an organization. This includes options such as remote work, participation in training programs, tuition reimbursement, and access to cutting-edge software. Embracing these diverse opportunities not only meets the evolving expectations of employees but also contributes to a dynamic and forward-thinking workplace culture.

Employees are looking for a hybrid remote work, which has become one of the top rated work environments to date. The modern employee no longer has to sit in traffic on a daily basis, go back and forth from the office, or worry about germs. Honestly, it causes less stress to work from home than working from the office. With the advancement of technology and changing employee preferences, organizations are embracing flexible work arrangements that combine remote work and in-person collaboration. Hybrid work models allow employees to maintain a better work-life balance, while organizations can benefit from increased employee satisfaction and potentially reduced operational costs. If you are unsure about a remote workplace or a hybrid model, consider the ramifications of turnover and lack of engagement if your employees seek this but you do not offer it. Remember, your employees know what they can do from home with technology and what requires them to be in office. These virtual environments enable employees to work flexibly, allowing them to access their work-related resources from any device and location.

Integration is another vital aspect of the modern workplace culture. Organizations are leveraging technology to integrate different systems and applications, allowing for smooth data flow and streamlined processes. Through access to these platforms and integration, data from various sources can be consolidated, providing employees with a holistic view of information and empowering them to make data-driven decisions more efficiently. Automation is also a significant component of the modern workplace, as organizations seek to optimize repetitive and time-consuming tasks. By automating routine processes, employees can focus on more strategic and value-added activities. Automation technologies such as robotic process automation (RPA) and AI are being implemented to improve operational efficiency, reduce errors and enhance overall productivity. With integrations and automations, your team can focus on less mundane tasks. This creates a culture derived from a higher level of thinking.

Employee Engagement

In the realm of employee engagement, particularly in today's dynamic global landscape, many businesses encounter challenges when it comes to HR practices. Employee engagement ties directly into employee culture and what employees are seeking in a career. It's crucial to recognize that each problem and every employee's situation is unique. Some issues may be rooted in personal matters unrelated to the company, while others might stem from policy or cultural factors. Ensuring that your HR team, or your designated HR person, is a perfect fit for this role in your organization is of paramount importance. They play a vital role in recruiting and retaining top talent for your company.

Employee engagement begins with the recruiting, hiring, and onboarding process.

"You need to understand what the trends are, understand what the issues are, literally what the challenges are of hiring and retaining talent and what you need to be competitive to be able to attract and retain top people because, again, your employees are the life engine of the success of your business. Don't take the excuse of 'I didn't know' or be naive because you didn't take the time to understand what's going on in society, whether it's in the United States or any other country where you may have employees."

Chuck Mollor, CEO, MCG Partners

To immediately capture your employees attention, include employee engagement tactics into your recruiting and assessment process. This could involve incorporating interactive elements such as gamified assessments, personalized onboarding experiences, or conducting team-building exercises during the recruitment phase. Additionally, showcasing the company's commitment to professional development and career growth during interviews can pique the interest of potential employees. Providing a glimpse into the positive work culture through testimonials or success stories can also be an effective way to engage candidates from the outset. These efforts should then be continued throughout the employee lifecycle, and upon termination an end of employment interview should be conducted to provide insight and feedback.

"One of the biggest mistakes I see with people in business is that they do not have an effective job description or hiring process for a position that they might be hiring for. If you don't tell the

world what you want in writing, you're going to get what you get. It is more than a skillset, culture is so vitally important. What are the core values in your organization and are those criteria spelled out also? Once you have a new team member, an intentional onboarding process is critical to success. If you do not have an intentional process about how you're onboarding a new team member you're, again, going to get what you get. The other mistake would be, once you have established team members, how are you communicating with your team and I'm not just talking about foosball and lunch on Fridays. You need frequent and structured communication, where you're not only communicating how the business is doing, what your business objectives are, and the most important part which most people are missing, how what the team member does on a day to day basis, their job description, affects the bigger picture, the organization, and the bigger mission. The other side of the equation is the metrics of all of that. There are a lot of parallels here for remote teams, the tools are the same. Mistake number one is not having an accurate job description. Mistake number two would be not setting the bar high enough. It feels almost incongruent to say these days when it's really hard to get good people but if you really want to get great people, you need to set a high bar. Shackleton led the first expedition to the South Pole back in the early 1900s. When he was trying to put a team together for that expedition. He put an ad in the paper, and it said 'Men wanted for a hazardous journey. Low wages, bitter cold, long hours of complete darkness. Safe return doubtful. However, if we succeed, you'll have a lifetime of notoriety and success.' He was painting a picture about what that mission was going to be, perilous. He was only looking for a select kind of people for his mission. So paint a more specific picture, and set a high bar for what you're looking for. Even though it's not a Shackleton expedition, take the tone of that and set the bar high for what you expect from your team.

One of the best leadership principles that I've ever heard and then employed was Dale Carnegie:

'Give people a reputation to live up to.'"

Jeff Eschliman, CEO

Cross-Generations and Fostering a Unified Workplace Culture

Diversity manifests in numerous dimensions, and one particularly impactful aspect is generational diversity. Today, the presence of baby boomers, Generation X, millennials, and Generation Z in the same workspace highlights the importance of comprehending and leveraging the unique strengths each generation brings. While challenges may arise, there are also opportunities for collaboration across generations, presenting effective strategies to bridge generational gaps, and establishing a workplace where diverse perspectives enrich the environment.

The generations and their characteristics in the workplace can be generally described as such:

- **Baby boomers (1946 - 1964):** Loyal, disciplined with a strong work ethic. They have decades of experience but may be reluctant to change.
- **Generation X (1965 - 1980):** Independent and adaptable, Generation X employees prioritize work-life balance, embodying pragmatism and resourcefulness.
- **Millennials (1981 - 1996):** Tech-savvy, collaborative, and purpose-driven, millennials actively seek meaningful work and value workplace flexibility and inclusivity.
- **Generation Z (1997 -):** The most recent entrants into the workforce, Generation Z is marked by a robust digital presence, an entrepreneurial spirit, and a fervent desire for rapid career advancement. They highly prioritize mental health, flexibility, and often have multiple streams of income (the "gig economy").

Each generation prefers distinct communication styles. For instance, baby boomers may favor face-to-face interactions, while millennials and Generation Z gravitate towards texting, using apps like Slack for quick communication.

Addressing generational diversity demands intentional efforts to bridge gaps and establish an inclusive environment. Here are two of our favorite strategies for fostering collaboration across generations, particularly in remote environments:

1. Assign a Buddy: Implement mentorship programs allowing seasoned employees to share experiences and insights with younger colleagues. Encourage reverse mentorship, enabling younger employees to share knowledge in specific areas. It can be a mutually beneficial relationship, as the mentor gains exposure to the mentor's experience and institutional knowledge, while the mentee gains fresh perspectives and insights. Reverse mentorship is particularly valuable in fostering cross-generational understanding and collaboration in the workplace.

2. Collaborative Projects: Collaboration across generations is a deliberate strategy for building a resilient and dynamic workplace. Understanding and appreciating the unique strengths of each generation enables organizations to create an environment where individuals of all ages feel valued, respected, and motivated to contribute their best. Bridging the generation gap isn't just a challenge but an opportunity to construct a unified workplace culture thriving on diversity and inclusion.

Team Atmosphere

Whether your employees are in the office or working remotely, a team atmosphere is important to allow a sense of belonging and loyalty to the company. Your best employees are those that

178

treat the company as if they are the CEO. Developing routine team processes and activities is going to mimic your employee culture, onboarding process, service details, and overall operational strategies. To bring home the ideas in this chapter and create a step by step guide, implement the following ideas:

Define Team Values: Again, go back to that list of what you'd like your culture to be. Clearly articulate the core values that define your team. Establish a shared understanding of the principles and beliefs that guide your collective efforts.

Encourage Open Communication: Foster a culture of open communication where team members feel comfortable sharing ideas, feedback, and concerns. Utilize both formal and informal channels to facilitate dialogue. Gain a guide from what your employees resonate most with.

Remote and In-Office Integration: Develop strategies to integrate remote and in-office team members seamlessly. Leverage technology for virtual collaboration and ensure that remote employees have equal access to information and opportunities.

Implement Regular Team Activities: Schedule routine team activities, whether virtual or in-person, to strengthen team bonds. This could include team-building exercises, social events, or collaborative projects that align with your company culture.

Align Team Processes with Culture: Ensure that routine team processes reflect and reinforce your desired employee culture. From daily stand-up meetings to project collaborations, these processes should embody the values and principles you want to promote. Once again, gain guidance from your team, if silent meetings are the key to their productivity, implement more of them.

Integrate Culture in Onboarding: Incorporate your team culture into the onboarding process for new members. Provide comprehensive insights into the team's dynamics, values, and expectations to help newcomers assimilate quickly and feel a sense of belonging. Seek that HR professionals help when necessary. Gain feedback from the candidates that are applying and look into your data.

Highlight Service Details: Emphasize the importance of service excellence within your team. Whether your team serves internal or external stakeholders, a shared commitment to delivering high-quality service contributes to a positive team atmosphere.

Adapt Operational Strategies: Regularly assess and adapt operational strategies to align with evolving team dynamics and goals. Flexibility in approaches ensures that your team remains responsive to changes while upholding the overall culture.

Professional Development: This is high on the list for employees, as turnover rates increase and opportunities for advancement and other employment opportunities become extremely competitive. Provide continued education courses relevant to your organization. Investing in your current employees is extremely more beneficial than hiring new ones. Invest in the employees who invest in your company.

Recognize and Reward Team Contributions: Acknowledge and reward individual and collective achievements within the team. Recognition reinforces positive behaviors and fosters a sense of pride and loyalty among team members.

Empower a CEO Mindset: Encourage every team member to adopt a mindset of ownership and accountability. When employees feel a sense of responsibility for the success of the team, it cultivates a strong team atmosphere where everyone strives for excellence. Listen to your employees' ideas. They are your greatest asset and resource.

By implementing these steps, you can create a team atmosphere that transcends physical boundaries, promotes a sense of belonging, and instills loyalty among your office or remote employees.

CHAPTER FOURTEEN

The Power of Delegation: Becoming a Better Leader

A GREAT LEADER
You Have to Delegate Well Today

To Be a Great Leader Tomorrow, You Have to Delegate Well Today. When you own your own business, no one is telling you what you have to do. You have the ability to set your own agenda.

The challenge with this ability is just how many projects you have on your agenda at time. When you have too many things on your to do list, nothing ever gets done.

Delegation is a critical skill for leaders who aspire to be successful in the long run. As a leader, it's important to recognize that you can't do everything yourself. This can be a tough realization, and letting go of some of the reins takes practice. But, delegating tasks and responsibilities is essential for effective team management and productivity. By delegating today, you set yourself up to be a great leader tomorrow.

Here are some additional benefits of delegation:

Showcase trust: When leaders delegate tasks, they convey confidence in their team's abilities, signaling trust in their capacity to deliver. This trust-building dynamic nurtures open communication, elevates morale, and fortifies the relationship between leaders and team members.

Focus on high-level tasks: Delegation allows you to focus on strategic planning, decision-making, and other high-level tasks that require your attention as a leader. When you delegate routine or less critical tasks to capable team members, you free up your time and energy to concentrate on activities that have a more significant impact on the organization. Conversely, if you could only work on tasks that bring you the most fulfillment and happiness – what would those be? How can you arrange your work so that you get to focus on more of those tasks and less on the ones that don't?

Find new perspectives: The best leaders and CEOs will surround themselves with those who have different perspectives, who have more experience in certain areas. By delegating your work, you remove your own blind spots and open yourself and your organization up to someone who can, perhaps, perform these tasks better, faster, or cheaper than you can on your own.

Improved productivity: Effective delegation can significantly enhance the productivity of your team. By distributing tasks among capable individuals, you leverage the strengths and expertise of each team member, leading to more efficient and timely completion of projects. Delegation also prevents bottlenecks and ensures that work is evenly distributed, preventing burnout, and promoting a healthy work-life balance.

Succession planning: Delegating responsibilities prepares your team members for future leadership roles. It allows you to identify potential successors and groom them for higher positions within the organization. By delegating strategically today, you are investing in the future of your team and building a strong leadership pipeline. Pay attention not only to the results, but the execution. Does the person execute it in such a way that is different from your own style, but that may be more beneficial to the organization? There's no room for ego here, so it is an important consideration.

To delegate effectively, consider the following tips:

Understand your team: Recognize the strengths, weaknesses, and interests of your team members. Delegate tasks that align with their skills and provide opportunities for growth. As a CEO, it may not be your direct responsibility to ensure every team member is ecstatic about their daily tasks, but fostering an understanding of what truly excites them work-wise can significantly enhance retention and job satisfaction. Encouraging open communication about what tasks invigorate them and actively channeling such work their way not only promotes a positive work environment but also harnesses the team's collective enthusiasm and expertise.

Provide support: Be available to answer questions, offer guidance and provide support to your team members as they work on their delegated tasks. Regularly check in on progress and provide constructive feedback to help them improve. And, when providing feedback, consider the Sandwich Method. This is a strategy used to deliver constructive criticism in a more balanced and palatable manner. The structure of the Sandwich Method typically involves presenting the feedback in three layers:

1. **Positive Feedback:** Start with a positive comment or affirmation. Acknowledge the individual's strengths, achievements, or positive qualities. This serves as the "top slice" of the sandwich and helps create a positive and receptive atmosphere.
2. **Constructive Feedback:** Insert the critical or constructive feedback in the middle layer. This is where you address areas for improvement, suggest changes, or provide specific feedback on performance issues. It's the core content of the feedback and represents the "filling" of the sandwich.
3. **Positive Feedback:** Conclude with another positive comment or encouragement. Reinforce the individual's strengths or express confidence in their ability to improve. This serves as the "bottom slice" of the sandwich and helps leave the recipient with a positive impression.

Empower decision-making: Delegate not only the tasks but also the decision-making authority that goes along with them. Encourage your team members to make independent decisions and take ownership of their work. Gradually increase autonomy over time. Start with smaller tasks and progressively entrust team members with more significant responsibilities as they prove their capabilities.

Delegation should not stop at task allocation; it should extend to decision-making authority. Encourage your team members to make independent decisions within their delegated roles. Empowering them to exercise judgment fosters a sense of ownership and accountability. It also promotes innovation and creative problem-solving.

Trust and accountability: Trust your team members to deliver and hold them accountable for their delegated responsibilities. Provide autonomy and freedom to complete tasks while establishing clear checkpoints for monitoring progress.

Clear Communication: Effective communication is the linchpin of successful delegation. Clearly articulate the expectations, desired outcomes, and deadlines associated with delegated tasks. Ensure that team members have a comprehensive understanding of their responsibilities, and be open to addressing any questions or uncertainties that arise. Provide guidance and resources as needed to set your team up for success.

Ongoing Assessment & Course Correction: Delegation is an evolving process that requires continuous assessment. Regularly evaluate your team's capabilities, strengths, and areas for improvement. Adjust delegated responsibilities as needed to align with changing circumstances or team dynamics. Encourage open feedback from your team members to refine the delegation process further. If the VA or employee that you're delegating to is veering off course or if there are misunderstandings, ongoing assessments provide an opportunity for course correction. This ensures that both parties are on the same page and working towards shared objectives. Moreover, if you schedule these ongoing assessments, it should be more well-received with the team member. They'll know to anticipate it, they'll be prepared, and they'll be ready to receive feedback.

Mastering the art of delegation is a critical step toward becoming a great leader. By delegating effectively, you not only optimize productivity but also nurture the growth and development of your team. Ultimately, leadership is about empowering others to excel, and delegation is a powerful tool in achieving this goal.

Remember that effective delegation is an ongoing process. It requires continuous assessment of your team's capabilities, regular communication, and adjustment of responsibilities as needed. By mastering the art of delegation today, you pave the way to becoming a great leader tomorrow.

Delegation is not merely a matter of assigning tasks to team members. It's an art form that, when mastered, can significantly enhance team efficiency and individual growth.

Understand that delegation is not a one-time task. It's an ongoing practice that requires finesse, adaptability, and a deep understanding of your team. By incorporating these principles into your leadership style, you can elevate your team's performance, foster individual growth, and position yourself as an effective and empowering leader in your organization.

Think about this way of categorizing the activities you need to do.

In the relentless world of leadership, the juggling act of tasks is a daily challenge, often dictated by the pressing demands of urgency and importance. We have spoken in previous chapters about the difference between urgent and important tasks, but let's break it down a bit further into categorizing activities to better understand where your focus should be as a leader.

Take one week and think about the variety of your tasks. You'll see that they fall into the following four quadrants:

1. **Urgent and Important:** These are the tasks demanding immediate attention, as neglecting them could lead to significant issues. The challenge here is misjudging urgency and importance, potentially placing tasks that are crucial for others, such as your Virtual Assistant, but not for you. Operating in this quadrant makes you reactive and can result in financial losses. It's the feeling of "always putting out fires." Tasks falling here include deadlines, urgent meetings, crises, and firefighting. Spending excessive time in this quadrant induces stress and burnout, as you might guess. Reduce time in this quadrant through one important method: delegation.
2. **Important and Not Urgent:** This is the optimal zone to inhabit. Here, you focus on important activities that can be done today – or tomorrow – without dire financial or operational consequences. The challenge is the tendency to procrastinate, risking the transition of once non-urgent but important tasks into urgent ones. Another pitfall is overloading this quadrant, hindering the quality of task completion. Strive to maintain a balanced workload in this quadrant by addressing one or two activities at a time. This in itself is difficult because any CEO knows, there are always more than one or two important activities at a time. Yet ask yourself, "What is important this week? What is going to move the needle if I do it in the next one to two days?"
3. **Urgent and Not Important:** This quadrant often involves others attempting to elevate the urgency and importance of their tasks to you. For instance, it might be urgent for your Virtual Assistant to do, necessitating their completion of the task or project. When you're

delegating effectively and efficiently, you don't spend any time in this quadrant because your VA or other team member has already taken care of these items.

4. **Not Urgent and Not Important:** If you find yourself in this quadrant, consider whether you need a break or if burnout is setting in. This quadrant signals a need for a pause, allowing you to recharge before returning to work. No CEO should be spending time in this quadrant.

Mastering the art of saying "no" is the crucial skill you must acquire to propel your leadership. The ability to say "no" where appropriate creates the necessary space for affirmatively saying "yes" to the endeavors that truly align with your priorities.

Having to say no might mean disappointing someone.

But time is a finite resource. Engaging in activities that fail to make a significant impact on your company means you won't have the time or energy to tackle tasks that genuinely contribute value.

The best system for avoiding burnout is called *now, soon, and later* and this is how it works:

1. Start by writing down all of the projects you have on your plate.
2. Put them into the Urgent Important Matrix.
3. Move all of your projects into the following three buckets: now, soon, and later.

"Now" is for things you have to work on right now. There should be no more than two items in this bucket. "Soon" are things you'll consider as soon as you complete the projects you have in the "Now" bucket. You can't consider them till you cross off something from your "Now" bucket.

If you do this system while hiring a Virtual Assistant, you'll avoid spinning your wheels, racing toward burnout, and bouncing from one activity to another. If you do these two things instead, you'll get your most important things done first and move faster than you thought possible.

This is really the secret sauce that keeps our clients focused on what's important and not urgent.

Using the following five powerful steps will increase your efficiency and put you on the path to mastering the art of delegation.

1. Demonstrate Your Willingness to Let Go

You have to be willing to let go of the tasks you are in the habit of performing in order to make room for bigger and better tasks. Start by evaluating which tasks hold the million dollar value and which do not. Understand that your delegation strategy may not be perfect all the time but the more you delegate, the better at it you will become.

Allow yourself to grow and expand. Those lower level tasks can often be a safety net and a comfort zone. Enabling others to assist you will open up time in your day to focus on strategy and growth.

Also, be willing to increase your self-knowledge. Ask yourself how you respond to conflict, what motivates you, what causes you stress, how you solve problems, and what your optimal communication style is. Answering these questions may help you find the answer to why you aren't able to let go.

2. Choose a Delegate

Juggling everything alone requires extreme dedication. Many of us pride ourselves on our ability to keep track of so many moving pieces. However, it is time to focus on tasks that are more *worthy of your attention*. Choose someone to help. Continuing to drag your feet digging through resumes and interviewing is not growth. Choose someone. If it doesn't work out, assign someone else. Remember, delegation is not only work on the part of your assistant or team member, but also work on your part. Our assistants can do their best to be mind readers, and try and project what you are looking for, but in reality this is an extreme expectation that will set you up for failure.

Building trust takes time and patience, but you need to start somewhere in order to know what is working for you and what is not. This will help you to hone in on the skill sets you require of your delegate.

3. Assign Tasks

Which tasks are priority tasks that require your direct attention and which do not? Make a list. Assign lower level tasks to others and keep the high strategic tasks on your plate. If you are unsure if the person you are assigning tasks to has the capability to execute it, just ask. Don't be afraid to present new tasks to others by simply asking. Often we do not know every single skill set that others around us possess.

Provide the opportunity for your team to speak up and show the skill sets in which they will truly shine. Play to your workers' strengths.

4. Set Expectations

Clear, concise instructions are imperative to delegation, especially when you are delegating to someone new. Setting clear expectations for the tasks or projects at hand is first and foremost. If applicable, establish KPIs that will be used to measure performance. This provides a clear benchmark for success. Also, consider documenting expectations in written form, such as in project plans, job descriptions, or task assignments. This serves as a reference point for everyone involved.

5. Be Adaptable

Not everybody is perfect. The art of delegation takes time. Be open to making changes and adapting your strategy. Everyone gives and receives information differently. Set a routine with your delegate. Listen to the feedback that your team is providing. Learn from the feedback provided and be open to suggestions on ways to improve.

As your vetted delegates prepare to take on new projects, keep the following key points in mind:

Provide your new delegate with hands-on training. This does not have to be in person, as a screen-sharing session will work to your advantage! Give step-by-step instructions to save time and record a tutorial. Recording a training session will allow your team to re-watch the video and follow side-by-side instructions. Doing this will free up your time, so you're not stuck answering questions multiple times, or re-training someone.

Be clear as to what needs to be done, and when it needs to be completed. Set hard deadlines for each task. If something needs to be done on a daily basis, make it known. Set the expectation of how long you think it should take to complete the task. We advise not getting carried away here as everyone works at different paces. For example, if you would like someone to complete a research task, set the expectation that you would like them to spend X amount of hours researching XYZ.

Creating a space in which tasks are assigned and reviewed will assist in developing a smooth machine of input and output of tasks. Your delegate will know where to look for tasks and how to submit them once completed. Establish a flow. Create a centralized location or system where tasks are assigned. This could be a project management tool, a shared document, or a task management platform. Having a dedicated space streamlines the process and avoids confusion. Clearly outline the process for submitting completed tasks. Specify the format for deliverables, any required documentation, and the preferred mode of submission. This streamlines the process and ensures uniformity in task submissions.

With some help from a few tech tools, delegation can begin to be a seamless process for you and your team.

Behavioral Assessments

Using behavioral assessments will give you deeper insight into what makes you and your team tick. Understanding yourself and your team will aid in adapting behaviors for maximum efficiency throughout your company. Assessments can improve working relationships by recognizing the communication needs of team members. Facilitate better teamwork and teach productive conflict. Manage more effectively by understanding the dispositions and priorities of employees and team members. Well-designed behavioral assessments have demonstrated predictive validity. They can indicate how a candidate is likely to behave in various work-related situations, offering valuable insights into their potential fit within the organization and specific roles.

Executive Tip: The Kolbe Index, developed by Kathy Kolbe, is an assessment tool designed to measure an individual's cognitive strengths. Conation refers to the natural instinctive strengths and approaches people use when taking action. The Kolbe Index focuses on an individual's instinctive or natural way of taking action, rather than learned or acquired behaviors. This provides insights into how a person is likely to approach tasks and solve problems in real-world situations. It also measures cognitive strengths – conative strengths are specific to how individuals initiate and handle tasks. The Kolbe Index identifies four Action Modes: Fact Finder, Follow Thru, Quick Start, and Implementor. Understanding someone's cognitive strengths helps match them with roles that align with their natural problem-solving and working styles.

When used properly in remote teams, the Kolbe Index can contribute to building well-rounded and complementary teams. Understanding the cognitive strengths of team members helps identify areas of potential synergy and potential sources of conflict, fostering more effective collaboration.

The Kolbe Index is designed to be non-judgmental and non-evaluative. It focuses on providing information about natural inclinations rather than labeling behaviors as "good or bad." This promotes a more positive and understanding approach to individual differences. The Kolbe Index is applicable across a wide range of industries and roles. Whether in creative fields, analytical roles, or leadership positions, understanding cognitive strengths can provide valuable insights into how individuals approach their work.

Project Management Software

Project management software can help to ensure everyone on your team is on the same page. These online programs can be accessed remotely and jointly by your team. They can help teams complete client requirements and manage time, budget, and scope constraints and much more! Each application is different so it is important to do your research before choosing one. Be open to the idea of new platforms as they are constantly being developed and improved.

Suggested platforms: Asana, Zoho, Trello, Monday.com, and Teamwork are popular project management tools, each with its own set of features and characteristics. Asana is good for collaboration features like comments, file attachments, due dates, and Kanban-style boards for visual project tracking. Zoho is great for task management and collaboration tools and one great feature is that it includes Gantt charts for project timelines. Visual folks love Trello because of the cards for task management and collaboration through comments, attachments, and due dates. While these project management tools share common features, the choice between them depends on your team's specific needs. Asana is suitable for goal tracking, Zoho offers a comprehensive business suite, Trello is simple and user-friendly, Monday.com provides flexible workflows, and Teamwork emphasizes project planning with Gantt charts. Consider the scale and complexity of your projects, team size, and desired features to make an informed decision.

Communication Platform

Effective communication is crucial for successful project management, and having a designated point and platform for communication can significantly enhance productivity.

A designated communication point provides a centralized space for addressing issues and solving problems. Quick and effective communication helps prevent misunderstandings and resolve issues promptly. Open and consistent communication fosters transparency. Team members can track progress, understand changes, and stay informed about the overall project status.

Selecting the right communication platform is essential. Here are three suggested platforms:

1) Slack features real-time messaging and collaboration. There are multiple channels for organization discussions by topic or team. Users love the instant, easy communication, quick file-sharing, and the fact that it easily supports both one on one and group conversations.
2) Chanty is a user-friendly team collaboration platform designed to streamline communication and enhance productivity. With a chat-based interface, users can create channels for organized discussions, fostering real-time communication among team members. Chanty goes beyond messaging by incorporating task management features,

allowing teams to create, assign, and track tasks within the platform. The platform also supports file sharing, audio, and video calls, and integrates with third-party apps, providing a comprehensive environment for team collaboration.

3) Microsoft Teams integrates chat, video conferencing, file storage, and application integration within the Microsoft 365 ecosystem. It provides a centralized hub for team communication, allowing users to organize conversations into channels, collaborate on documents in real-time, and conduct virtual meetings. Teams offers seamless integration with other Microsoft 365 apps and third-party services, fostering a unified workspace. With features like threaded conversations, direct messaging, and customizable channels, Microsoft Teams aims to enhance team collaboration and productivity across various industries and work scenarios.

Once you select a platform, how do you establish it as an effective hub?

1. Define Channels and Topics: Create channels or threads for specific topics, projects, or teams to keep discussions organized. Set clear guidelines for channel usage and etiquette to maintain a focused and professional environment. Encourage team members to use threads for in-depth discussions to avoid clutter in the main channel.

2. Clarify Communication Norms: Establish communication norms, such as response times and the use of specific channels for different types of communication. Use @ mentions appropriately to direct messages to specific team members. Consider using @channel sparingly to avoid unnecessary notifications for the entire channel. Encourage team members to set status updates to inform others about their availability. Utilize custom statuses to provide more context, such as "In a meeting" or "Working on a deadline."

3. Training and Onboarding: Ensure that team members are trained on the chosen communication platform. Provide guidelines for effective use and onboarding for new team members. It can be helpful to designate one employee to stay ahead of best practices and updates in the platform, and communicate those to the other team members. This person can also be in charge of creating user-friendly documentation, guides, and video tutorials that team members can refer to at their own pace.

A designated communication point, supported by platforms like Slack, Chanty, or Microsoft Teams, acts as a hub for collaboration, knowledge sharing, and problem-solving, ultimately enhancing productivity and project success.

CHAPTER FIFTEEN

Maximizing Efficiency and Productivity: Guide to Leveraging Virtual Assistants

MAXIMIZE EFFICENCY
The Power of Utilizing a Virtual Assistant

CEOs are constantly juggling an array of responsibilities and demands. From strategic decision-making to managing teams and staying informed about industry trends, the CEO's role is multifaceted and, most days, overwhelming. In this chapter, we explore how CEOs can take advantage of the power of Virtual Assistants to optimize their time, enhance productivity, and focus on what truly matters.

Not Your Average CEOs are acutely aware that time is their most valuable resource.

Every minute spent on administrative tasks or routine activities is a minute taken away from strategic thinking, innovation, and building relationships. Virtual assistants offer a strategic solution to this challenge, allowing CEOs to reclaim their time, profitability, and allocate it more effectively.

Unlocking the Power of Delegation

Delegation is a cornerstone of effective leadership, and Virtual Assistants serve as the ultimate delegation tool for CEOs. By entrusting specific tasks to VAs, CEOs can free up mental bandwidth and channel their energy towards high-impact activities. This shift from being a hands-on manager to a strategic leader can yield profound results for both the CEO and the organization.

Is It Time?

Deciding when to hire a Virtual Assistant is a strategic decision that depends on various factors related to your workload, business needs, and overall organizational dynamics. Here are some indicators that suggest you may be ready to hire a virtual assistant:

Overwhelmed with Routine Tasks:

- If you find yourself spending a significant amount of time on repetitive, administrative tasks that don't necessarily require your expertise, it may be a sign that you could benefit from a Virtual Assistant. Delegating these tasks can free up your time for more strategic activities. Go back to the executive tip in our previous chapter on reviewing your calendar and where your time is best spent.

195

Consistent Workload:

- A consistent and growing workload can indicate that your responsibilities are becoming more demanding. If you're struggling to keep up with the day-to-day tasks, a Virtual Assistant can manage routine activities, allowing you to focus on high-level priorities.

Frequent Task Redundancy:

- When you notice that certain tasks are becoming redundant, such as scheduling appointments, managing emails, or report generation, a Virtual Assistant can handle these routine activities, streamlining your workflow. In fact, email triage for CEOs is one of the most popular requests for a VA to tackle.

Expansion of Business Operations:

- If your business is expanding, whether in terms of clients, projects, or geographical reach, the increased workload likely necessitates additional support. A VA can be a scalable solution to accommodate growth without immediately adding to on-site staff.

Desire to Focus on Core Competencies:

- As a CEO, your time is valuable. If you feel that your core competencies lie in strategic decision-making, business development, or other high-level tasks, hiring a VA enables you to concentrate on activities that directly contribute to the growth and success of your business.

Increasing Communication Overload:

- Managing emails, scheduling meetings, and handling communication can become overwhelming as your network grows. A Virtual Assistant can assist in organizing your inbox, scheduling appointments, and maintaining correspondence in a timely manner.

Limited Budget for Full-Time Staff:

- If your budget doesn't currently allow for hiring full-time on-site staff, a VA can provide cost-effective support. Virtual Assistants often work on a flexible, part-time, or project-based basis, allowing you to access assistance without the overhead of a full-time employee, such as things like worker's compensation insurance, employer taxes, and payroll systems.

Need for Flexibility:

- Virtual Assistants offer flexibility in terms of working hours and tasks. If you require support during specific seasonal periods or for particular one-off projects, a Virtual Assistant can adapt to your changing needs without the long-term commitment associated with traditional hires.

Evaluation of Personal Well-Being:

- If you find that your work-life balance is suffering, and you're constantly feeling overwhelmed, a Virtual Assistant can play a vital role in alleviating stress, improving work-life balance, and enhancing overall well-being.

If you find that administrative tasks are hindering your ability to focus on critical aspects of your role, it is definitely the right time to explore the benefits of Virtual Assistance.

You Need a Virtual Assistant But Are You Ready?

There is a distinct difference between knowing that you need to hire a Virtual Assistant and being in a place to hire one.

You know that you may need a VA when you:

- Find yourself spending more time on administrative work than growing the business and engaging in strategic planning
- Your loved ones are complaining that they never see you
- You've lost the excitement and zest for being a CEO, and feel that you might just be going through the motions
- Important tasks are falling through the cracks or not being completed in a timely manner, due to your own competing priorities and/or overwhelm
- You're doing tasks or projects that you know someone else can do better or faster than you can because it's not in your area of expertise, such as bookkeeping or writing social media posts
- You feel like you can never actually catch up on work

However, there's an important distinction between needing a Virtual Assistant and being ready to hire one. Consider these important rules:

197

- Your business generates enough revenue that this will not be a financial strain. Several Virtual Assistant companies offer flexible plans so that you do not need to commit to a certain number of hours each month, so they can be more budget-friendly.
- You're ready to let go – at least a little bit. You have to be ready to give up on the idea that you need to have your hand in every little detail of the business. If you're not sure you can give up even a little bit of control, you're probably not ready to hire a Virtual Assistant.
- You have to have existing processes and SOPs in place, or be open to developing them. If you don't have a standard operating procedure, a good, experienced Virtual Assistant can help you develop one to protect the integrity of your brand.

A Virtual Assistant is a valuable asset for businesses of any size but especially for small scale enterprises where resources are scarce and access to funds are limited. CEOs need to manage their time effectively and focus more on activities that translate faster to business development and growth.

The Versatility of Virtual Assistants

A Virtual Assistant is not a one-size-fits-all solution; rather, it's a versatile tool that can be customized to meet the specific needs of a CEO. Here are some key areas where VAs can make a significant impact:

1. Administrative Support

CEOs find themselves inundated with emails, scheduling conflicts, task management and administrative tasks. Virtual Assistants excel in handling these routine activities, managing calendars, scheduling meetings, and triaging emails to ensure that the CEO's time is used efficiently.

But, delegating administrative work is not just about lightening the CEO's workload; it's about optimizing your role as a leader. It allows CEOs to be more strategic, productive, and effective in guiding their organizations toward success. Effective delegation is a hallmark of strong leadership and is key to achieving long-term business objectives.

Case Study: Laura's Email Overhaul

Laura, the CEO of a marketing agency, was overwhelmed by her overflowing inbox. Her Virtual Assistant implemented a robust email management system, categorizing messages, prioritizing communication, and drafting responses for routine inquiries. This email overhaul not only saved Laura hours each day but also ensured that important messages received prompt attention.

2. Research and Data Analysis

Staying informed about industry trends, market conditions, and competitors is vital for CEOs. Virtual Assistants can conduct research, compile reports, and provide data analysis, enabling CEOs to make informed decisions and stay ahead of the curve. VAs can conduct market research to gather data on industry trends, consumer behavior, competitor strategies, and emerging markets. They can compile comprehensive reports and summaries to help CEOs make informed market-related decisions.

Other tasks a VA can do in this realm include:

- **Competitor Analysis:** Analyzing competitors' strengths, weaknesses, opportunities, and threats (SWOT analysis) can provide valuable insights. VAs can gather data on competitors' products, pricing, marketing strategies, and market share.
- **Industry Benchmarking:** VAs can collect data to benchmark the company's performance against industry standards and best practices. This can help CEOs identify areas for improvement and set realistic goals.
- **Customer Surveys:** VAs can design, distribute, and analyze customer surveys to gather feedback on products, services, and customer satisfaction. This data can guide product development and customer retention strategies.
- **Financial Analysis:** VAs can assist in financial data analysis by preparing financial reports, tracking key performance indicators (KPIs), and conducting profitability assessments. They can help CEOs monitor financial health and make data-driven financial decisions.
- **Data Visualization:** Creating clear and concise data visualizations, such as charts and graphs, is essential for presenting complex information. VAs can use tools like Microsoft Excel or specialized data visualization software to create compelling visuals for reports and presentations.
- **SWOT Analysis:** VAs can help CEOs perform SWOT analyses by gathering data on internal strengths and weaknesses, as well as external opportunities and threats. This analysis aids in strategic planning and decision-making.
- **Feasibility Studies:** When considering new projects or investments, VAs can conduct feasibility studies. They gather data on project costs, potential returns, and risks, helping CEOs assess the viability of initiatives.
- **Product Research:** Researching new product ideas or improvements to existing products is crucial for innovation. VAs can collect data on market demand, competitive offerings, and customer preferences.
- **Data Mining:** VAs can mine large datasets for valuable insights. They can use data analysis tools to identify trends, patterns, and correlations within the data, providing CEOs with actionable information.

- **Statistical Analysis:** For more complex data analysis, VAs with statistical expertise can perform regression analysis, hypothesis testing, and other statistical techniques to uncover meaningful relationships in the data.
- **Social Media Analysis:** Monitoring social media platforms for brand mentions, customer sentiment, and trends is essential for reputation management and marketing. VAs can use social media analytics tools to track and report on these metrics.
- **Industry Reports:** VAs can subscribe to industry-specific publications and compile reports on relevant news, research findings, and regulatory changes that may impact the company.
- **Data Validation:** Ensuring the accuracy and reliability of data is critical. VAs can perform data validation and cleansing tasks to maintain data integrity.
- **Risk Assessment:** VAs can assist in assessing business risks by gathering data on potential threats, vulnerabilities, and mitigation strategies.

Case Study: John's Competitive Edge

John, the CEO of a beauty products retailer, relied on his Virtual Assistant to monitor competitors' pricing strategies and consumer trends. The VA's comprehensive reports allowed John to make timely pricing adjustments and adapt marketing strategies, giving his company a competitive edge in the market.

3. Travel Planning and Logistics

Travel is a fundamental aspect of a CEO's role, whether it involves attending conferences, meeting clients, or visiting global offices. Virtual Assistants can take charge of travel planning, booking flights and accommodations, and ensuring smooth logistics, leaving CEOs free to focus on their objectives during the trip.

Case Study: Maria's Global Expansion

Maria, the CEO of an international consulting firm, expanded her business into new markets. Her Virtual Assistant played a pivotal role in coordinating travel arrangements for Maria and her team, ensuring seamless transitions between time zones and cultures. As a result, the company's global expansion efforts progressed smoothly.

4. Task Prioritization

VAs can assist CEOs in prioritizing tasks and managing workflows. By helping identify high-impact activities and delegating routine tasks, Virtual Assistants ensure that the CEO's attention is directed toward strategic initiatives.

Case Study: Michael's Strategic Focus

Michael, the CEO of a tech startup, was often overwhelmed by the day-to-day demands of running the company. His Virtual Assistant helped him implement a task management system that categorized activities based on strategic importance. Michael could then allocate his time and energy to critical projects, propelling the company's growth.

5. Communication and Follow-Up

Maintaining effective communication with stakeholders, board members, and team members is essential. Virtual Assistants can draft and proofread emails, prepare presentations, and follow up on action items to ensure that nothing falls through the cracks.

Case Study: Sarah's Boardroom Mastery

Sarah, the CEO of a financial institution, entrusted her Virtual Assistant with preparing concise and compelling board meeting presentations. The VA's attention to detail and data accuracy earned Sarah praise from the board and bolstered her reputation as a capable leader.

Building a Symbiotic Partnership with Your Virtual Assistant

To fully leverage the potential of hiring Virtual Assistants, CEOs should establish a strong working relationship built on trust and clear communication. Here are some strategies to make this partnership successful:

1. Define Expectations

Clearly define the tasks and responsibilities you expect your Virtual Assistant to handle. Set expectations for response times, availability, and quality of work to ensure alignment. Oftentimes we think we are setting clear expectations but we are not taking into account how the other person is perceiving it. The best way to set your assistant up for success is to schedule out time to work one on one with them. A recorded screenshare typically works most effectively here. Videos and procedures that your VA can revert back to will be extremely helpful in learning your techniques. Providing detailed examples and constructive feedback will help set any expectations that have gone array.

Assuming that you are being clear and concise is a mistake in defining your expectations. Lastly, you can ask questions to ensure that your VA understands what outcome you are looking for.

2. Communicate Effectively

Establish regular check-in meetings or communication channels to discuss priorities, provide feedback, and address any questions or concerns. Effective communication is key to a productive partnership. A cadence for this can be a weekly phone meeting and a daily email check-in at the end of each workday. This will be different for everyone in varying industries but the idea is that you are establishing consistent touch points.

3. Empower Decision-Making

Encourage your Virtual Assistant to make decisions within their designated scope of work. Empowering them to take ownership of tasks can lead to more efficient execution.

4. Invest in Training

Invest time in training your Virtual Assistant about your organization, industry, and specific preferences. The more they understand your business and your work behavior, the more valuable they become. Being transparent with your VA about your own pet peeves and working style is helpful here.

5. Continuously Optimize

Regularly assess the tasks your Virtual Assistant handles and identify areas for improvement or additional support. Adapt and refine their role as your needs evolve. Keep a living document with your assistant that details advancements and milestones.

Case Studies: CEOs Embracing Virtual Assistants

To illustrate the real-world impact of Virtual Assistants on CEOs' lives and businesses, let's explore two case studies:

Case Study: Lisa's Strategic Transformation

Lisa, the CEO of a healthcare startup, faced the daunting task of expanding her company's reach. Her Virtual Assistant took charge of market research, identifying potential partnership opportunities, and streamlining communication with potential investors. Her assistant even drafted an outreach email, and created a partnership spreadsheet to monitor responses and follow ups. Lisa's strategic vision for the company was realized and implemented with the support of her VA.

Case Study: James' Digital Delegation

James, the CEO of a digital marketing agency, embraced Virtual Assistants as a core part of his team. His VAs managed client communications, social media scheduling, and content creation, allowing James to focus on business development. The agency's client base grew significantly as a result of James's ability to dedicate more time to strategic initiatives.

A Powerful Partnership

CEOs must maximize their efficiency and focus on strategic priorities. Virtual Assistants serve as invaluable partners in achieving these goals. By entrusting administrative tasks and routine operational responsibilities to VAs, CEOs can optimize their time, enhance productivity, and devote their energy to steering their organizations toward success. Embrace the potential of Virtual Assistants, and watch as your role as CEO becomes not just manageable but truly transformative. With the support of a skilled Virtual Assistant, your capacity for leadership and strategic thinking knows no bounds.

CHAPTER SIXTEEN

Silent Meetings:
Amplifying Productivity

SILENT MEETINGS
The Conundrum of Traditional Meetings

Meetings are a double-edged sword. While they are essential for collaboration, decision-making, and knowledge sharing, they can also become a source of frustration due to inefficiency, domination by a few voices, and a lack of inclusivity. This chapter introduces the concept of silent meetings, a groundbreaking approach that leverages written communication to enhance productivity, foster inclusivity, and streamline discussions, particularly in large group settings.

The Conundrum of Traditional Meetings

Before we dive into the transformative potential of silent meetings, let's first understand the limitations of traditional face-to-face gatherings:

Dominance of Verbal Communication: In many conventional meetings, a handful of assertive individuals tend to monopolize the conversation. Their dominating presence often drowns out the voices of quieter, yet equally valuable, participants.

Time Inefficiency: Meetings are notoriously time-consuming, with discussions meandering off-topic, lengthy monologues, and repetitive conversations that seem to drag on endlessly. This squanders valuable work hours that could be spent on productive tasks.

Inequality of Participation: Traditional meetings may not create a level playing field for all participants. Introverted team members, who often have valuable insights, might hesitate to speak up, missing opportunities to contribute.

Multitasking and Distraction: Participants often multitask during meetings, checking emails, scrolling through their phones, or mentally disengaging. This multitasking diminishes the quality of discussions and decisions.

Decision Fatigue: An overabundance of meetings can lead to decision fatigue, where participants become mentally exhausted and make suboptimal choices.

The Silent Meeting Revolution

Silent meetings represent a paradigm shift in how organizations approach gatherings. Instead of relying on verbal communication, participants use written communication, such as typing on a keyboard or using messaging apps, to engage in discussions. This transformative approach can significantly improve the efficiency, inclusivity, and overall effectiveness of meetings.

Benefits of Silent Meetings

1. **Equitable Participation:** Silent meetings democratize the discussion process. By eliminating the immediate pressure to speak, they ensure that every participant, regardless of their communication style or personality, has an equal opportunity to contribute their thoughts and ideas.

2. **Enhanced Focus:** Without the distractions of verbal interruptions and side conversations, participants can engage more deeply with the subject matter at hand. This enhanced focus often results in more meaningful and productive discussions.

3. **Mitigation of Dominant Voices:** In silent meetings, the absence of vocal dominance tends to reduce the problem of a few individuals monopolizing the conversation. Written contributions tend to be more balanced, concise, and respectful of others' opinions.

4. **Inclusivity:** Silent meetings are particularly valuable for introverted or reserved team members who might find it easier to express themselves in writing. This inclusive approach ensures that their valuable insights are not overlooked.

5. **Time Efficiency:** Silent meetings are often shorter and more focused than traditional ones. With written communication, discussions stay on track, making better use of everyone's time and reducing the likelihood of off-topic tangents.

Implementing Silent Meetings

To successfully incorporate silent meetings into your organization, consider the following steps:

1. **Set Clear Objectives:** Begin by defining the purpose and desired outcomes of the meeting. Ensure that written communication aligns with these objectives and fosters productive discussions. Limit the objectives in each meeting so that it is not overwhelming, as a best practice. Your agenda should have a narrow focus. If you find that you're listing too many objectives or that the agenda is too long, consider breaking the meeting up into several separate ones.

2. **Choose the Right Tools:** Select digital platforms or collaboration tools that facilitate written communication. These could include shared documents like Google Drive, messaging apps, or specialized silent meeting platforms designed to streamline the process.

3. **Establish Communication Guidelines:** Create clear and practical guidelines for written communication during silent meetings. Specify expectations such as word limits for contributions, deadlines for responses, and the use of respectful language.

4. **Preparation Is Key:** Encourage participants to prepare in advance. Provide relevant materials and information before the meeting to ensure that all attendees are well-informed and ready to engage in meaningful discussions. It's important to consider your attendees' schedules when you're asking them to prepare in advance. Perhaps it is not best to stack one meeting after another and ensure that the meeting doesn't take place on a day with a lot of competing priorities.
5. **Moderation:** Designate a moderator or facilitator for the silent meeting. This individual oversees the meeting, ensuring that it remains focused, respectful, and on track. The moderator can also summarize key points and guide the flow of the discussion.
6. **Follow-Up and Documentation:** After the silent meeting, compile the written contributions and summarize the decisions made. Share this summary with participants to maintain transparency and accountability.

Silent Meetings in Action: Real-World Examples

To illustrate the practical application and success of silent meetings, let's explore how various organizations have integrated this innovative approach into their corporate cultures:

1. Zapier: The Remote Work Pioneer

Zapier, a strong advocate for remote work, heavily relies on silent meetings to coordinate its globally dispersed teams. Using digital communication tools and collaborative platforms, Zapier conducts daily stand-up meetings, decision-making sessions, and brainstorming discussions. This approach ensures that remote employees, regardless of their time zones or communication styles, can actively participate in meetings and contribute meaningfully.

2. GitLab: Embracing Asynchronous Collaboration

GitLab, a leading name in the world of software development, has fully embraced silent meetings as part of its asynchronous work culture. Teams within GitLab use written communication to discuss code reviews, project updates, and strategic planning. This approach fosters in-depth technical discussions and allows contributors from around the world to collaborate effectively, unburdened by the constraints of time zones and synchronous communication.

3. Basecamp: Simplifying Communication

Basecamp, a company specializing in project management software, incorporates silent meetings into its daily operations to streamline decision-making and reduce the need for lengthy in-person gatherings. Written discussions enable teams to clarify objectives, address concerns, and document key decisions efficiently. This approach aligns with Basecamp's broader philosophy of minimizing unnecessary work and optimizing productivity.

Overcoming Challenges

While silent meetings offer numerous advantages, they also come with their own set of challenges. Here are some strategies to address common issues:

- **Resistance to Change:** Introducing silent meetings may encounter resistance from team members accustomed to traditional meeting formats. To overcome this resistance, provide training and demonstrate the advantages of this approach through real-world examples. Understand your teams behavioral styles will also help you predict which team members may struggle with this idea, due to their high need for interpersonal skills and over communication.

- **Technology Barriers:** Ensure that all participants are comfortable with the chosen digital tools. Offer training and technical support as needed to ensure a smooth transition to silent meetings. Ask for feedback from all team members and participants on their experience and how you can optimize it moving forward.

- **Ensuring Engagement:** Maintain engagement by setting clear expectations, enforcing communication guidelines, and recognizing and rewarding active participation. Encourage all participants to contribute thoughtfully. Provide examples of engagement and as always, lead by example.

- **Balancing Inclusivity and Efficiency:** Strive for a balance between inclusivity and time efficiency by fine-tuning the format and duration of silent meetings to match the specific goals and needs of your organization.

Enhancing Creative Thinking

Silent meetings also hold great promise for enhancing creative thinking within organizations. The act of putting thoughts into writing encourages participants to think more critically, formulate ideas more clearly, and even challenge their own assumptions. In the absence of immediate verbal feedback, individuals have the space to ponder and refine their contributions, leading to more well-rounded and innovative solutions.

Moreover, silent meetings allow for parallel idea generation. Participants can simultaneously brainstorm or provide feedback in a structured and focused manner. This simultaneous input can lead to the rapid generation of ideas and solutions, making silent meetings particularly effective for creative or design-focused discussions.

Boosting Accountability

Another beneficial aspect of silent meetings is the accountability they bring to the table. In traditional meetings, it can be challenging to attribute specific contributions or decisions to individuals, leading to a lack of accountability. In contrast, silent meetings leave a written record of each participant's input and commitments.

This written record serves as a valuable reference point. It allows for easy tracking of action items, decisions, and the progression of discussions over time. Team members can refer back to the written record to ensure that tasks are completed, deadlines are met, and agreements are honored. This enhanced accountability streamlines project management and ensures that everyone is on the same page.

Optimizing Hybrid and Remote Work

The rise of hybrid and remote work arrangements has accelerated the adoption of silent meetings. In a dispersed workforce, silent meetings bridge the geographical gap, enabling team members from different time zones and locations to engage meaningfully. They become a cornerstone of asynchronous communication, facilitating collaboration without the need for synchronous meetings that can be challenging to coordinate across time zones.

Silent meetings also offer a solution to the common problem of "Zoom fatigue." Video conferencing, while essential, can be mentally exhausting. Silent meetings provide an alternative mode of collaboration that allows team members to contribute at their own pace and during their most productive hours.

Embracing Silent Meetings as a Tool for Transformation

Silent meetings represent a promising evolution in the way organizations communicate, collaborate, and make decisions. By replacing traditional verbal exchanges with written contributions, these meetings empower every team member to share their insights, promote inclusivity, and streamline decision-making. As you consider integrating silent meetings into your organization's culture, remember that the key to success lies in setting clear objectives, thoughtful preparation, effective use of technology, and the willingness to adapt to this transformative approach. Embrace the silent meeting revolution, and witness how your organization's productivity and collaboration soar to new heights, leaving behind the inefficiencies of traditional meetings.

211

CHAPTER SEVENTEEN

Navigating the New Normal

NAVIGATION IS KEY
A New Workforce Normal

Leadership has undergone significant transformations.

It can be hard as a leader to make adjustments. Change does not always come easy or happen overnight. It often requires leaders to rethink traditional leadership models and embrace new ways of working. This includes fostering a culture of trust and collaboration among teams, finding innovative ways to communicate and connect with employees, and leveraging technology to enhance productivity and efficiency.

To reflect on leadership overall, leading can be a deeply fulfilling, extremely impactful and an ever-changing experience. Yet, it can also be emotionally challenging and unpredictable. Throughout this book, we've emphasized the importance of self-awareness, adaptability, and tact. These qualities and attributes are essential as you progress in your leadership journey.

The world is constantly evolving, and having the skills and resources to feel confident and lead with intention is invaluable, not just for yourself but also for those you lead. Navigating this new normal can be difficult but leadership can leave a lasting impact, and it's within your power to shape what that impact will be.

The New Shift

With the shift to remote and hybrid work setups, leaders are faced with unique challenges. Adapting to this new environment can be challenging, requiring leaders to make significant adjustments to their approach.

One of the most notable changes in leadership practices is the way technology has revolutionized the recruitment process. With online job boards and the use of social media for professional networking, CEOs now have access to a large pool of talent from all corners of the globe. This has not only expanded the possibilities for finding the right candidates but has also increased competition among organizations to attract top talent. The use of artificial intelligence and machine learning algorithms has further streamlined the hiring process. These technologies can analyze vast amounts of data to identify the most suitable candidates based on specific criteria. This has significantly reduced the time and effort required for recruitment.

For example, platforms like LinkedIn allow you to target specific audiences based on their profiles, ensuring that your job openings reach the most relevant candidates. LinkedIn Groups and Communities provide a platform for professionals with similar interests to connect and share insights. By joining relevant groups and actively participating in discussions, recruiters and/or CEOs can establish themselves as industry experts and build relationships with potential candidates. Additionally, these groups can serve as a valuable source of talent, as members often share job opportunities or refer candidates to each other. LinkedIn also offers virtual recruitment events where companies can connect with potential candidates in real-time. Participating in these events can be an effective way to engage with job seekers.

But it's not only CEOs and recruiters who are utilizing technology for hiring – it's the candidates themselves. Candidates are not only looking for a job but also seeking a company that aligns with their values. Therefore, it is essential to build a strong employer brand on LinkedIn. This can be achieved by encouraging your employees to update their LinkedIn profiles with accurate information and link to your company. Their networks can be valuable sources for referrals. Leverage recommendations and endorsements on LinkedIn profiles to highlight the skills and expertise of your current employees. Positive testimonials can attract potential candidates. By showcasing your organization as an attractive employer, you can attract top talent and increase the likelihood of successful recruitment.

As technology continues to advance, leaders must adapt their management styles to effectively lead a tech-savvy workforce. The younger generation, in particular, has grown up in a digital age, where technology is an integral part of their lives. CEOs must embrace this reality and leverage technology to enhance communication, collaboration, and productivity within their organizations.

Business has also become more than just a strategy plan.

And yet, the role of emotional intelligence has become increasingly important in this context. While technology has undoubtedly improved efficiency and productivity, it has also created new challenges in maintaining human connections. Leaders who possess high EI can navigate these challenges by fostering a culture of empathy, understanding and open communication. By recognizing and addressing the emotional needs of their employees, CEOs can create a positive work environment that promotes loyalty and job satisfaction.

Challenges in the Labor Market

The labor market is constantly evolving, presenting new challenges for CEOs and organizations. In a post-pandemic world, society's values and expectations have evolved, influencing the labor market. Employees now prioritize work-life balance, flexible schedules, and a positive work environment that emphasizes mental health. CEOs need to understand these changing dynamics and create a culture that attracts and retains top talent. Emphasizing employee well-being and providing opportunities for growth and development can help address these challenges. The labor market is highly competitive, with employees having access to a wide range of opportunities because of the increase of remote work. This has led to a decrease in employee loyalty and an increase in job hopping. CEOs must recognize this trend and focus on creating a compelling employee value proposition. You can do this by providing opportunities for skill development and career growth, offering flexible work arrangements, and promoting work-life balance.

So what about shifting social mores and leadership? What is expected of today's leaders?

The societal expectations of leaders have experienced a significant shift in recent years. Today, leaders are expected to be more inclusive, diverse, and socially conscious. The traditional hierarchical leadership model is gradually being replaced by a more collaborative and participatory approach.

Leaders are expected to be:

- ☐ **Flexible and adaptable:** The ability to adapt to changing circumstances is crucial. Remote leaders should be flexible in accommodating diverse working styles, time zones, and personal situations that may affect team members.
- ☐ **Empathetic with a high emotional quotient (EQ):** Remote work can amplify feelings of isolation or stress. Leaders are required to be highly empathetic to understand the unique challenges and emotions team members may experience. The scientific underpinnings of empathy and EQ provide neurobiological insights into how leaders navigate the complexities of remote work. These attributes are not merely soft skills but are rooted in the intricate workings of the brain, influencing social dynamics, stress responses, and adaptive behaviors in the context of distributed teams.
- ☐ **Results-Oriented:** Remote leaders are expected to focus on outcomes and results rather than micromanaging processes. Measuring performance based on outcomes and providing autonomy are key aspects of results-oriented leadership.

Celebrating employees is also critical. Good news not only boosts employees' mental health but also reinforces a sense of purpose and resilience. For example, companies like Best Buy have adapted their communication methods, transforming physical bulletin boards into digital platforms to share uplifting stories and achievements. By actively promoting positive news, CEOs can foster a sense of optimism and motivation within the workforce.

Companies are increasingly expected to contribute to the common good and make a positive impact on people's lives. CEOs should define and communicate how their company's activities align with these expectations. By highlighting the ways in which the organization supports the local community, leaders can inspire employees and reinforce the company's values. This not only enhances the company's reputation but also fosters a sense of pride and purpose among employees.

Job Turnover: Proactive Steps

CEOs and leaders can take proactive steps to address the lack of loyalty and the prevalence of job hopping in the modern workforce.

Why is job turnover so high these days?

People changing jobs more often can be boiled down to a mix of seeking fresh challenges and adapting to the changing work scene. Nowadays, folks are on the lookout for opportunities that promise career growth and personal development, leading them to jump between jobs for a shot at new experiences and quicker career climbs. The rise of remote work and the gig economy has also made it easier for people to switch things up. With the freedom to work from anywhere, individuals feel more inclined to explore different roles without being tied to a traditional office setup. Add to that the evolving vibe in workplaces, which now values personal fulfillment, work-life balance, and aligning your job with your values. This shift encourages folks to actively search for workplaces that match their goals and preferences, making job hopping a common strategy to find the right fit. So, in a nutshell, it's about chasing opportunities, adapting to the times, and finding workplaces that vibe with personal aspirations.

As discussed, the gig economy and the widespread adoption of remote work have ushered in an era of increased employment flexibility. This flexibility empowers individuals to explore various roles and organizations without the constraints of traditional office-based employment. The accessibility of remote work options has particularly contributed to the ease with which individuals can navigate different professional avenues.

Employees often struggle to comprehend the decisions made by leadership or the intricacies of business operations. As a leader, it's crucial to recognize that they may not always be capable or inclined to understand these decisions. They might harbor unrealistic expectations and overlook the fact that leaders, too, are human and can make mistakes.

The workforce can sometimes be unforgiving towards leaders. It's important not to take this personally. Instead, take a step back and pause before reacting. This pause is a crucial step in navigating today's work environment. One helpful tactic is to put yourself in the employees' shoes to better understand their actions. It's important for leaders to acknowledge the gap in understanding between themselves and their employees, not take criticism personally, and approach situations with empathy and understanding. This approach can lead to more effective leadership and a more harmonious work environment.

The post-pandemic years have witnessed a profound transformation in leadership.

The advent of technology, shifting social mores, and the growing importance of emotional intelligence have reshaped the expectations placed upon leaders.

Additionally, the availability of alternative opportunities and the rise in competition have posed challenges in the labor market, leading to a lack of loyalty and increased job hopping. By embracing these changes and implementing strategies to address these challenges, CEOs and leaders can navigate this evolving landscape and foster a more engaged and committed workforce.

"Leadership itself is not just something we, it's not a title. It's a craft. It's a profession that has to be developed and needs to continue to be developed."

Chuck Mollor, CEO, MCG Partners

Steps to Crafting Your Leadership

We have touched upon many areas in this book on how you can begin to evolve as 'Not Your Average CEO', but let's take another look at this for greater clarity and overall leadership.

Self-Assessment: As if we haven't said it enough throughout the book, begin by assessing your current leadership style, strengths, and areas for improvement. Reflect on your values, beliefs, and goals as a leader. Take a look back at your feedback from the most objective standpoint.

Authenticity: Clarify your vision and values as a leader. What do you stand for? What principles guide your decisions and actions? What does your company stand for? And ask yourself does this trickle down and reflect throughout how your employees view their vision of the company and its leaders?

Goals and Skills: Define clear, achievable goals for yourself and your team. Set hard expectations to ensure these goals align with your vision and values. Continuously work on developing these goals and skills, but evaluating and improving communication, conflict resolution and emotional intelligence.

Loyalty, Trust, and Build Relationships: Cultivate strong, positive relationships with your team members and colleagues. Show empathy, respect, and appreciation for their contributions. Building trust and loyalty will go a long way for everyone involved.

Executive Tip: Loyalty Exercise.

Reflect on your current team or those who surround you.

Whom do you feel loyal to and why?
What attributes do you see in them that make you feel loyal to them?

Secondly, reflect on those that you think are loyal to you?
Write down what makes you feel this way?
What hard and soft skills do they possess?

Lastly, do all of your team members possess these similar qualities? Do you reflect or look for these qualities in your hiring processes?

Lead by Example: Demonstrate the behaviors and attitudes you want to see in others. Your actions will set the tone for the team. Make sure to understand every aspect of the company. In order to lead you have to fully understand each role and its entirety. Spend time executing your team's tasks, you may find new ways to process their role and simplify things as technology changes.

Encourage Their Success: Let your team define their own success. Seek interest in what makes them successful in their role. Allow for growth opportunities and advancements in their education.

The outlook on leaders and what societal expectations are will be forever shifting. It is imperative to recognize the current norms and values of the workforce in order to adapt your leadership style accordingly. Staying attune to new technologies and implementing processes to help organize and be aware of available resources will contribute to your leadership goals and lasting legacy on those you lead.

CHAPTER EIGHTEEN

Shaping Your Company's Future

CHOOSE YOUR NEXT CEO
Where Your Company Goes After You

Having the wrong CEO can lead to disastrous consequences, regardless of how much mentoring, executive coaching or team engagement is provided. Yet if you have a long term vision for your company, there's eventually going to be a CEO who isn't you. It is interesting to note that CEOs often struggle when it comes to hiring for their own leadership role, despite their ability to assemble a great team of operations, finance, and marketing professionals.

Selecting a future CEO holds immense importance due to the profound impact it can have on the organization. Drawing insights from our interactions with CEOs over the years, we've distilled some guiding principles for executives involved in the executive-succession process.

1. **Acknowledge that individuals are the ones who shape strategy – not merely a mission statement on a website.** As Yogi Berra, the American baseball legend, wisely cautioned, "If you don't know where you're going, you might not get there." This underscores the correlation between incomplete strategies and ineffective leadership. Executives and directors who possess a clear vision for the company are better positioned to steer it toward success.

2. **Establish an evaluation system that aligns the company's strategic needs with the individual capabilities and performance of potential candidates.** Focus on attributes such as integrity, ethics, team building, execution excellence, personal gravitas, and their ability to contribute to the growth. Think strategically about your company culture and where you want it to go in the future. Will the new CEO be able to drive that forward? It would be wise to also ask your existing team for the qualities they want to see in their future leader. You can ask questions from a prospective like: *What aspects of the company culture are most important to you, and how can a leader contribute to or enhance these cultural elements? What approach to conflict resolution do you find most effective, and how would you like a leader to address conflicts within the team?*

3. **Integrate succession planning into corporate culture.** Develop a culture that incentivizes executives to contribute to the system, provides widespread development opportunities, offers coaching and mentoring, and remains open to both internal and external candidates. Implement a structured process for identifying high-potential employees early in their careers. This involves assessing not only current performance but also leadership potential, adaptability, and strategic thinking. Active collaboration between other managers and executive team members and the CEO is crucial to ensuring a full and upwardly developing talent pipeline.

222

4. Companies should recognize that no candidate is flawless. The key is to comprehend the trade-offs between candidates' strengths and weaknesses and ensure that any deficits do not significantly impact critical areas for company performance. The fate of the enterprise hinges on this thoughtful consideration.

Quality Control in Succession Planning

There are certain essential qualities that must be considered when selecting the next CEO. It is necessary to meticulously define the qualities required for success in the role. Additionally, it is important to keep an open mind regarding where the best candidate may come from. Thoroughly understanding and evaluating each candidate to determine the best fit is also essential. Lastly, it is important to acknowledge that imperfections may exist in the chosen candidate. And that's okay!

While rigorous succession planning is crucial, it can only take an organization so far. Eventually, a decision must be made, and in such situations, judgment plays a significant role. To ensure sound judgment, it is important to have a clear understanding of both the current and future requirements of the job. As the current CEO, you possess valuable insights into these requirements. It is important to identify the critical capabilities that can make or break the company. This is not about creating a generic list of leadership traits or focusing on a single aspect. Instead, it involves identifying two or three tightly interwoven capabilities that are crucial for the new leader's success. This is what ultimately differentiates one candidate from another.

When making the final decision, it is important to consider the fit of the candidate. Each situation is unique, and it is crucial to consider the future as well. A CEO in any industry should possess the ability to focus on the end-to-end consumer experience, have a deep understanding of digital innovations, and be capable of shaping the ecosystem of vendors, resources, people and consultants. Taking the time to fully comprehend the company's specific current challenges and the changing external context is vital. This can be achieved by reading reports, consulting with insiders, and seeking advice from external experts. It is important to delve deeper and broaden your perspective beyond what is typically done when hiring for other positions. This is not a typical hiring situation and it is crucial to not overlook complexities or contradictions. Instead, it is important to cut through them and determine the essential skills and capabilities through an iterative process until the right combination is found.

You've undoubtedly heard all of the standard interview questions – and you've probably even asked most of them yourself. But what about some of the less common questions? The ones that really show you about the candidate's ability to think strategically, execute with confidence, and willingness to be the future of the company.

Here are some important questions to ask:

1. "How well do you know yourself?" The best CEOs are always keenly aware of their own flaws and blindspots. You want to have a CEO that recognizes their own shortcomings but is dedicated to rounding out a team.
2. "What are the limits of your knowledge and skills?" The most successful CEOs will have the humility and knowledge to surround themselves with people smarter than they are. They want to be aware that they don't have all of the answers but that they can work to deepen the team's experience.
3. "What will help you in the future?" This will give you insight as to whether a CEO candidate is forward-thinking enough to be looking down the road.
4. "What is your natural thinking style?" Diversity plays a crucial role in another aspect: thinking style. If you tend to be a spontaneous and decisive CEO, it's essential to complement that with individuals who approach situations with caution and analytical rigor. Even though these individuals may be challenging to deal with on occasion, their perspective might also prevent impulsive decisions that could jeopardize the company's future.
5. Ask the candidate, "As advancements in AI and automation impact industries, how do you envision integrating these technologies into your organization while considering the impact on the workforce?" It prompts the candidate to consider the human element and the potential impact on the workforce. A thoughtful response will address not only technological implementation but also strategies for workforce development and support.
6. Ask the interviewee, "What initiatives have you implemented to support employee well-being, especially considering the challenges brought about by remote work and the blurring of work-life boundaries?" A CEO who recognizes the impact of well-being on retention and productivity understands the long-term benefits of work/life balance. Organizations that prioritize employee well-being often gain a competitive advantage in attracting and retaining top talent. The CEO's initiatives can contribute to the overall employer brand and market positioning.

Forming an exceptional leadership team is a challenging – but necessary – task. It requires the application of critical thinking, effective recruitment strategies, and the courage to make tough decisions. Additionally, it demands a considerable investment of time and patience. When mishandled, it has the potential to inadvertently steer a company in the wrong direction, impeding growth. However, when executed correctly, it has the power to propel the company to increasingly higher levels of performance.

When creating the final shortlist of potential candidates, it is advisable to start with a clean slate. It is important to recognize that a company's needs can change suddenly, rendering the candidates identified in an earlier succession plan irrelevant. It is also crucial to challenge hidden assumptions and biases, both your own and those of others, as you narrow down the prospects to two or three and ultimately make a final choice. Often we form a definite opinion about a person after the first encounter and fail to change our views, even when presented with contradictory evidence. Think about it – CEO performance is often evaluated over the long term. Success in this role involves navigating challenges, steering the company through changing landscapes, and achieving sustained growth. Initial impressions may not capture a CEO's ability to deliver consistent, long-term results. It's more often than not worth giving someone a second or third look in this type of search.

It is also important not to assume that an insider or outsider is the best choice. Many companies engage headhunters to include external candidates in the final list, even if it is just for the sake of due diligence. However, this step should not be perfunctory. The search firm must understand the specific requirements to avoid presenting the usual accomplished CEOs.

While interviews are a standard part of the selection process, there can be significant variation in the depth of these conversations. One way to ensure thoroughness is to not only conduct interviews yourself but also involve other team members in the process. This is particularly important because these team members will be reporting to the CEO. It is crucial to gather input from everyone and consider their perspectives when making the choice. There's a benefit to the team members here as well. It's not just about making your own job easier. Communicate how participating in the interview process can contribute to their professional growth. Mention that this experience provides insights into leadership evaluations, decision-making, and exposure to strategic discussions. Lastly, this is a good opportunity to reflect with the COO and gain insightful feedback that aligns with the criteria and expectations for the new CEO. This collaborative effort from all levels within the organization ensures a comprehensive evaluation process, ultimately leading to a well-informed and strategic decision that benefits both the organization and its team members.

Hiring From Within – Does It Make Sense?

At a certain stage in every business's life cycle, the matter of succession becomes a prominent consideration.

Many businesses default to hiring an executive recruiter to seek external candidates, but statistics show only a 50-50 chance of finding an ideal fit who stays in the job. This means a 50 percent risk of hiring someone who could potentially cause significant damage, costing the business millions of dollars in a short period if they aren't the perfect fit for organizational growth.

In our experience, promoting someone from within the company, if feasible, offers better odds of success, with research indicating an 80 percent probability of success in such cases. The challenge lies in identifying the right internal candidate.

Your Executive Team

Examine your executive team to identify individuals with the ambition and potential to ascend to the CEO position. Consider their cross-functional experience within the organization and mentoring both internally and externally. Ideally, limit the number of candidates directly reporting to you for succession planning to avoid internal competition.

Adding Candidates to the Pool

Evaluate whether there are "blockers" among your executive team, meaning individuals impeding those with higher succession potential. Consider replacing blockers with internal or external candidates. This move can be particularly effective in unleashing the potential of high-performing individuals lower in the hierarchy, motivating the entire executive team.

The Best Candidates Are Already in Critical Roles

When forming a succession inner circle, focus on candidates from core business areas where value is created. For instance, if you're in product sales, look to your sales team for executive talent. Align the strengths of potential successors with the center of your business. Consider this perspective for your own career goals within the business to ensure alignment with the core functions of the company.

The Traits to Look For

Do you want to ensure the enduring success of your organization? If so, the next CEO must embody four crucial traits: a relentless focus on the long-term future, an inherently entrepreneurial mindset, a solid grounding in business fundamentals, and the behavior of a consummate diplomat.

CEOs come and go, with some, like Apple's Steve Jobs, Amazon's Jeff Bezos, and Virgin's Richard Branson, standing out as exemplary leaders who "get it." Others, such as Microsoft's Steve Ballmer, GE's Jeff Immelt, and Lehman Brothers' Dick Fuld, fall short in understanding the essential dynamics of their roles.

The distinguishing factor between successful and less effective CEOs lies in possessing these four vital traits. To ensure your organization thrives in the face of evolving challenges, seek a CEO who embodies these characteristics.

A Relentless Focus on the Long-Term Future

The most successful CEOs are visionary leaders with a clear understanding of where the organization needs to go, grounded in a purpose that extends beyond short-term gains. These leaders focus on a vision spanning 25 to 50 years, acknowledging the volatile and uncertain nature of the world. Founders often excel in this role due to their long-term, transformative visions. Effective CEOs are attuned to emerging trends, understanding that aligning strategies with these trends is crucial for success. They actively shape the future, recognizing the need to be proactive and preemptive in steering the organization toward desired outcomes. You can ask interview questions like:

How do you proactively shape the future of the organization rather than reactively responding to challenges?

How do you measure success in the context of a long-term vision?

What is the overarching purpose that drives your leadership decisions?

An Inherently Entrepreneurial Mindset

Great CEOs embrace entrepreneurship, recognizing the value of experimentation to shape the future. They operate parts of the organization like startup studios, conducting lean and intelligent experiments to learn about emerging market needs and reactions. This approach, exemplified by companies like Amazon and Starbucks, allows organizations to identify winning strategies and discard unsuccessful ones. The entrepreneurial CEO thrives on experimentation, understanding that failure is an inherent part of the innovation process.

Questions to ask could be:

1. Can you share a specific instance where you demonstrated an entrepreneurial mindset in a leadership role?
2. How do you approach risk-taking in decision-making?
3. Can you provide an example of how you maximized resources to achieve strategic goals?
4. Can you share a specific failure and discuss the lessons learned?

Solid Grounding in Reality and the Fundamentals of Business

Effective CEOs rely on facts and data to drive decisions. They maintain objectivity and lack bias, understanding the importance of ongoing analytics to evaluate the success of strategies. This trait is inseparable from an entrepreneurial mindset, as both are necessary for organizational success. Objective CEOs are honest about the organization's performance, ensuring that underperforming aspects are addressed promptly. This trait is critical for preventing the organization from descending into irrelevance due to self-deception.

Some examples of interview questions are:

1. Can you describe your decision-making process and how data plays a role in it?
2. How do you ensure that relevant data is accessible to the appropriate teams and individuals within the organization?
3. In what ways does data inform your approach to risk management?
4. What measures do you take to ensure the quality and accuracy of the data used for decision-making?

Behavior of Consummate Diplomat

A prospective CEO must be diplomatic, treating employees, investors, customers, and the public with respect. Even with the aforementioned traits, a lack of diplomacy can undermine the organization's success. The right CEO will create organizational culture, fostering autonomy and accountability for long-term success. Diplomacy ensures that relationships with all stakeholders are maintained, contributing to a positive workplace and sustained results.

You can interview with questions like:

1. How do you approach resolution, and what strategies did you use to maintain positive relationships?
2. Describe a decision you made that faced resistance, and how did you communicate and navigate the aftermath to maintain trust?
3. Can you share a successful experience in managing cross-cultural dynamics?

Finding a CEO who embodies these traits ensures that your organization will continue to thrive and succeed for years and decades to come.

When devising a succession plan, prioritize building a strategy around executive team members whose talents and strengths align with the core of your business. Without individuals fitting this description, your succession plan remains nothing more than a dream.

Lastly, it is important to acknowledge that no CEO selection is without risk, and it takes time to see the results. However, by focusing on the pivot, avoiding favoritism, thoroughly understanding candidates' strengths, and allowing for imperfections, those responsible for the decision can avoid common pitfalls and increase the likelihood of making an excellent choice.

CHAPTER NINETEEN

Charting the Path for the Company in a Remote Environment

COMMUNICATION THAT CONNECTS
Leaders as Enablers, Not Enforcers

For the book, we researched how effective managers engage people and drive performance while working from home. The key finding was subtle, yet illustrated an important shift in how employees expect their managers to work with them. They want their managers to be present, hands-on, and operationally vigilant without being intrusive. In other words, employees don't want their managers to *micromanage* them, but they want their managers to *micro-understand* their work.

Micromanagement is restrictive. Heavy managerial meddling undermines trust, disempowers employees, and manifests itself in the form of exhaustive reviews, checklists, and levels of approval. Micro-understanding is about better integrating yourself into your team's workflow and problem-solving remotely. The micro-understanding manager can identify vulnerabilities and construct a radar for potential trouble spots. Micro-understanding is about trusting while making sure there are no unanticipated bumps. This requires delegating but being there to keep workers from stumbling. Balance being flexible, while heeding any warning signs.

Leaders as Enablers, Not Enforcers

Remote or in-person, the role of a leader at its core remains the same: motivate employees and organize resources to drive performance excellence. What managers and leaders do remains the same when working remotely, but "the how" changes. Many CEOs and leaders are concerned about how to manage their staff when they can't see them. Presenteeism, or the need to show facetime at work, is often assumed to be necessary for productivity.

However, productivity data during the COVID pandemic demonstrated that people could perform just as productively – and sometimes even more so – without being monitored for time spent at work or being physically present in an office. Anecdotally, in our work running a Virtual Assistant company, we know that our team members believe that having a manager is a positive thing, provided that their managers or supervisors shift from managing time and activity to managing results and outcomes.

In our experience, employees consider their supervisors and managers to be even more of a key resource in getting the job done remotely. They expect their managers to devote more time and effort to removing interpersonal and work barriers, coordinate among many stakeholders, as well as coach and orchestrate their performance. In a virtual or remote setting, good managers act as enablers and not as enforcers.

Being in the Game Without Being on the Field

Managing remotely is a delicate balance. Leaders are accused of micromanagement when they exert excessive oversight. In our company, we have to monitor employees clocking in and out so that we know they are doing their work when they're supposed to be doing it and that we're accurately accounting for client billables. However, doing this too closely can impair employees' productivity and morale. This is where micro-understanding comes in. It's like being a coach who is very much in the game but not on the field.

A present leader generates better organizational outcomes and increased employee engagement in a virtual environment. Presence here entails being approachable, visible, mindful, and having frequent individual and team check-ins, as well as being a valuable resource to employees in accomplishing their tasks. It's important that employees don't feel that you're monitoring them. Instead, they should see you there as a resource.

Here are some examples of situations where micro-understanding is necessary:

- **Setting priorities and clarifying.** A remote work environment calls for ruthless prioritization. Everyone on the team needs to understand what needs to be done when it needs to be done, and by whom. Micro-understanding entails understanding how detailed priorities work together to produce the intended product on time and with the required level of efficiency.
- **Problem solving.** In a remote context, problem-solving involves setting up alert mechanisms for potential problems and timely fixes as they appear. This means that managers must develop an ability to scan constantly and instantly know vulnerabilities and obstacles. This is true not only with security measures but also as far as the company's whole process is concerned. In a remote environment, we are limited in what we can visibly see on a day-to-day basis. Setting up alert mechanisms such as weekly reminders to do quality checks in multiple areas of the company, such as invoicing, customer services, or monthly checks on platforms that you know have a tendency to glitch. Foreseeing the problem or taking proactive corrective steps will set the tone for easier remote management and operations.
- **Checking in and showing compassion.** Checking in is about interpersonal trust and connection. Remote work lacks opportunities for spontaneous connection and coaching. They need to be created. While checking in was popular in the initial days of the pandemic, it has gone down in importance and frequency over time, with managers feeling exhausted by the emotional drain it causes. However, check-ins are necessary in a remote working environment since most employees view their immediate managers as the most important link they have with their organization.

Managers, whether they like it or not, are often required to provide "emotional first aid" to employees in times of distress. Unskilled managers often end up making check-ins look like check-ups, making employees feel that they are being monitored. Others never show empathy and compassion and alienate the team. We've seen, on our team, that most team members are appreciative of their managers' ability to connect with them. A random email saying, "I'm thinking of you and am grateful you are on my team," contributes a lot more to trust than any formal program. Humanizing the remote workplace is a special art for the remote leader, and it happens in non-obvious but conscious ways.

Leading with empathy is a foundational principle that becomes even more crucial in the context of a remote workplace. As teams operate from dispersed locations, the traditional cues of an office environment, such as face-to-face interactions and nonverbal communication, are often replaced by virtual connections. In this scenario, empathetic leadership becomes a cornerstone for fostering a positive and productive remote work culture.

Empathy begins with a deep understanding of the unique challenges and experiences that remote team members navigate. Leaders need to recognize that each individual may be working from a distinct environment with its set of complexities. Some may be juggling family responsibilities, while others may be dealing with feelings of isolation. Acknowledging and empathizing with these diverse circumstances forms the basis of effective leadership.

Communication that Connects

In a remote setting, where face-to-face interactions are limited, the way leaders communicate becomes paramount. Empathetic leaders prioritize clear and compassionate communication. They actively listen to their team members, encourage open dialogue, and create a virtual space where individuals feel comfortable expressing their thoughts, concerns, and ideas.

Regular check-ins, both one-on-one and in group settings, provide opportunities for leaders to connect on a personal level with their team. Understanding the unique context of each team member's work environment and life situation fosters a sense of camaraderie and trust.

Flexibility extends beyond just work hours. Empathetic leaders are attuned to the fact that remote employees may face interruptions, such as family obligations, or technical issues, such as Wi-Fi disruptions. Instead of fostering a rigid environment, they encourage adaptability and understanding, ensuring that team members can navigate their responsibilities without added stress.

Leading with empathy involves creating a culture where care for the well-being of team members is embedded in the organizational DNA. This can be achieved through initiatives that

234

prioritize mental and physical health. Encouraging breaks, promoting self-care, and offering resources for managing stress contribute to a workplace where employees feel seen and supported.

An empathetic leader understands that each team member has unique needs, both professionally and personally. By acknowledging and addressing these individual needs, leaders demonstrate a commitment to the holistic well-being of their employees. Whether it's providing additional support for professional development, adjusting workloads based on personal circumstances, or offering resources for skill enhancement, leaders actively contribute to the growth and fulfillment of their team members.

Research affirms that cultivating compassion in the workplace as a leader doesn't demand significant time investments. Studies, such as one from Johns Hopkins, reveal that just 40 seconds of compassionate engagement can notably reduce another person's anxiety. Additionally, dedicating time to serving others, as indicated by a University of Pennsylvania study, enhances one's subjective sense of time "affluence."

Embracing an "attitude of gratitude" has proven benefits. Meta-analytic research indicates that gratitude amplifies our focus on others and motivates us to be of service. A University of Toronto study suggests that gratitude keeps us attuned to these changes.

When colleagues face personal challenges, it's crucial to ask the right questions; instead of binary inquiries that might elicit a negative response, frame questions positively. For instance, inquire about specific ways to offer support or inquire how to make their day better.

Highlighting instances where employees go above and beyond creates a culture that recognizes and encourages compassionate behavior.

Recognizing compassion and empathy as an evidence-based skill integral to effective leadership is crucial for talent retention and organizational performance, particularly in challenging times. Compassion is not merely a trait that's nice to have; it is firmly grounded in both the art and science of leadership.

Leading with empathy in a remote workplace involves a holistic understanding of the individual experiences of team members and a commitment to fostering a culture of care and connection. Empathetic leaders recognize that the success of a remote team is not solely measured by productivity but also by the well-being and satisfaction of each team member. As organizations continue to embrace remote work, the principles of empathetic leadership will undoubtedly play a pivotal role in shaping positive and thriving virtual work environments.

CHAPTER TWENTY

Founder to CEO

FOUNDER TO CEO
Beneath the Layers

Becoming a CEO is a significant milestone for any founder. This marks a transition from being solely focused on the creation and growth of a company to assuming the responsibility of leading and guiding a company in a specific direction.

Have you found yourself not having time to just *think*? This is the moment when you're so involved in the day-to-day running of your company that you no longer have the big picture in sight. CEOs more easily achieve success when they work on functions they're good at and have an eye on the company's overall growth.

Beneath a CEO, there are five layers of the business:

1. **Administration:** This layer includes paperwork, report generation, correspondence, scheduling, travel planning, and market research. These are usually tasks that a founder isn't necessarily passionate about. The good news is that some people are passionate about this type of work – Virtual Assistants. The first hire you should make is someone who can take the administrative tasks off your plate.

2. **Delivery:** Remove yourself from production work and delegate all that behind-the-scenes work that doesn't deal directly with your growth or revenue generation. Let your Virtual Assistant or another team member handle the backend service or product delivery tasks. And if you find yourself spending a lot of time on one side of your business, consider that as a warning sign. Look for ways to delegate that work to somebody else. If that specific work can be broken down into a series of tasks, have several Virtual Assistants or team members work on them at the same time. This will not only speed up production, delivery, and operations but will also increase your capacity and lead to greater sales numbers.

3. **Marketing:** A lot of businesses get *stuck* on marketing. Certainly, it's a significant and important cog in the wheel, but when someone isn't a marketer by training or education, it takes much more time than necessary. Marketing your business effectively takes a lot of time and a lot of brain power. Free up mental space by outsourcing or delegating to a professional.

4. **Business Development:** Business development is the most critical piece for a growing company. This is about cultivating relationships, developing new business, and closing deals. This is where the most successful entrepreneurs live. The only way you can live here is when you've got the other stages under control.

238

5. **People:** A strong company is an environment where people thrive professionally and personally. To do that effectively, you need someone in charge with experience in both personnel management and organizational development. This layer of the business involves hiring new employees or consultants, developing training programs, and improving employee retention rates. This role serves as a steward of human capital.

As a founder, you love the company you invented, the company that you started. You want to be the CEO that pilots it to sustain success and growth. Looking at your business through the lens of the above stages will help you transition from the early days of building a product or service to the later days of managing a growing organization.

You're going from being a founder – someone who is solely focused on building a great product or service – to a CEO, where your role is about building an enduring and sustainable company. When you break down your business into stages and delegate effectively to professionals you trust, you can make that leap successfully.

Perhaps you've already hired more people, brought on a COO, and advanced to the next phase in your business. But many entrepreneurs find themselves still struggling to step back and let go of the day-to-day tasks.

As a founder, your primary focus to this point has been on innovation, product or service development, and establishing a strong foundation for your company. However, as a CEO, your role expands to encompass strategic decision-making, team management, and long-term planning.

Transitioning to becoming a CEO requires sharpening your leadership skills. There are several key competencies necessary for effective leadership, including communication, delegation, decision-making, and creating a strong company culture.

Behind the Scenes Team

One of the most critical aspects of being a successful CEO is assembling and nurturing a high-performing team. These individuals are motivated, skilled, and aligned with the company's mission, which leads to better results. High-performing teams are more innovative and adaptable. They quickly respond to changes in the market, industry, or business environment, helping the company stay ahead of competitors. A skilled team brings different perspectives and expertise to the table, leading to more effective problem-solving and decision-making processes. CEOs should be able to rely on their teams to provide insights and recommendations. A high-performing team is efficient in using company resources. They can maximize productivity, reduce waste, and control costs, contributing to the organization's financial health.

High-performing teams are better equipped to identify and mitigate risks. They are vigilant about potential issues and can proactively address challenges before they become significant problems.

A CEO's success is intricately linked to the performance of their team. By assembling a high-performing team and nurturing its growth, a CEO drives the organization forward and ultimately achieves sustainable success in today's competitive business landscape.

CEO Role: Strategic Planning:

Strategic planning in a CEO role involves considering the long-term sustainability and growth of the organization. This may include exploring new markets, diversifying products or services, or investing in innovation. The CEO is also responsible for defining the company's vision and mission. The vision outlines the desired future state of the organization, while the mission defines its purpose and reason for existence.

Team Role: Execution

Teams are responsible for translating the CEO's high-level strategies and plans into actionable tasks. They execute day-to-day operations, ensuring that the company is moving towards its strategic goals.

CEO Role: Managing Stakeholder Relationships:

CEOs must navigate complex relationships with various stakeholders, including investors, executive board members, employees, and customers. In this role, CEOs should be actively engaged with stakeholders to understand their perspectives, needs, and expectations. When conflicts arise between stakeholders or between the organization and stakeholders, the CEO plays a leadership role in resolving disputes. Effective conflict resolution contributes to maintaining positive relationships.

Team Role: Engaging Stakeholders:

Teams serve as the frontline communicators with stakeholders. They interact directly with clients, suppliers, and other external parties, conveying information, answering queries, and addressing concerns. They play a vital role in ensuring client satisfaction on the front lines, addressing issues promptly, and enhancing the overall client experience.

CEO Role: Embracing Continuous Learning and Growth:

The journey from founder to CEO is a continuous learning process. Transitioning from founder to CEO is a transformative journey that requires adaptability, resilience, and a commitment to continuous improvement. By embracing the mindset shift, developing essential leadership skills, building a high-performing team, and effectively executing strategic plans, you can navigate this transition successfully and lead your company to new heights of success. Remember, the path to becoming an exceptional CEO is a continuous process of learning, growth, and embracing the challenges that come your way.

Team Role: Participating in Growth

Teams should actively engage in training and development programs offered by the CEO or organization. This includes workshops, seminars, online courses, and other learning opportunities that enhance skills and knowledge relevant to their roles. Teams can form learning communities or interest groups where members with similar learning objectives collaborate, share resources, and support each other's growth. Teams should actively stay informed about industry trends, market changes, and emerging technologies. This awareness helps the team anticipate future challenges and opportunities, prompting proactive learning initiatives.

The Journey of a Not-Your-Average CEO

After nearly two decades in business and working with thousands of business owners, we've found there exists a breed of CEOs who defy traditional norms and challenge conventional expectations. These trailblazers, the Not Your Average CEOs, possess a unique blend of qualities, experiences, and approaches that set them apart from their peers. Let's explore the key traits and lessons that define their journeys.

Embracing Authenticity

Not Your Average CEOs are unafraid to be their authentic selves. They shatter the mold and refuse to conform to preconceived notions of what a CEO should be. Historically, CEOs were typically rigid, ego-driven in their decision-making, and authoritative. By embracing their true identities, they cultivate a sense of transparency and trust within their organizations. They lead with honesty, vulnerability, and genuine passion, allowing their authentic selves to shine through and inspire those around them.

Cultivating a Growth Mindset

Not Your Average CEOs have an insatiable appetite for growth and learning. They cultivate a growth mindset, embracing challenges and viewing setbacks as opportunities for improvement. These leaders encourage their teams to adopt the same mindset, fostering a culture of continuous learning and development. It's important to view your abilities as developable. Instead of viewing your abilities and intelligence as fixed traits, CEOs with a growth mindset understand that these qualities can be developed over time. They believe in the potential for improvement. By prioritizing personal and professional growth, they inspire their organizations to reach new heights and adapt to an ever-changing business landscape.

Disrupting the Status Quo

Conventional thinking rarely piques the interest of Not Your Average CEOs. They thrive on disruption, seeking new ways to challenge the status quo and drive innovation. These leaders encourage their teams to question existing norms and explore unconventional solutions. By encouraging calculated risk-taking and embracing failure as a catalyst for growth, they inspire breakthrough thinking and spark transformative change within their organizations.

Balancing Purpose and Profit

For Not Your Average CEOs, success is not solely defined by financial gains. They understand the power of purpose and strive to make a meaningful impact beyond the bottom line. These leaders align their organizations with a higher purpose, with a sense of shared mission and social responsibility. By prioritizing both profit and purpose, they create sustainable businesses that positively influence their communities and the world at large.

Nurturing Emotional Intelligence

Not Your Average CEOs possess a high degree of emotional intelligence, as we've discussed in other areas of the book because it's just that important. They recognize the importance of understanding and empathizing with their teams, cultivating strong relationships built on trust and mutual respect. These leaders excel in communication, active listening, and conflict resolution, creating an environment where everyone feels valued and supported. By nurturing emotional intelligence, they create a positive and collaborative culture that drives organizational success.

Embracing Agility and Adaptability

Not Your Average CEOs excel at embracing agility and adaptability. They anticipate change, stay ahead of trends, and swiftly adjust their strategies to capitalize on emerging opportunities. These leaders encourage agility within their organizations, empowering their teams to embrace change, learn quickly, and pivot when necessary. By staying nimble and adaptable, they navigate uncertainty with grace and turn challenges into triumphs.

Being a Not Your Average CEO is not for the faint of heart. It requires courage, authenticity, and a relentless drive for growth and innovation. These visionary leaders challenge norms, break barriers, and inspire others to embrace their uniqueness. They understand that true success lies inside.

The Remote Revolution: Unleashing the Power of Remote Work

In today's digital age, the way we work is undergoing a transformative shift. Remote work, once considered a rarity, has now become a powerful force that revolutionizes how businesses operate. As CEOs, you have the opportunity to harness the advantages of remote work and unlock its vast potential. Let's explore the persuasive case for embracing remote work and discuss strategies to maximize its benefits for your organization.

The concept of remote work has evolved from an occasional perk to a fundamental shift in the way we work. Enabled by advanced technology and a changing workforce mindset, remote work has become more than a response to global events—it is a long-term strategy that can reshape the future of work. The remote work revolution is not simply a passing trend – it's a transformative shift that offers immense opportunities for businesses to thrive in a dynamic world. By embracing remote work strategically, CEOs can unlock the potential for growth, innovation, and resilience while creating a more flexible and fulfilling work environment for their teams.

Embracing a New Paradigm

Remote work offers a paradigm shift in how work is conducted. By breaking free from the confines of a traditional office space, you can tap into a global talent pool and access the best minds regardless of their physical location. Embracing remote work enables you to build agile, diverse, and dynamic teams that bring fresh perspectives and innovative solutions to the table.

Empowering Productivity and Improving Work-Life Balance

Remote work empowers employees by providing them with the freedom to work from anywhere, at any time.

Does it matter to you as a CEO where your employee sits as much as it matters what the quality of their work is?

This flexibility enhances productivity and work-life balance, leading to increased employee satisfaction and engagement. By trusting your team members to manage their time effectively, you create an environment of autonomy, motivation, and a sense of ownership.

Attracting Top Talent

Talent knows no geographical boundaries. With remote work, you can attract and retain top talent regardless of their location. By offering remote work opportunities, you position your organization as a forward-thinking and inclusive employer that values flexibility and work-life integration. This competitive advantage allows you to attract highly skilled professionals who may otherwise be inaccessible due to geographic constraints. Some remote workers who enjoy traveling may opt for "workations" – a combination of work and vacation. This allows individuals to maintain their professional responsibilities while enjoying a change of scenery and exploring new destinations during downtime.

Cost Savings and Operational Efficiency

Remote work presents significant cost-saving opportunities for your organization. By reducing or eliminating the need for a physical office space, you save significant money on rent, utilities, and other associated expenses. Moreover, remote work eliminates time-consuming and costly commutes, allowing employees to dedicate more time and energy to their work. The increased efficiency and reduced overhead costs drives bottom-line growth for your organization.

Leveraging Technology for Collaboration

Advancements in technology have made remote collaboration seamless and efficient. By leveraging communication tools like Slack and sharing tools like Google Drive, you create a virtual workspace where teams can collaborate effectively, irrespective of their physical locations. Embrace video conferencing, instant messaging, and cloud-based platforms to facilitate real-time communication, collaboration and maintain a strong sense of connection among team members.

Navigating Challenges

While remote work offers numerous advantages, it also presents unique challenges. As a CEO, address these challenges proactively. Provide clear communication channels, establish transparent performance metrics, and foster a sense of camaraderie through virtual team-building activities. By nurturing a remote culture centered around trust, accountability, and effective communication, you can overcome challenges and unlock the full potential of remote work.

The era of remote work is upon us, offering a wealth of opportunities for your organization. By embracing this transformative shift, you can tap into a global talent pool, enhance productivity, attract top talent, reduce costs and foster diversity and inclusion. However, success in remote work requires strategic planning, effective communication, and a strong remote culture. Embrace the remote revolution, adapt to the changing landscape and leverage what is at your disposal.

Unleashing the Leader Within: A Journey of Inspiration and Empowerment

In life, we are all bestowed with the capacity to lead, to make a difference and to leave a lasting impact on the world. The journey towards leadership is not merely a pursuit of power or authority; it is a transformative path of self-discovery, growth, and empowerment.

1. Embrace Your Purpose

Every great leader begins their journey by discovering their purpose – the driving force that ignites their passion and fuels their actions. Reflect on your values, aspirations, and the positive change you wish to create in the world. Embrace your purpose as the guiding star that navigates your path, inspiring you to lead with conviction and authenticity.

2. Cultivate Self-Awareness

Self-awareness is the cornerstone of effective leadership. Take time to introspect, understand your strengths, weaknesses, and triggers. Embrace your authentic self and recognize the unique qualities you bring to the table. Embrace your vulnerabilities, for they can be the source of strength and relatability. By cultivating self-awareness, you lay a solid foundation for personal and professional growth.

3. Embrace Continuous Learning

Leadership is an ongoing journey of growth and learning. Embrace a thirst for knowledge and seek opportunities to expand your horizons. Engage in continuous learning through reading, attending workshops, seeking mentors, and exposing yourself to diverse perspectives. Remember, wisdom is not confined to a single source – it is found in the collective wisdom of others.

4. Develop Resilience and Courage

Leadership is not without its challenges and setbacks. Develop resilience, for it is the armor that protects your spirit in the face of adversity. Embrace challenges as opportunities for growth and learn to adapt and overcome them. Cultivate the courage to take calculated risks, challenge the status quo, and persevere even when faced with uncertainty. Believe in yourself and your ability to navigate through storms, emerging stronger on the other side.

5. **Develop Empathy and Emotional Intelligence**

Great leaders connect with others on a deep and empathetic level. Cultivate empathy by actively listening. Seek to understand and consider diverse perspectives. Develop emotional intelligence, understand the emotions of others, and manage your own effectively. By fostering empathy and emotional intelligence, you create an inclusive and supportive environment that inspires and motivates those around you.

6. **Build Meaningful Relationships**

Leadership is not a solitary endeavor; it thrives on the power of relationships. Cultivate meaningful connections with others, foster a culture of collaboration, and surround yourself with individuals who complement your skills and share your vision. Invest in building strong and authentic relationships based on trust, respect, and mutual support. Remember, the collective strength of a team far exceeds the capabilities of any individual.

7. **Lead with Integrity and Ethical Values**

Leadership carries with it the responsibility to uphold integrity and ethical values. Lead by example. You may wish to make a list of your personal core values so that you can reiterate them to yourself and your team as principles for you to live by. In our team, for example, some of our core values with leadership are honesty, transparency, humility, and balance. Make decisions guided by principles rather than short-term gains. Your commitment to ethical leadership will inspire trust and loyalty among those you lead.

By embarking on this transformative journey, you unleash the leader within you, capable of inspiring others, driving positive change, and leaving a lasting legacy. Embrace the challenges, celebrate the victories, and remember that leadership is not a destination but a journey.

Practical Steps to Becoming Not Your Average CEO

Nontraditional CEOs stand out by taking unconventional approaches to leadership and business strategy. Here are some things that you can put into practice immediately as a Not Your Average CEO:

1. **Implement Flexible Work Policies:** Going beyond the standard 9-to-5 workday, a forward-thinking CEO might adopt flexible work policies, allowing employees to choose when they work to provide a better work-life balance and increase productivity.

2. **Encourage Risks:** Encouraging a culture of experimentation and risk-taking can set a CEO apart. This involves allowing employees to test new ideas without fear of failure and promoting a mindset that views failures as valuable learning experiences.
3. **Invest in Continuous Learning:** Recognizing the importance of adaptability, a Not Your Average invests in continuous learning opportunities for employees, encouraging the development of new skills and knowledge. This can be done by selecting certain employees to lead Lunch and Learns, as an example, where employees are encouraged to showcase their skill sets and teach others in a training yet relaxed environment. Offering continuous education and training in relevant areas to your business also invests in your team and your company's future.
4. **Encourage Unconventional Collaboration:** Actively seeking collaborations outside the industry or partnering with unexpected allies, a Not Your Average CEO may foster innovation through unconventional partnerships.
5. **Rethink Traditional Compensation Models:** Exploring alternative compensation models, such as profit-sharing, equity options, or unconventional bonuses, can set a CEO apart and align employee interests with the company's success.
6. **Personalize Customer Experiences:** Instead of following a one-size-fits-all approach, a Not Your Average CEO might prioritize personalized customer experiences, leveraging data and technology to tailor products and services to individual preferences.
7. **Institute a Four-Day Work Week:** Going beyond flexible work hours, a Not Your Average CEO might experiment with a shorter workweek, believing that increased employee satisfaction and productivity can be achieved in fewer days.
8. **Implement a No-Meeting Day:** Recognizing the impact of constant meetings on productivity, a Not Your Average CEO might designate specific days as "no meeting days" to allow employees uninterrupted time for focused work.
9. **Encourage Reverse Mentorship:** Instead of traditional mentorship structures, a Not Your Average CEO may implement reverse mentorship programs, where younger or less experienced employees mentor senior executives, fostering cross-generational knowledge exchange.
10. **Host Unconventional Team-Building Events:** Moving beyond traditional team-building activities, a Not Your Average CEO might organize unconventional events or retreats that challenge employees, promote creativity, and strengthen team bonds. If you're virtual, these can be a team happy hour over Zoom or a trivia night. If you're in person, perhaps you can get together to do an Escape Room or arrange for an artistic workshop like a painting night.
11. **Adopt a "Fail Fast, Fail Cheap" Mentality:** Embracing a culture that accepts failure as a natural part of innovation, a Not Average CEO may encourage rapid experimentation, provided lessons are learned quickly and at a minimal cost.

There are many ways and practical steps to becoming a Not Your Average CEO. As we showcased in earlier chapters, the important thing is not to get overwhelmed but to break your action steps down into manageable steps. You don't need to dive in headfirst and do each item on the list right away, but it is more important to just start.

CHAPTER TWENTY ONE

Beyond the Book:
Where You Go From
Here

NOT YOUR AVERAGE CEO
An Opportunity to Contribute a Lasting Effect

As we conclude this journey into the world of being a Not Your Average CEO, let's reflect on the fundamental concepts we explored throughout this book. From the outset, we stated the importance of the power of setting clear and ambitious goals – goals that are not merely benchmarks but that give the steps toward the path toward extraordinary leadership. We dissected the art of time blocking, recognizing that how we allocate our most precious resource – time – ultimately shapes the narrative of our success.

The information presented may seem intense, one that could potentially overwhelm even the most seasoned leader. However, as we've consistently emphasized, the key lies in the art of chunking it down. Much like the way we approached goal setting and time blocking, the journey to becoming a Not Your Average CEO requires breaking down complex tasks into manageable, actionable steps.

Actionable items to begin at a high level. We recommend placing time on your calendar, multiple sessions in some cases, to complete these tasks. Set reminders that will nudge you to complete these tasks:

Discover a deeper self awareness.

1. **Actionable Next Steps:**

   - Set aside dedicated time for self-reflection.
   - Start journaling or seeking feedback from mentors and colleagues.
   - Conduct an anonymous survey from your team.
   - Research and engage in personal development activities like workshops or coaching/training sessions.

2. **Dedicated Time on Calendar:**

   - Schedule recurring sessions for self-reflection over the next six months.
   - Schedule to attend a personal development workshop or training.
   - Review survey results.
   - Take a behavioral assessment such as DISC.

Assess the harmony of your executive team.

1. **Actionable Next Steps:**
   - Develop agendas for one-on-one meetings with each executive team member.
   - Research team-building sessions or seminars.
   - Review and analyze team dynamics and communication channels.

2. **Dedicated Time on Calendar:**
   - Schedule individual meetings with each executive that occurs at regular intervals.
   - Plan a team-building session or quarterly meetings.

Consider the technology you currently utilize.

1. **Actionable Steps:**
   - Create a spreadsheet with a comprehensive audit of your current technology stack.
   - Assess the efficiency and effectiveness of each tool.
   - Research and explore new technologies that align with your business goals.
   - Reach out to your team to find out what technology they are currently using.
   - Sign up for one or maximum of two technology newsletters to keep you current.

2. **Dedicated Time on Calendar:**
   - Allocate a week for the technology audit and assessment. Set a recurring follow up for every six months.
   - Schedule a one hour time block for a research session for potential new technologies.

Schedule time to assess your marketing strategy and customer journey.

1. **Actionable Steps**
   - Review and analyze current marketing campaigns and their performance.
   - Collect customer feedback and conduct surveys to understand their journey.
   - Identify areas for improvement and innovation in your marketing strategy.

2. **Dedicated Time on Calendar:**
   - Set aside two sessions for marketing strategy review in the upcoming weeks.
   - Schedule customer feedback sessions and surveys over the next month.
   - Schedule time to make adjustments after the surveys have been completed.

Assess your brand and culture. Get to know your team and your audience.

1. **Actionable Steps**
   - Conduct employee engagement surveys and gather feedback. Use 360 surveys as well.

- Analyze brand perception both internally and externally.
- Foster open communication channels within the team. Set up multiple group chats.

2. **Dedicated Time on Calendar:**
   - Schedule a team-building session to strengthen internal culture.
   - Set aside time for employee surveys and brand perception analysis. Set this as a recurring task for every six to 12 months.

Gain your time back today. Start time blocking.

1. **Actionable Steps:**

   - Identify key priorities and allocate specific time blocks for focused work.
   - Minimize multitasking and distractions during dedicated time blocks.
   - Regularly reassess and adjust time blocks based on productivity.
   - Set reminders and alert mechanisms to proceed to the next goal.

2. **Dedicated Time on Calendar:**
   - Schedule a time-blocking session to plan the upcoming week.
   - Implement and adjust time-blocking techniques daily for the next month.

Schedule time to assess your strategies, profit margins, and future goals.

1. **Actionable Steps:**

   - Analyze financial reports and assess current profit margins.
   - Review and refine business strategies based on market trends.
   - Set specific, measurable goals for the upcoming quarter or year.

2. **Dedicated Time on Calendar:**
   - Allocate a full day for a comprehensive financial review.
   - Schedule quarterly strategy sessions to align with the business calendar.
   - Schedule a year out worth of financial planning and review sessions with appropriate team members.

Develop a remote piece to your company

1. **Actionable Steps:**

   - Assess the feasibility and benefits of remote work for your team.

- Implement remote work policies and technologies to support virtual collaboration.
- Provide training on remote work best practices for your team.

2. **Dedicated Time on Calendar:**
   - Schedule a series of meetings to discuss and plan the remote work transition.
   - Implement remote work policies and conduct training over the next several months.

Delegate

1. **Actionable Steps:**

   - Identify tasks that can be delegated to team members.
   - Communicate expectations clearly and provide necessary resources.
   - Monitor progress and provide feedback regularly.
   - Create video training and operating procedures – store them in appropriate team folders.

2. **Dedicated Time on Calendar:**
   - Schedule delegation sessions to identify tasks and communicate expectations.
   - Set up regular check-ins to monitor progress and provide feedback.

Shaping Your Company's Future

1. **Actionable Steps:**

   - Conduct strategic planning sessions with key stakeholders.
   - Identify emerging trends and innovations in your industry.
   - Develop a roadmap for the future, including growth and expansion plans.

2. **Dedicated Time on Calendar:**
   - Schedule strategic planning sessions with stakeholders over the next month.
   - Allocate time for ongoing market research to stay updated on industry trends.

It's important to recognize that the road to success is not a sprint but a series of intentional strides. Each chapter, each concept, serves as a stepping stone, laying the foundation for transformative and unique leadership. As you embrace the principles shared here, remember that the journey is as crucial as the destination. Remember the resources available to you, reflect on your experiences, and keep your vision manifested.

It's perfectly acceptable to acknowledge that, at times, the load may seem daunting. Yet, the secret lies in understanding that it's not about doing everything at once. It's about recognizing the power of focused, deliberate action.

In the future, as you navigate the complexities of the business world, envision the success that awaits. Picture the ripple effects of your unconventional leadership – a team that thrives on innovation, a workplace where top talent stays and a company that not only meets but exceeds its goals. The journey to being a "Not Your Average CEO" is a dynamic process, one that evolves with each strategic decision, every empowered team member, and all the milestones achieved. A lasting impression on the world through the remarkable impressions you have made along the way.

As we part ways, remember this: You are not alone in this journey. The insights, strategies, and perspectives shared in these pages are your companions on the road to success. You possess the capability to lead in a way that transcends the ordinary and leaves an indelible mark on the world of business. Embrace the challenges, celebrate the victories, and always remember that being a nonconventional CEO is not just a role – it's a mindset, a commitment to continuous growth, and a legacy in the making.

Beyond the balance sheets and profit margins, your story as a Not Your Average CEO is written in the lives you touch, the clients and communities you uplift, and the positive change you inspire.

To your unconventional success,

Nicole Gallichio-Elz and Danielle Julia Cuomo, MBA